Beyond Road's End

Beyond Road's End

LIVING FREE IN ALASKA

Janice Schofield Eaton

ALASKA NORTHWEST BOOKS®

Anchorage, Alaska • Portland, Oregon

LIBRARY OF CONGRESS CATALOGING-IN-PUBLICATION DATA

Eaton, Janice Schofield, 1951-
    Beyond road's end : living free in Alaska / Janice Schofield Eaton.
        p. cm.
    ISBN 978-0-88240-754-8 (softbound)
    1. Eaton, Janice Schofield, 1951- 2. Eaton, Janice Schofield, 1951—Marriage.
3. Frontier and pioneer life—Alaska—Kachemak Bay Region. 4. Outdoor life—
Alaska—Kachemak Bay Region. 5. Women—Alaska—Kachemak Bay Region—
Biography. 6. Kachemak Bay Region (Alaska) —Biography. 7. Kachemak Bay Region
(Alaska) —Social life and customs. I. Title.

F912.K26E37 2009
979.8'3051092—dc22
    [B]   2008043277

Alaska Northwest Books®
An imprint of Graphic Arts Center Publishing Co.
P.O. Box 10306
Portland, OR 97296-0306
(503) 226-2402 * www.gacpc.com

President: Charles M. Hopkins
General Manager: Douglas A. Pfeiffer
Associate Publisher, Alaska Northwest Books®: Sara Juday
Editorial Staff: Timothy W. Frew, Kathy Howard, Jean Bond-Slaughter
Editor: Laura O. Foster
Cover design: Elizabeth Watson
Interior design: Andrea Boven Nelson
Maps: Marge Mueller, Gray Mouse Graphics
Production Coordinator: Susan Dupèrè

Printed in the United States of America by Lightning Source

In memory of Ed
who taught me to "Live Now."

To Barry for his unending support during fulfillment of the promise

and to Ellie
and the campfire of friends.

~ Introduction ~

Promises are easy to make in times of crisis. "I'll go to church every Sunday. I'll quit drinking." My promise was to tell this story, if only . . .

When "if only" finally happened, I set out to fulfill my pledge. I'd breeze through beginning chapters, then hit discomfort zones and crash. My notes would retreat to the top drawer and hibernate, then reignite like those joke birthday candles you extinguish and then burst back into flame.

"I'd rather write about my friends' Alaskan adventures," I'd argue with myself. "They climb Mount McKinley, captain boats in Prince William Sound, race the Iditarod, fly planes to the Arctic. Mine's an ordinary life, and what it's like to shift from the Lower 48 to Alaska."

"You're right, Jan," a voice replies, its Boston slur strangely like my husband Ed's. "And that's why it's important. Living our dream didn't require outrageous abilities. Besides, this story's far bigger than us. It's about an entire community, and what working together can achieve."

Still I dawdled and evaded my vow. I'd make sporadic attempts, beginning anew to tell the tale. Then life, spinning its wheel of change, would sidetrack me. More than a decade later, with Ed passed on and me living in a new hemisphere remarried to a New Zealander, the promise and Ed's voice still nagged in the ether. "Tell the story, Jan. Write about Alaska."

"Oh Eddie," I reply silently, "I hate writing when we're central characters. It's like letting a stranger into our bedroom."

"Jan," his spirit says. "No excuses."

Fire burns me to action. A log rolls out of the fireplace and knocks over the screen. Embers ignite the carpet. My Kiwi spouse walks into the dining room in time to save our home, and my manuscript notes. My resistance turns to ash.

The next morning I face the blank page, feeling more naked than when in a sauna. What do I say?

"Write like you're talking around the campfire," coaches friend Ellie. "I've heard bits of the story over the years, I want to hear the whole thing. Tell me again about that gold bar. Whatever became of it?"

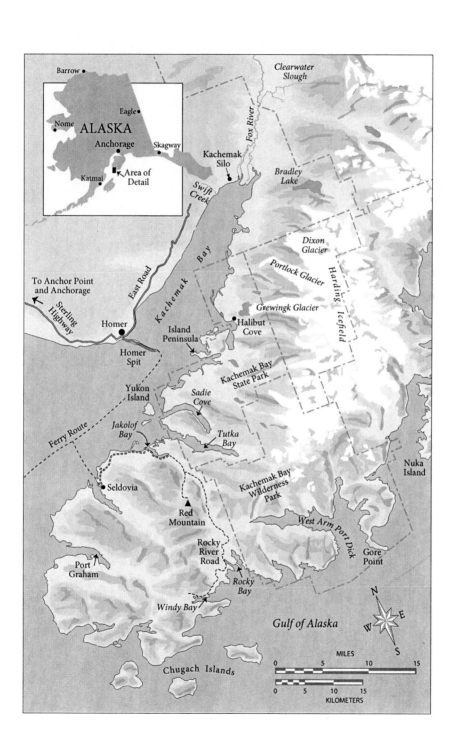

Barrow •

Eagle •

Nome • ALASKA
Anchorage •
                Skagway •

Katmai • ■ Area of
              Detail

Clearwater
Slough

Fox River

Kachemak
Silo

Bradley
Lake

Dixon
Glacier

Portlock Glacier

Harding Icefield

Swift
Creek

Kachemak Bay

East Road

To Anchor Point
and Anchorage

Sterling Highway

Homer •

Grewingk Glacier

Halibut
Cove

Island
Peninsula

Homer
Spit

Kachemak Bay
State Park

Yukon
Island

Sadie
Cove

Ferry Route

Jakolof
Bay

Tutka
Bay

Nuka
Island

Seldovia •

Kachemak Bay
Wilderness
Park

Red
Mountain ▲

West Arm Port Dick

Gore
Point

Rocky
River
Road

Port
Graham

Rocky
Bay

Windy Bay

Gulf of Alaska

N
W   E
S

Chugach Islands

MILES
0   5   10   15

0   5   10   15
KILOMETERS

PART ONE

Lady's slipper
(Cypripedium candidum)

"How do you picture Alaska?"
"I see us in a log cabin by the sea,
with a snowcapped mountain view."

Good as Gold ⟲

The bar is the size of a Hershey's chocolate bar, the weight of a quart of orange juice. The color is molten gold, and gold it is, solid and pure. I heft big yellow in my hand, feeling strange. Everything feels strange.

Tony, Ed's friend from the construction industry, kneels before us. Besides the gold bar is another strange sight: American greenbacks march like soldiers across our living room floor. Tony points at the stacks of hundred dollar bills secured with elastics. It's more money than I've seen in twenty-eight years of living. He counts aloud.

One thousand, two thousand, three thousand . . .

Ten thousand, eleven thousand, twelve thousand . . .

The piles are like Monopoly money. But these are genuine, green dollars. The stacks of thousands spread.

Seventeen thousand, eighteen thousand, nineteen thousand. Still Tony counts. With each wad I feel odd, like I'm part of a heist scene. People I know don't have money like this. We've never had money. All ours?

Twenty-three thousand, twenty-four thousand, twenty-five thousand.

I look at Ed as the magic number is reached. Twenty-five stacks of hundreds, plus thirty-five ounces of gold.

Three months ago our north-to-Alaska future felt like a fairy tale. Now we've no excuse and no choice. We've just swapped our log home on Blueberry Hill in New Hampshire along with its forty-six acres, its organic garden, its riding ring, and its barn for wads of green paper and a chunk of metal.

Are we crazy, surrendering our bucolic lifestyle for a vague dream? We've no work to head to, no friends waiting to greet us, nothing certain. Will we even like Alaska, we wonder, or find a niche in a state bigger than Texas, Montana, and California combined?

Henry David Thoreau's counsel beats in our ears: "Sim-pli-fy, sim-pli-fy. Follow your drummer, follow your drummer." The books of wilderness survival author Bradford Angier bait us with promises of living richly in the wilderness on ten dollars a day. We're hooked by images of freedom, freedom from financial stress and crushing East Coast taxes.

But doubts pinch, coupled with warnings from family. "You don't even know where you're going—some vague somewhere in Alaska. Why don't you visit first? Why sell everything you love?" they sanely suggest.

"Because it feels right," I answer. "I'm following my intuition. But my answer sounds strange. Everything about Ed and our getting together is strange, the most bizarre event of my entire life.

The Other Life ⁓

Bizarre began with New Hampshire in a January cold snap, me grumpier than a bear with a toothache. Every single chore is hard going. The barn's water buckets are rock solid. The track's glaciated and horses skate precariously to the turnout paddock. The only warmth is steam from their nostrils and their fresh deliveries of hot buns.

In the barn, I'm shoveling shit and feeling shitty. Each toss stirs daydreams of palm trees and escape from bone-numbing winter. I'm cold and cranky. Judy, the farm's owner, has been out of commission since knee surgery. Solo, everything's far more of a chore.

The shovel tip catches the side of the cart and dumps a soggy load in my lap. My jeans reek. I grizzle, re-scoop, and heft again.

"You do that like a pro, Jan."

I jump. It's Ed. Ed Schofield is a regular around Mirither Farm, partnered with Judy's hubby in a concrete business.

"Hi Ed. Steve's at the shop for another pack of cigs."

Ed leans against the stall door. "It's not Steve I came to see."

"What's up?" I pause, shovel in mid-air.

"Been watching you around the farm for quite a while, Jan. The way you carry a bale of hay in one hand, saddle in the other. I'd like to get to know you better."

My mouth flaps like a fish yanked from a stream. I gasp for air. Ed? Wants to know me better?

Judy's always telling me about Ed's life, the Schofield Saga, she calls it. Some days she blurts about his past with wife Lucia, in the sixties when Ed and Steve ran Minuteman Floors Corporation. Or his seventies drama, building his log home solo on Blueberry Hill in Maples, and how he did everything by hand, even dug the cellar hole. "Ed hates plumbing," says Judy, "so he subbed out that one job. But when he came home, the plumber was gone, along with Ed's jeep and girlfriend."

The saddle soap opera continues. "Now Ed's with Sue," Judy says, "She thinks Ed's log home is only a holiday camp. They're staying in her suburban house by the highway. Ed hates it, Jan. If only he was with you. You and Eddie would get on so well together." I tell Judy to shut up. I'm married. I'm not available.

Standing there, with soiled jeans and Ed in front of me, I finally get my tongue untied. "I'm married," I stammer to Ed.

He spins to leave and glances back over his shoulder. "If you want to talk, I'll be at the cabin."

I bang my shovel, matted with urine and sawdust, into the corner. "Stupid," I mutter to the wall. "Don't even think about it."

But my heart's a jackhammer. My head feels faint. I grab the cart for balance and collapse on the edge. I sit on a pile of shit and brood.

Derailed ～

Every decision's a mixture of who you were and who you could be. My whole life has been the New England truism: "The apple doesn't fall far from the tree." Like my parents, I was born in this town, bred in this town. Happy or not, we stay married. We do what's expected.

Sitting on the cart, my mind rewinds time, wanders dusty roads, and remembers: the day driving under the overpass during the commute to my teaching job. A bored kid tosses a rock, shatters my windshield. The next day, the district supervisor watches as I teach seventh graders about hidden sugars in food. I hold my poster, showing the number of sugar cubes in soft drinks, donuts, and snack foods.

The kids are impressed, but the supervisor rants. "Don't you know anything about nutrition? Sugar gives energy." The following week the district implements a breakfast program for low income students. Trays of free sugar donuts lay next to the soda machine.

Then comes a citywide teacher strike for higher wages. We strike out. "Back to work," the judge orders, "or face fines or jail."

We refill the trenches, discouraged with still being the forty-ninth lowest-paid teachers in the nation. Zombielike, I rise daily. Commute forty minutes. Teach teens. Deal with bureaucracy. Commute home. Make dinner. Clean up. Grade homework. Prep classes. Do it all again.

Each night I unload on my husband Gary as he unwinds with his telly. I time my talking to commercials. "The kids are great, Gary, but the bureaucracy drives me nuts. And commuting is worse than ever with these gas shortages and crazy oil prices. Did you hear President Carter on the radio, talking about Americans losing faith in their future? I'm starting to wonder about mine. I'm getting fed up with this rubbish and never having enough money. Perhaps I need a new budget," I conclude.

I grab the calculator. From my salary I subtract income tax, commuting costs, teaching materials, work expenses. I calculate hours: time readying for work, commuting, teaching, after-school duties, class prep. My bottom line shatters like the rock. "This works out to three dollars an hour, Gary. All this hassle for a crappy three bucks an hour."

Commuting home the next day, my mind is stuck. One way or another I have to end this dead-end path. "Do I drive off the bridge?" I muse out loud. I'm shocked by how appealing it sounds.

I take the long way home and stop to watch a horse jumping fences. I chat with its owner, Judy, and sign on for what I always yearned for as a kid—a weekly riding lesson.

A year later, with me jumping fences and winning blue ribbons, I resign from my job. I work now for Judy, teaching beginning riders, and training equines. My commute is a ten minute walk, my hourly wage ten times higher than when I taught. There are no school politics, simply shit to shovel and subzero weather. Most days, life's easier than ever.

Then heaven laughs.

"Ed wants to get to know me better."

Meltdown 〰

The next day, I bump into Ed at the farm and ask if we can chat. I climb into his rusty pickup and we drive on back roads to the Skowhegan River. Ed cuts the ignition. We stare at the river.

"If I wasn't . . . ," I stammer.

"Yes?" Ed leans forward intently to catch the end of my sentence.

"If I wasn't married, I'd love to get to know you better. But I'm married."

"Oh Jan, I don't want to disrupt anything in your life if you're happy with Gary. But sometimes people grow in different ways and end up on different tracks and are ready to move on."

"I'm happy," I insist. "But maybe someday we'll meet again down the road."

"Yeah, maybe."

Ed drops me back at the farm, back to normal life. But life's no longer normal. I don't want food. Pounds melt like hot butter. I don't want sleep. My mind's a hamster wheel. I've a gut-ache, a yearning for new life, knowing all the while it is a mission impossible. I, Janice, have taken vows. I'm married, for life, the Catholic life.

Ten sleepless nights, ten lean days later, exhausted, I doze off. A voice startles me.

"If you want to grow, go with Ed."

"What?" I ask, not sure the voice is real.

The voice repeats, clear and definite. "If you want to grow, go with Ed."

I inhale the words and feel waves of peace. I argue with them and war erupts. But they make no sense. The idea of going with Ed is irrational. I have to ignore this craziness.

"If you want to grow, go with Ed." The voice is a mantra, insisting, unchanging, unrelenting. Peace surges with the surety of the voice.

"If you want to grow, go with Ed."

But how would I do such a thing, if I were even to consider it?

The voice resonates again.

Morning brings quivers of apprehension. How do I tell Gary? I can't cheat on Gary, nor can I cheat myself. Do I really leave my marriage and plunge into Ed's life? Is Ed willing to be more for me than 'a date'?

Restless, I rise, make tea, sit at the kitchen table. To still the mental roaring, I open junk mail and mutter, "Ha, another sweepstakes I've won." But this letter is different. I've truly won the Farnam Companies' sweepstakes. A shipping container full of products is heading my way. Is this my dowry for a new life: cases of mink oil, bug dope, hoof dressing, horse shampoo? Is this a sign from the heavens?

The voice hits again. "If you want to grow, go with Ed."

With my hands warmed by my mug of tea, I remember . . . seven years ago before Gary and I got engaged, I was meditating by candlelight. The flame flickered and words came: "Love Gary well. You won't be with him forever." I shivered then, thinking it a portent of a fatal accident, never imagining I'd be the cause of the crash.

At the breakfast table, I pen Gary a letter. When he rises, I read it to him: "I'm leaving you everything: bank accounts, house trailer, furniture. I'll only take my clothes, personal stuff, and the last five hundred I made teaching riding. I can't explain what I'm doing. I haven't been having an affair but I know I have to go." We cry and hold each other.

Afterward, I call Ed and ask if we can meet. We take a drive. "I'm leaving my marriage, Ed. I can't cheat on Gary. I'm now homeless." I tell Ed about the voice and ask if I can move in.

"Yes," he replies with no hesitation. A warm yes, a comforting hug, and a kiss on the side of the cheek. We will begin our new life together.

Day One ~

I return to the trailer while Gary's at work. Sleepwalking, I pack my clothes in boxes. The steadying influence is the calm mantra. "If you want to grow, go."

In the den, I stare at the sewing machine, Gary's Christmas present to me. That doesn't feel right to take. Neither does the stack of journals of our life together. Now I am boldly—or foolishly—stepping into another lifetime, an orphan future.

The former me has died, and I'm cleaning up the remains, things strewn everywhere, fringed with memories. Most things I leave as is. It is enough that I am leaving, I don't want to shatter Gary's life.

I drive to my winter work, teaching women's fitness classes, and give my two week notice, telling my boss I'm moving and it's too far to commute. Afterwards, traffic is snarled; I'll be late for my three o'clock rendezvous with Ed. I hate to start life with Ed on a sour note, with him waiting in the cold.

I check my map, glance at the X where I'm to park, and replay Ed's voice directing me to my new life. "Drive to the end of the state-maintained road, Jan. Leave your car in the plowed spot by the pond." At last, I pull in. Ed is waiting, huddled on his snowmachine. A beagle jumps off and races toward me. Ed strides forward, arms open wide.

"Welcome, woman," he says, in his Boston accent. I melt into his hearty embrace.

"I tried to call," I stammer. "I'm so sorry I'm late."

"You're a big girl, Jan. Knew you'd be fine; figured you must have hit snags. This is Princess."

The beagle ignores me. Her eyes are glued on Max, my Doberman, who's clacking against the car window for release.

"Let him out so they can get acquainted."

My hand freezes to the door handle. "Max was given to me because his owners wanted a watchdog. But all he does is watch people and wag his stump of a tail."

"Great," says Ed, reaching for the door.

"It's a different story with dogs. But he's usually okay with girls. And Princess is pretty . . . stout." How can I tell him she's the fattest beagle I've ever seen?

"Princess is big-boned, Jan. And good at taking care of herself."

"Okay." I open the door. Max dives out. Princess marches up, hackles up. Max sniffs her butt. She bangs her head against his privates. Tails switch from stiff poles to waving flags. Princess sticks her nose in a track, and races between trees. Max tags behind.

"We'd best get loaded up, Jan. It'll be dark soon."

I open the hatchback. In the car, boxes are crammed to the ceiling. Ed loads the snowmachine sled and fastens all with bungee cords. Ed straddles the machine. I mount behind and wrap my arms around his waist. His broad back blocks the cold but doesn't stop my shivering. I wonder if we'll have anything to say. Through Judy, I've caught glimpses of Ed's life on the hill. But is it Ed or Ed's lifestyle I'm attracted to? What if we're not compatible? I've burned my bridges and jumped, all because of a voice in the night.

My breath forms frost on Ed's coat as he steers the snowmachine over dips of the snow-packed trail. We head deeper into the woods. The track weaves between stone walls in a forest of maples, oaks, and white pine.

Ed veers left, on yet another track that curves round a bend, then dead-ends. Logs gleam golden in winter sun. I gasp. This is the exact image I always doodled when bored: a log home on a knoll with a curved drive, but oh, with a center chimney. No chimney on Ed's house.

Ed pushes the wrought-iron latch on the hand-crafted door, scuffs his boots over the plywood floor, and points to a gaping opening in the center of the house. "Watch out for the hole. Chimney's going there." My forearms prickle with goose bumps.

Welcome Home ⁓

Fate leads up the spiral stairway, past shelves stuffed with books into the bedroom. I stiffen. Bedroom. I've never been with any man other than Gary. Whatever am I doing? Who is this stranger who's showing me shelves where I can put my things, and who is showing me his bed?

"You okay, Jan?" Ed pauses. "Let's go downstairs, have tea."

"Fine," I stammer. I sit on the couch while Ed brews drinks. My stomach rumbles.

"After our cuppa, let's go dine at the Depot. We'll take my last twenty and celebrate our togetherness."

My mind's rivets on the word "last." Gary paid bills months in advance. Is Ed saying he's stone broke?

After tea, we head out for dinner. In the snowmachine's headlamp, the trees look skeletal. At trail's end, we transfer to Ed's truck and drive to the restaurant. "Steaks here are great," says Ed. "Especially the T-bones."

"Fine."

"Wine?"

I squeeze my purse; do I have enough if we go over that last twenty?

The steaks arrive. Ed saws a juicy chunk and smacks his lips. I sip wine and worry. "Your last twenty?"

"Winter," says Ed, as he inhales another morsel. "Usually have savings, but this year work is as dry as an old boot."

"Hope we don't end up living in a shoe."

"Nah," Ed laughs. "Got the cabin. It's just tough saving with this recession. Newscasters are saying it's the worst since the Great Depression."

"Gary's workplace was having record profits. Folks keep their cars running longer when times are hard."

"Great for auto parts, but not for building. It's only February, and the phone bill's overdue, and the mortgage; no work likely 'til April."

Crap. Why'd I quit my winter job at the spa? I nervously fork beef into my mouth. We chew ideas on how to get by 'til the spring thaw.

"I can mortgage the old pickup—maybe get a thousand," Ed proposes.

"I've my teacher's retirement fund, Ed; that's another eight hundred dollars."

"Not going there. That's yours."

"Ours."

"We'll see . . . There's a white-tail in the freezer, so we've got meat."

"I can bake bread; buy a bag of rice."

"Or potatoes, Jan. I love potatoes . . . We've wood for the stove, so we won't be cold."

I reach across the table and take his hand. "No . . . I don't think we'll be cold."

We throw down the last of his money for a tip and drive to the skidoo. Back at the cabin, my eyelids droop. "I'm knackered."

"It's been a huge day, Jan."

Life shattering, I think.

"You can use the bathroom first."

I brush my teeth, my heart racing and then stand in the steamy shower, struggling to breathe. I dry myself and emerge, wrapped in a thick towel.

"Why don't you head up to the loft, Jan. I'll be up in a few." As I pull on a T-shirt, the phone rings.

"Can you get that please, Jan?" Ed shouts.

"Is Eddie there?" asks a shrill voice.

"He'll be here in a moment."

"I want Eddie now. Get me Eddie, Sue."

"I'm not Sue, I'm Jan."

"Jan? Who the hell are you? I want Eddie."

"Ed . . . ." I shout. "You'd better get this." Ed takes the phone.

"It's some cranky woman," I whisper.

"Oh hi, Mom . . . No, Mom. I'm not with Sue any longer . . . Jan . . . I'm with Jan." Ed holds the receiver away from his ear. I hear garbled words and a piercing tone.

"Thanks for the offer, Mom. But, no. I don't go to those kinds of places. . . . No, Mom. I can't live with you. . . . I live with Jan." Ed puts a finger in his ear. "Yes, Mom . . . I'll talk with you later."

Ed hangs up and sighs. The phone rings.

"Hi Mom . . . Oh . . . Hi Sue . . . That's good Sue . . . I'm glad you're feeling better about things . . . No, Sue, we can't try again . . . . Why not? Because I'm living with Jan."

Ed winces and sets the phone down sheepishly. "Sorry about that, Jan. Sue's upset."

Now I want answers. "I thought you two were totally done."

"We are . . . but Sue forgets; she wants to try again . . . but it never works."

I take a deep breath. What have I gotten myself into?

"Come on, Jan, let's get some sleep. I'd love to merely hold you. This is new for both of us, you know."

I snuggle into Ed's arms, focus on my breath, and shift from shallow worried breaths to belly breaths. My mind settles as the deeper breathing calms me.

Smoke ∿

In the morning, I waken groggy and try to remember where I am. I sniff the air; it's thick with . . . "Fire!" I bolt upright, hear a sound, and spin around in bed. Ed. Smoking a cigarette in bed.

There are moments you are too far down a trail to turn back and you discover the truth of the trail. The truth is I've teamed up with a smoker. Memories flood—Mom and Dad clouding the kitchen with puffs of their Lucky Strikes; brother Jim hiding firecrackers in Mom's cigarettes. Dad quitting while Mom persists. Family feuds over cigarettes and their stink. Now I'm in bed with stink.

Do I raise a stink? Or allow Ed total freedom? But cigarettes affect me and not only Ed.

"Ed," I launch, "how'd you start smoking?"

"High school. It was hot to have Kools rolled up in T-shirt sleeves. Grown up. The ads swore 'Smoking is healthy—opens up the lungs.' I smoked cigs during my army years but then got bored, switched to a relaxing pipe now and then. Sue's a smoker," he says as he takes another drag. "Got back on the cigarettes to keep her company."

"It doesn't keep me company, honey," I say sweetly. "In fact, the smell's rather a turn-off. And I'd much rather a turn-on."

"Me too, Jan." Ed stubs out the half-smoked cigarette. "Done." He pauses. "Wouldn't mind keeping the pipe though."

"I like the smell of pipe smoke . . . except in bed."

"Deal."

In a Muddle ⟞

Each day after breakfast we now walk down Blueberry Hill to the row of mail boxes. "A letter from my sister," I say excitedly. It's my first personal letter since moving in a week ago. I rip it open.

> *Dear Jan.*
>
> *I'm still in shock. What can I say? I want you to be happy but I don't see happiness as the basic value in life. Our present philosophies are miles apart. I'm afraid you're going to be really hurt. I'll say not much more but I must say this: Ask yourself what you'll do if he dumps you or runs around on you. Do you have the strength to survive such a crisis? I don't think you've been much without a significant other in your life. Look at the possibilities no matter how absurd it sounds now. Gary was dependable. That is so rare in this value-less world.*

This whole thing is ugly for me. It has blown me apart. I feel like there is nothing to believe in anymore except God, death and suffering. I have no desire to meet your friend. That's how I feel. I don't say this in anger or revenge . . . just emptiness.

I pray you know what you're doing. Keep your possessions in your *name.*

God bless. Doris

I sob; Ed holds me, strokes my back. "It'll be okay, honey. Our families will come around soon."

I pray that Ed is right but even his beagle hasn't taken to me. When I walk around the cabin, Princess broadsides me. Then she lures Max to the woods and races home solo.

Ed is philosophical. "Oh Jan, she's always been queen of the hill here. She shadowed me during the cabin's construction. She'd even sit on the chair at the kitchen table and eat with me. That stopped when Sue came along, so Princess helped end that relationship by terrorizing Sue's cat. Now she's trying to get rid of you."

"Me and Max."

"She'll get over it."

"Hope so. She nearly flattened me today; smacked my shins full force."

"Not good. Neither is my next news. Mom's coming this weekend."

"So?" I say. "I need to meet your mother."

"Mom has never liked anyone I'm with; don't take it personally."

"No problem."

"She *is* a problem. At my wedding with Lucia, she made a toast."

"That's normal."

"Not this toast. Mom got on the microphone and told the Italian contingent how sad she was that her son was marrying a no-good guinea. You could've heard a pin drop."

Ellen, Ed's mom, arrives, quiet as a firecracker. She greets Ed and ignores me. "Damn dogs!" she screams. "Get on the damn floor where you belong." The dogs slink from couch to floor. "You," she shouts to me. "Get me tea." I slink to the kitchen.

Ellen heads to the bathroom. Princess follows her to the bathroom door, stops a moment there, and returns to reboard the couch.

I carry tea and snacks to the living room. "Something stinks."

"Ah, crap. Princess pooped, right where mom will step in it." Ed grabs a shovel. "You'd best put her out 'til Mom leaves."

"I'll go too; it will give you time alone with Ellen. Tell her I had an appointment."

I drive to road's end and play with the dogs for two hours. Max woofs as a car exits Blueberry Hill. The coast is clear. "Home guys."

The dogs scramble happily onto the couch. Ed hands me a wine. "To us."

"To us," I respond.

Princess looks at me and wags. Now that she and I have a mutual foe, I am part of us.

Moving Mountains 〜

"Where will we put my colt?" I ask Ed. "I need to get Good Vibrations home from Judy's."

"Can't build a barn until we've more money, Jan. But you could use that backyard shed meanwhile."

I empty the shed of clutter and cobwebs, hauling mildewed boxes to the dump.

"Now," Ed says, "we'll move the shed to the paddock."

"But it weighs a ton."

"No problem. We've got these." Ed holds two long poles. "You'll see." He wedges the poles under the building.

"Now push," he commands. We lean our shoulders into the corners. The poles rotate; the building slides. As the rear pole emerges from the bottom of the shed, Ed leapfrogs it forward.

"Like a miracle, Ed."

"Together, babe," Ed winks, "we can move mountains." He pauses and puffs his pipe. "That, Jan, and the power of leverage; always use brain, not brawn."

Good Vibrations arrives in Judy's trailer. I lead Vibes on the snow-packed track to his stall. He stands, bewildered by his cramped quarters and strange surroundings.

"We'll build him a proper barn soon. Meanwhile, let's clear pasture." Ed hoists his chain saw and fells an oak. I drag branches to piles for burning. He bucks hardwood into four foot lengths and demonstrates how to heft the chunk to my shoulder, and how to stack a woodpile. Tree by tree, a clearing emerges.

Our life swings into winter's rhythm: pastures by day; evenings by the fire. We discuss the day's progress, listen to music, rub sore shoulders. Cuddles lead to loving. We fall asleep wrapped in each other's arms.

The sun grows stronger. Frosty nights give way to warming days. Maples run sap. Asparagus shoots up in the garden. The phone rings with the first work of the season. Ed commutes to job sites. Mostly I stay home and ready the garden for planting and do home chores.

"I love you, Eddie," I tell him. "I love our life too; this is my dream come true. What about you? What's your fantasy?"

Ed's eyes flicker left and get a funny look. "Alaska. I want to show you Alaska, Jan. Visited there briefly a decade ago; have ached to return ever since." He rambles about salmon teeming in the streams, mountains tall as skyscrapers, the feeling of freedom. "I want you to see Alaska with me."

Taxing Times ⌒

Work goes well, but money vaporizes like steam. The barn needs nails, lumber, roofing, hay racks, horse bedding, grain. There's the mortgage, utilities, groceries, insurances, loan payments. And now the unbelievable lies in my hand.

"How can this be, Ed? Is this a misprint?"

"No, that's what we owe. Three thousand dollars in property tax."

"For a hand-built cabin in the woods? I thought this was the 'live free' state."

"You forget the rest of the state motto, Jan. It's 'live free or die.' Here you have to keep working 'til you croak."

"I hope we manage to get to Alaska before that happens."

As the season passes, we save pennies, fork out dollars. The mail bears yet another ominous envelope. I rip it open.

"The IRS says you didn't file."

Ed grabs the form and prints GONE TRAVELLING across the top.

"You can't do that, Ed."

"Just did. Did it before, too."

"What happened?"

"They sent it again. Wrote it larger. Then they left me alone. There's far bigger fish to fry than me."

My eyes glaze like a dead trout. "Priests preach about fearing God. I fear the IRS more. What got you started?"

"Long story."

I uncork a chardonnay and pour; Ed leans back and lights his pipe.

"Back in the sixties we had a hard winter. My buddies and I were broke as skunks. So we pooled our efforts and launched a concrete corporation, Minuteman Floors. Within a year, we had more than a million dollars' worth of business."

"In the sixties?"

"Yep; huge money back then. We worked Boston's Prudential Tower, all the skyscraper projects. Grabbed any contract that turned a buck. I was corporate director, drove a Cadillac."

"You?" My Ed's bearded, with blue jeans and a rust-bucket truck.

"We played the game, Jan, did the whole nine yards. Had employees on the payroll, lawyers, accountants. But the bottom line had us bummed. So the pencil-pushers had us create a second corporation and rent equipment to the first corporation to save taxes. Accountant and legal fees went up; life got even more convoluted. Finally I had enough. Told the guys I wanted out of the corporation. Said I could make more money jobbing, with no headaches. But when I went home I got a surprise. Lucia wanted out of our marriage."

"Just like that?"

"Like a bloody sledgehammer. Next day after work, I was crying in my beer. A buddy told me he'd heard rumors that my kids were going to have a new dad soon. All I knew for certain was that Lucia wanted out, and wanted everything: house, pool, car, and our three young daughters."

"What'd you get?"

"Screwed." Ed tenses and takes a puff. "Judge said I could see my kids one lousy hour each month, plus pay Lucia a monster alimony."

"That's not fair."

"No kidding. But back then, judges believed mothers knew best to raise kids. And he based alimony on my peak summer earnings. When I told him I couldn't pay that amount year-round, he told me to work three jobs if I had to.

"So here I am, my life gutted, and this old fart telling me I can see my girls once a month. I lost it. Told him he was a bald-headed bastard. Next thing, I'm in the air, lifted by two court gorillas, my legs dangling, lungs bellowing, and they hauled me from court. Another workmate, Carlo, saw how bummed I was. Said he owed me a favor, so he'd fix my problem no charge. Finally figured out what he was talking about. His work finishing concrete was simply a cover for his main job as a Mafioso hit man. Told him to forget it, to stay away from Lucia, that my kids needed a mom. That I'd sort things out my way.

"At the same time, my lawyer told me to take some time away from court to cool off. Told me to go on holiday, and put some fear about my whereabouts into Lucia and her lawyer. So I did. Called my lawyer two years later. Asked him if he thought they were scared yet. He asked me how I was doing, and I said okay. 'Don't try to do any better,' he warned, 'and don't tell me where you are. You're in deep trouble if you come back.' So I've stayed away these ten years."

"But I don't understand, Ed, these are your girls. How could you stay away?"

Ed shrugs and averts his eyes. "All options sucked, Jan. Felt wedged between a rock and a hard spot. I grew up without a dad, and it's awful. But I couldn't imagine seeing the kids an hour a month. And with my oldest only four, and believing Lucia was getting remarried, I thought they'd adjust easier to a solid family, rather than having me flit in monthly. So I left and headed to Alaska. But things didn't come together to settle there."

Ed pulls on his pipe; I take another sip of wine. How many aspects are there, I wonder, to Ed Schofield?

"Wait here a minute, Jan." Ed climbs to the loft and returns with a safety box. He dials the combination, leafs through documents, and lifts out photos. "My three daughters," he says. "Aren't they beautiful?"

"Gorgeous," I say. "And did Lucia ever remarry?"

Ed nods.

"It'd be great if you could reconnect with the girls."

"I'd love to Jan, but it'll probably have to be when the gals are grown. Trying to do that now would open Pandora's box."

Spring Thaw ⸺

Spring brings financial relief; Ed gets a contract to build a log home. We burn with excitement: for his labor Ed's promised $10,000. Our Alaskan dream reignites.

We migrate north to the building site and hire neighbors to care for the animals back home. I become gofer, going for materials and tools and helping lift logs into place. Day by day the home grows. Night by night we study Alaska maps. As the roof rises, Ed's neck bleeds. The vampires are black flies, scourge of the New England spring woods. As he sits in our camper, I smear salve on his wounds. "Damn bloodsuckers," he winces.

"Does your neck hurt that much?"

"This does," he says, handing me the paper he's reading. "Another property tax bill." He grabs a pencil and jots columns of figures then shakes his head. "We still won't have money for Alaska, Jan. It'll have to be another year."

"How badly do you want to go, Ed? Maybe we need to simplify."

"How, Janzie? We drive an old truck, don't take flashy holidays, rarely go out to eat. How else?"

"What if we let go of it all and sell everything?"

We decide then and there. Our home's for sale. We'll swap Blueberry Hill for a new life, cash in our stakes, and go to Alaska.

But deciding, we learn slowly, is the easiest bit of all.

"Moving is like eating an elephant," says Ed. "The only way to do it is bite by bite."

Our first mouthful is selling our home. "Looks bad with this recession, Jan. Real estate sales are down. And who'll want a property you can't drive to year-round?"

"Oh Eddie, look at your craftsmanship. This isn't an ordinary stick-built house. It's a lifestyle we're selling."

Ed calls seven realtors and lists with them all but insists, "I want the right to sell the house myself." The realtors balk, but they're hungry for listings, even odd listings like this.

"What is this place worth?" Ed asks the first realtor.

"$200,000," is the answer. We puff with excitement. We tell the second realtor to list it at $200,000. "No way," he protests. "Sorry, but with the unmaintained road, all you've got is a hunting camp. I could get you $50,000, maybe." Value estimates settle at $80,000.

The first prospective buyer is a fat man in shorts. Ed leads him up the spiral stairs. I follow. With each step, the man toots. Noxious gas wafts in my face. Ed is telling the man, "You can't drive the road in spring, and you've gotta lock out hooligans in their four-wheel drives. They tear up this road something awful. Last year they hack-sawed the chain, buried their truck in the mud, and had to be towed out. Took me all summer to get rid of the ruts."

In the cellar, Ed points at the sump pump. "Water pours in during spring melt; you could raise goldfish down here. Make sure you hit that switch."

The man's not into goldfish, mud, or hooligans. He drives away.

"Why'd you do that Ed?" I ask, as the tail lights vanish. "You drove him right off."

"He's not right for the place, Janzie. I want someone who will love this house."

The realtors bring more people by. There's always an excuse. Our cabin's too small, too dear, too remote. Or the buyer is "not right" to Ed.

Months pass. Leaves turn gold. Maybe Ed's right. Our place is hard to sell. A knock interrupts my thoughts. It's Tony, Ed's associate in the concrete trades, here to show off his new gal—Sweets. Sweets has legs like telephone poles, made even longer by stiletto heels. Her pants are leather, spray-painted on, her blouse sheer and revealing. I chuckle, imagining fancy Sweets prancing up our road in heels during mud season.

Tony hands Ed an envelope.

Ed lifts out a folded note. "A wedding invitation!"

We congratulate the couple. Ed reads on . . . "Come in costume?"

"My associates, Eddie. There'd be deep shit if they saw each other's faces. With masks they can all party."

I'm puzzled. I thought Tony did construction.

Tony describes the Halloween wedding-to-be, the lobster banquet that will follow. The phone interrupts the conversation for the third time since Tony and Sweets arrived.

"What's up with the phone, Eddie? You that busy with work?"

"Nah. It's realtors. I'm selling the place. We're going to Alaska."

"You're shitting me, Ed. I love this. I'll buy it. How much?"

"Eighty thou."

"How do you want the money? Cash and gold okay?"

"Amazing," I think to myself. "Sweets *will* be walking up this road. Hope she buys mud boots."

"I want to assume the mortgage, Ed. Bank money's cheap money. There's more profit this way."

"Can't, Tony. No mortgage transfers, except to another realtor."

"No problema. Sweets, you call Pencil tomorrow. Have him form a realty company for us. Let's see, what'll we call it?"

"Acme comes first in the phone book."

"Good work, Sweets. That'll do. Acme Realty."

"But you're not really going to buy and sell realty, Tony, are you?"

"I'm going to buy this house, Ed. And sell my other house."

"I thought you renovated the whole thing; got it exactly the way you wanted it."

"Yeah, but . . . " Tony leans and whispers to Ed, as Sweets asks if she can tour the house. Her heels click across the plywood behind me.

A week later, Tony drives us to Boston, swapping lanes like an Indy driver. My nails claw Ed's knee. Is Tony puffing on a joint? "Ass-wipe," Tony screams, as he rips past a driver doing ninety. We reach the attorney's office, sign papers, and redo the wild ride home. At Blueberry Hill, Tony peels down his sock and extracts wads of green wrapped in elastic. From the other sock he pulls out a black bag and slides out the gold. We stare dumbly at the piles. Our dream come true now sits here on our living room floor: Alaska—north to our future.

Stuffed ⟿·

"I still have to sell my place in the city," Tony says. "You two can stay here until then."

Tony leaves. We look around. Stuff. We've got to get rid of stuff. We run ads. Vibes goes to the Quaker community in Canterbury, the geese to a neighbor's pond. We make a pile of loved items and set them aside. In November, we bake a turkey in the wood-fired cookstove and call family. "Come share our last Thanksgiving on Blueberry Hill." We surprise everyone with Thankschristmas—wrapped presents next to a decorated tree: our horse-collar mirror, the handmade pine coffee table, the cane rockers, and Ed's favorite deer head mount.

The truck sells. We buy a van, a Ford Econoline, that we christen "Greenie." Ed custom-builds bed and cabinets into Greenie. We wean ourselves of possessions, down to what fits inside, and what we imagine we'll need in Alaskan life. Ed's chain saw crams under the bed, near my typewriter and Nikon camera. The canoe gets strapped on top, filled with fishing poles and fillet knives.

We let go the old and buy the new. We order a feather and down mattress and comforter from a Vermont artisan. Ed gags at the $600 price. "We'll be warm, Eddie," I console him. "No matter where we end up in Alaska."

As we load the van, readying for a "ride," Max wags his tail like a windshield wiper. Princess frets. She disappears solo to the woods, arriving home at dusk coated in porcupine quills. We rush her to the vets.

"This isn't like her," says Ed, as we anxiously wait. "She's far too woods-wise to roll on a porky. It's beagle suicide. She doesn't want to leave Blueberry Hill."

Despite the surgery, broken quills from her chest continue their journey, penetrating organs, and exiting through her back. In the morning, Princess lies under a pine, and sleeps. She's to remain guardian of her beloved Blueberry Hill.

More "to do's" strike from our departure list; we say good-byes to people and places. We book tickets to hear a concert by Bill Staines, a folksy New Hampshire singer and songwriter highly acclaimed by friends.

Details unfold with ease, except for the Staines concert. The venue is overbooked the first night he plays. Then I have the flu. "Third try's a charm," predicts Ed. We leave early, with abundant leeway for flat tires or detours. On the narrow road out, we pull onto the verge so our neighbor can pass, and roll down the window to say hi. "My girlfriend left me," he moans. "I could really use someone to talk to." Ed and I pause and turn around. We spend the evening consoling our neighbor.

"So much for Bill Staines," says Ed.

"Mustn't be important . . . Maybe someday."

The Great Stone Puzzle ~

Tony drops in to visit. "You've got to do something 'bout that hole," he says, pointing to the fireplace foundation pit.

"No problem, I'll cover the floor and lay new carpet before we go."

"No way. Sweets and I want a fireplace. You and Jan are living here rent free; you could mason up a fireplace."

"We could pay you rent," evades Ed. "You should build it, Tony; it's your house. I'll show you what I had in mind." The men scour the drawings. "This is a Rumford design," explains Ed, "with a shallow firebox. Pumps heat into the room, not up the chimney."

"What are the dimensions?"

"Four feet wide, eight long, two stories plus high."

"And this third flue?"

"For a bake-oven."

"This is your creation, Ed. It needs your touch. You're a perfectionist," Tony cajoles, "perfect to do it."

"Yeah, Tony but it'd be a full-time job."

"So? Got anything else to do this winter?"

Tony leaves. Ed springs to action. "Okay, Jan, you get the rocks, I'll get the mortar. I'll show you what's needed." At the stone wall, Ed hefts a rock, big as a sack of spuds. "See the square sides, flat bottom? This is a corner rock."

"Want me to get the wire brush and scrape off that flaky stuff?"

"Oh no, Jan. I want rocks with these lichens."

"You like lichens? Why?"

"Color, texture. More interesting than a plain old rock. Lichens are weird. In school they taught us about Fred and Alice."

"Who?"

"Fred the fungus lives with Alice the algae. Fred builds the house; Alice cooks."

Ed has really lost it, prattling on. The nuns never told me about Alice in bed with Fred.

"Lichens are two plants living as one, Jan. Alice algae does the chlorophyll; Fred fungi does the structure."

"Okay," I surrender. "You want rocks this size, covered with Fred and Alice?"

Ed nods.

"And how many do I need to haul?"

"Thousand would be good."

"Good joke; how many do you really need?"

"A thousand, Jan. We need plenty to select from, so they can nest naturally. I hate stonework with fat gobs of mortar as glue."

"Every rock has to have Fred and Alice?"

"Yep."

"And we can't go to Alaska 'til this is done?"

"Let's get started; I'm off to town. I'll haul this one back to the house."

I scout the wall. Rocks the wrong size, wrong shape. Ah, a perfect stone, but no lichen. Six feet along the wall, I find the first suitable stone. How many miles of stone wall did Ed say we have on our land, three? I fear I'll need to visit every foot of it.

Each day, I search while Ed concretes. He builds the guts of the firebox. Each rock is a quarter my body weight. I squat, lift, clutch the stone to my chest, slog over hill, through the bog.

Ed transforms the rock heap into a functional sculpture, with mortar seams tinted a shade darker than the stones. I stand back and anticipate the rocks for the next layer while Ed fine-tunes every stone, shaping them with a chisel. Stones dovetail perfectly. He makes it look easy. "Let me try, Ed." I whack; the stone shatters like glass.

"Watch for the seam. Try like this." Ed whacks. Perfection.

I whack. Rubble. Ed's progress stirs wonder. "You're like Michelangelo, releasing figures from marble."

"Nothing like that," protests Ed.

"You're too modest," I argue.

Ed pauses and lights his pipe. "I've got an idea. Let's get a piece of granite from the quarry and shape it like the state of New Hampshire. We'll set it there," he says, pointing to the upper third of the fireplace. "It'd be a nice tribute to this state, and a great homecoming present for Tony and Sweets." A week later, Ed scrambles up the scaffolding and sets the carved granite. Stones nestle around it like a picture puzzle.

The fireplace finally kisses the ceiling. Below, Ed installs bake-oven doors, bolts a log mantel above the firebox, and chisels block letters into the top of the flattened log.

I stand on tiptoes to see the words.

"Live now."

"My motto," says Ed. "What we're doing now, Jan. Living our dreams. It will be awesome to experience Alaska with you. But is this your dream too, or only mine?"

"I've never hung a place name on my dream, Ed. But as kids, Dad had a tarpaper-covered camp out in the woods near Washington, New Hampshire, sixty miles from Nashua. We'd go there on weekends, haul water in buckets from a stone well, read by candles and Coleman lights. The best family times I remember. I always imagined more life like that."

"How do you picture Alaska?"

"I see us in a log cabin by the sea, with a snowcapped mountain view. What about you?"

Ed answers with a smile.

Golden Quandary ~

"What do we do with Tony's gold bar?" I ask Ed as we lie in bed at day's end. "It's the size of a candy bar; how about if we get a Hershey wrapper and carry it in our back pocket?"

"I'd feel like a target, Jan. Don't want to walk around with a $25,000 wedgie in my jeans."

"We could stuff it in the van and take it with us."

"Remember when we went to register Greenie? And learned that she'd been stolen once? I'd hate Greenie to vanish with the gold bar inside."

"What about a safe-deposit box?"

"Recession's sending banks belly-up, Jan. And I don't like . . . "

"Institutions. I know. Got a better idea?"

"No, but let's review. What do we know?"

I tick the no's off on my fingers. "No bank. No van ride. No pockets. What else is there?"

"Don't know. Let's sleep on it. Let the answer come to us. Maybe it'll pop in, like Tony did when we had the house for sale."

"Okay, Ed. We're not solving it any other way."

"Let's let go of trying. Focus. We have the perfect solution. We have the perfect solution. . . ."

We drift to sleep, the mantra echoing.

With winter days lengthening toward spring, Ed announces that we'd best pay a final visit to neighbor Oscar. "He's one of the old-timers around here, Jan; in his seventies and as crusty as stale bread, but don't mind him. He has a good heart, and a good eye for the ladies." We drive the two miles over to the cabin, where Oscar sets in a corner chair by a roaring log fire, newspapers on his lap. Ed does intros. "Kettle's over there," Oscar points to me. "Make yourself at home. I'll have tea, two sugars." I head to the stove.

Oscar takes a pull on his pipe and passes it to Ed. I sniff the air: cannabis.

"What's that sporty thing you drove up in?"

"Jan's Starfire. She's got it for sale."

"You don't say." Oscar takes another puff of the funny tobacco. "The quack tells me I'd best get South next winter. Says the sun will help my lungs, put more strength in my bones. And," Oscar pauses, "I've got a new gal down in Florida I'd like to see. But my truck's tired. Now if I had that there car," he points out the window.

"We'd be happy to sell it to you."

"Wallet's dry," says Oscar. He scratches his chin. "What ya think 'bout a trade; that car of Jan's for a chunk of land?"

Land? Did Oscar say land? If we had land we could bury the gold. And we could build something later if we didn't like Alaska. I'm ready to shout, "Yes!" Of course we'll do the trade. It's a no-brainer. No one wants the car. Land is investment. But a glance at Ed stalls me.

He chews the stem of his pipe. "Where's the land?" he asks.

"Yonder about a mile; take your first left. Section starts by the fallen pine. Two acres with a stream," Oscar tempts.

"Well, I suppose we could look at it," Ed drawls.

We follow Oscar's directions and stand in snowy hardwoods, surrounded by stone walls and a frozen brook.

"She'll be mighty pretty after snowmelt," I coax Ed. He squeezes my hand and nods. He calls Oscar. "Deal."

We now have a place to bury the gold. But there's a new problem. I stand on a snow mound and twirl a strand of hair. "Four feet of frost, Ed. It will be impossible to dig."

"Spring's coming early, Jan. But first we have to go back to Blueberry Hill."

Ed heads to our woodpile and nods to me to load up our sled. "I'll be back," he tells me. "I've got to get something at the cabin." I stack and bungee and hitch the sled to the snowmachine. Ed returns wearing a full backpack.

We snowmachine to the gold burial site. Ed opens his pack and removes newspaper, a thermos, a grill, venison, spuds wrapped in foil, marshmallows, and a crowbar. He builds a fire. We sit on insulated camp mats and sip cocoa, watching the flames. We toss taters on the coals, sizzle steaks, roast marshmallows. Afterwards, Ed grabs the crowbar, scrapes two inches of thawed soil from the fire pit, then piles embers back on top.

We return the next day with more food fixings, plus a pick ax and shovel. We repeat the process and scrape away three more inches. Ten days later, Ed tucks the gold in a glass jar. We bury it and make a treasure map. Another issue resolved.

We return home to a visitor: Tony. "Good news. My place sold. Sweets and I want to move in."

Trials with Tony

"It's only March, Tony," Ed says. "Alaska's far too cold for camping. We can't leave yet."

"There are two bedrooms," Tony counters. "Sweets and I don't mind your being here."

"Suppose that'd be okay; it's only six weeks 'til Jan and I go."

"Look at the bright side, Eddie: with your stuff gone, this place is like a Buddhist center. Nothing to sit on but stumps. We'll fix you right up."

The next day Tony and Sweets arrive, bearing couches, chairs, tables, a boom box, Sweet's collection of stiletto heels, and his bottle of laughing gas. Every day, the phone rings incessantly.

"Message for you," Ed tells Tony. "Someone called Fuckface said to give him a call or else."

Tony frowns. "Always remember, Ed, where lies the risk lies the profit."

Two weeks later, I'm solo with Sweets. The door crashes open. Tony's face is as white as yogurt. "They're after me," he screams. "There's a roadblock at the bottom of the hill!"

Sweets rolls her eyes. "And you came here, Antonio? That's dumb."

"I've got to dump it, got to dump it." Tony thrashes around in his and Sweet's bedroom and emerges, arms full. He kicks the bathroom door open and drops the load. The toilet flushes. It flushes again. And again.

I panic. Drug bust? Hard drugs in our house? I race outside and dash to the woods. I'll cut down the backside of Blueberry Hill, to where Ed's visiting the neighbors. I can't go down the road with a roadblock waiting.

Our forty-six acres are a maze of stone walls and hardwoods. All I see are trees, trees and walls running hither and yon. I set off to the neighbors, then stop, unclear which way to go. In my panic over Tony, I didn't even grab a coat. I'm freezing already. I'd best return while I can, get something warm, then take my chances on the road. After all, I haven't done anything.

Back at the cabin, I suit up and trot to the mailboxes. There's no roadblock, no sign of Tony being chased. At the neighbors' house, I tell Ed our dilemma.

"Tony's paranoid, Jan. Last week Sweets told me they passed an accident scene. He wouldn't believe Sweets that the crashed cars and ambulance were real. Says cops were spying on him. Says dealers are after him too, and he might not be wrong there. Things are hot and heavy on both sides."

"Maybe that's why he was so fired up to move in, to use our place as a hideaway. Perhaps we'd best go, Ed. We don't want to get nailed because of Tony."

"Roads are too bad, still, to head north."

"What about south? We could head to Virginia and the Carolinas, and see part of the country we've never been to. Spring is kick-started there."

"Great idea, Jan. South to Alaska."

The Detour ⌒

We load the van and wave good-bye to Tony and Sweets. New Hampshire rural roads give way to highway hustle. Drivers blat horns on the Boston beltway. "This is chock-full of nuts, Ed. Everyone's trying to get nowhere faster."

"Did this daily for years," he says, "commuting to Boston for high-rise work."

"Hard to imagine, honey, you in a zoot suit living this; I prefer your woodsman persona."

We motor Interstate 95 through Connecticut to the New York gauntlet. "Yonkers," I say. "Well named. Can't see a happy face anywhere."

"Another toll booth," sighs Ed. "Worse than slot machines, not even a chance to win." We toss quarters to the ravenous beast and finally cross into New Jersey; more four-lane highway, bordered by industrial plants belching black smoke.

Trenton gives way to Philadelphia; we race onward round Baltimore. We stop only to fill the Ford and empty our bladders.

The Blue Ridge Parkway welcomes us with rumpled rug mountains. New life begins; we camp by night along the ridges and creep with the camera to photograph deer. On rainy evenings, I kneel on the floor of Greenie and cook on the propane stove. Everything inside is sized for dwarfs. I reach the sink, stove, pots and pans, cutlery, water jug, and ice chest all without shifting my knees.

In fine weather, we light a fire and roast chicken and veggies over the grill. I wrap dough around a stick and toast the bread over the coals. Ed tears off hunks and smothers it with butter and honey. "Yum. Where'd you learn to make this?"

"I got the idea from that Bradford Angier book we read. The ingredients are flour with baking powder, salt, and butter. Angier called it bannock; supposed to be a classic wilderness bread. Some people think that Scottish fur traders brought it to North America."

"I never had fresh-baked bread camping before. What a great idea, Jan."

Ed's praise fires me to action; while he washes dishes, I drag out the typewriter.

"Who are you writing to?" he asks.

"*Field and Stream* magazine. I'm writing up our bannock experience. I've always wanted to see if I could get published, and with our new life starting this might be an easy way to make money."

"But *Field and Stream* does fishing and hunting stories."

"Don't you think other outdoor folks might like it too?"

"If you really want to write, why don't I take you to the National Geographic Society office in D.C.? It's only two hours back. You can tell them about our move to Alaska. Perhaps you can get an assignment."

"*National Geographic* magazine might be more than I'm ready for."

Ed insists. The next day we're on the beltway, following hordes to the nation's capital. A uniformed attendant at the *Geographic* offices insists on parking our van. He peers at our Doberman. "His name is Max," I tell him. "He's friendly."

At the head secretary's office, we wait and flip through stacks of familiar yellow magazines. I rehearse what I'm about to say. The secretary ushers us into the editor's lair. The editor rises, smiles, shakes our hands and listens politely to my story ideas. But no, no assignment at this time. I'm red-faced as we depart. "That was a bit over the top."

"Doesn't hurt to start at the top, Jan. Bet you'll be writing for *Geographic* some day."

Our parking attendant calls a younger man over. "Go get that green van," he drawls. "Talk nice to that dog in there; his name's Jaguar."

"The Doberman's name is Max," I pipe in. "If you knock on the van, he'll click his teeth. Say, 'Hi Max!' friendly-like, like you belong, and he'll wag and want you to pet him." The guy shuffles to the van, shuddering.

We reload into Greenie and head south again, back to the quiet of the Blue Ridge. Daily we hike in the hardwoods. We motor along the ridges listening to John Denver promising a Rocky Mountain high. We meander down country roads in Virginia, sleep in downy comfort, and waken to loud honking. A V-formation quacks north.

Ed climbs out of the van and walks to its dusty rear window and scratches three words.

"It's only late April," I frown.

"I'm antsy."

I squeeze his hand. "Me too."

We do a one-eighty-degree turn: "North to Alaska."

Five Thousand Miles

Quebec: tidy as starched shirts, roof edges curled provocatively like a Mona Lisa smile. I copilot, scan for wildlife and points of interest. In the cobweb of Montreal, I shout lane changes to keep us westward bound. Ontario's hills and dales, lakes and forests go on and on. I recheck the map. We've still endless hours of Ontar-eye-o-eye-o.

We camp in provincial parks. My five-foot frame shoehorns into the bed. Ed lies at an angle. We nestle like spoons in a drawer. Max snuggles by our feet.

At lakeshores we untie the canoe and float still water. My arms mirror Ed's strokes. We inhale earthy aromas of fiddleheads unfurling and leaves rotting.

We hit the plains, the interminable, plain plains; nothing to see but flat fields and grain silos. My bladder frets from morning coffee. There's nary a bush to hide behind.

Ed pulls over, jumps out the driver's side, and discreetly unzips behind the open door. I silently slide out my side, undo my belt, and drop my drawers; I use the sidewall as a road screen. Ed hops aboard and assumes I'm back getting snacks. He mats the pedal. I grab my pants with one hand and bang madly on the departing van. Ed brakes, hits reverse, laughs.

The landscape shifts oh so slowly; a white haze dusts the horizon. The further we drive, the taller the haze soars. "Rockies," says Ed.

"Unbelievable."

"You ain't seen nothing yet. Wait 'til Alaska."

"Can't imagine anything more beautiful than this." Even road signs ballyhoo beauty. Beautiful British Columbia. "Photo stop," I cry again.

"We'll never get north."

"So? This is sooo beautiful. Going somewhere?"

We stop, take walks, take pictures. We camp and while away hours with retirees in their RVs; they send us on side trips. We stand on a small bridge, watching salmon the size of breadboxes.

"Check out Kootenay Lake," salmon watchers tell us. "Ringed by snow-caps but ice-free all winter; it's the fruit oasis of British Columbia." We detour, canoe, camp, explore. Inside a Kootenay cave, hot springs soothe our travel-weary bodies. Outside, cascades of blossoms perfume the air. "Is Alaska better than this?" I ask Ed. "Why not Canada?"

"My Dad's from Nova Scotia," he muses.

"My grandparents were born in Quebec," I say.

"If Alaska doesn't suit, we'll recheck Canada."

"Deal."

Soon I see my first glaciers. "Glaciers were empty words before this," I tell Ed. "Something I studied in science class. I had no idea they were so blue. So big. I feel like an ant next to a dinosaur." My voice subsides, like in church. I stare through the viewfinder. Impossible. I let the glacier carve memories in my mind.

Back on the highway, I scream. A bighorn sheep is silhouetted against a Rocky Mountain backdrop. Ed stops the van. "Shh, Jan. Follow me," he whispers. I mimic Ed's step, quiet as cat's paws. We slip behind a rock, shoot body shots of the sheep in its mountain habitat. We advance and click head shots, the sheep chewing, yawning.

Brakes squeal. We and the sheep all cock our heads and glance roadward.

Jabbering Japanese tourists exit a bus and run at the sheep like wolves. I retreat and photograph the photographers shooting the sheep.

"Damn. My Nikon froze."

"No worry. We'll hit the next big town." Ed studies the map and frowns. "Nothing looks promising until we reach the Yukon. Whitehorse the capital must have a repair center."

In the Whitehorse camera shop, I share my tale of woe and get laughter.

"What's so funny," I say, miffed.

"I should pay that sheep; great for business. Yesterday, some American told me how he'd stopped to photograph a bighorn. He clicked away while his wife stayed in the car, hand outstretched pretending she had treats. Sheep walked up, sniffed, backed up, then roared forward with full curl lowered. Stove in the side door. Husband kept shooting to prove what happened to the insurance, but his camera quit. Shutter stuck, exactly like yours."

Repairs complete, we continue to Carcross, watch waterfalls plummet off cliff faces, and cross Klondike Pass. One hundred ten miles later, we kiss the border. Alaska at last.

PART TWO

Forget-me-not
(Myosotis alpestris)

"Go to the dump," Fred tells us.
"The dump?"
"Yes, find a few metal rods. Then go to the valley
and pick out the land you want.
Stake the corners. Make a map.
Then come back and we'll sign the papers."

In the Panhandle ⁓

Skagway, at the north end of the Alaska panhandle, is Tlingit for "the place where the North Wind blows." The town looks like a television Western, complete with false storefronts, funky logwork, and a dusty main drag. Dolly's Bordello now serves as saloon; its sawdust floor catches chew spit by the mangy crew at the bar. In the street, ladies trot their pony-trap. My unstuck shutter gets a workout. Even the café signs deserve film, like the one where Skagway gangster Soapy Smith advertises square deals at Northern Lites Café. Ed heads inside.

"We already ate," I protest.

Ed points to the fine print. "Pie. One of the four food groups, Jan. Haven't had my fruit yet."

After apple pie, we head to Liar's Camp. A policeman raps on the van door. "You can't camp here."

"It's a campground, isn't it?"

"Yes, but Governor Hammond's coming in the morning with the legislators to dedicate the official opening of the Klondike Highway. Everyone has to exit so we can set up pavilions."

"What about over there?" Ed points to the campground edge. "We'll camp out of the way."

"Suppose so."

"And could you give us a wake-up call in the morning," asks Ed, "so we can attend?"

At seven, the cop knocks. We breakfast, then dress in our Sunday best, and join the festivities. Politicians celebrate completion of the highway linking Alaska and Canada, then shift discussion to relocating Alaska's capital city. Juneau, they say, is the only American capital inaccessible by road. "The legislative offices should move to Willow, forty miles north of

Anchorage, so that there's easy highway access," a senator explains.

Hammond has a different take on things. "Rather than move the capital," he says, "let's have a moving capital. Put it on a ferry, so everyone has access."

We warm to the governor's wit. "Some of the politicians look snarky," says Ed, "but Hammond's a good egg. The kind of man you'd like to have over for supper. Genuinely seems to care about this state."

Post-ceremony, we wander through town, then board the Malaspina for transport across Lynn Canal to Haines. The 400-foot, 8,000-horsepower ship is one in Alaska's floating highway fleet, moving people, vehicles, and goods to three dozen Southeast communities.

We drive onto the ramp, squeeze into the hold, then scramble upstairs to buffet restaurants, viewing lounges, a solarium, and educational displays. During the two-hour crossing, I keep wiping my eyes. "All this . . . eagles, whales, mountains. My eyes keep leaking. I'm so glad we're living now."

In Haines, we camp at Chilkat Lake. "Exactly how I imagined Alaska," I say. "Picture perfect peaks, wildflowers against snow, glassy lake."

"Grab a paddle. Let's do the lake."

At lake's end, we park the boat and scout the beach. "These plants look a bit like garden peas," I muse. "I wonder if we can eat them."

"We'd best grab a book in town; make sure," Ed counsels.

"That author we read, Angier, insisted there were lots of great wild foods up north. Didn't have much motivation to learn them in New Hampshire with our big garden, but perhaps now we'll have time. It would be great to have some fresh greens in our diet."

"And fresh fish," adds Ed.

"Now that looks promising. Look at these fish heads on this beach."

Ed peers closer. "Check out these tracks next to them; they're big as dinner plates."

"Plates with claws. Doesn't that mean . . ."

"Grizzlies. Let's boogie."

We race to the canoe. On the water, the wind is nervous. Whitecaps crest. We power into the strokes. "I feel like one of those cartoon characters, Ed. Going full tilt and going nowhere."

"Paddle harder."

Waves roil and crest over the bow. Ed leans forward like a jockey and paddles furiously. Our canoe creeps, gains an inch, and then another. I swear my arms will fall off. We keep at it. The green dome of our tent appears. Max wags us welcome.

We rest and then head to town for supplies. At the harbor, I photograph a fisherman hefting king crab from his skiff. "I'd give anything for one of those," I tell him.

"Got ten bucks?"

Next stop is butter and beer, then the campfire, with water on the boil. "Can life be any finer, Ed?" I ask, stuffing a final buttery morsel.

Haines holds us for a week. We chat up locals at the sourdough pizza parlor, find hot spots for fishing Dolly Varden, a Northwest cousin to our favorite Eastern brook trout. In Charles Dickens's *Barnaby Rudge,* Dolly Varden was a flirt who loved green dresses with pink dots. The fishy Dolly Varden sports a greenish body with pink dots. "Fish and Game once had a bounty on Dolly Varden tails," we're told, "to exterminate Dollies 'cuz they eat salmon eggs. Well hell, salmon eat salmon eggs. Bounty stopped in 1941, after they killed off more than six million."

At our Chilkat Lake campsite, we fish and feast on Dollies, rest and relax. We lean back on our blanket and gawk at mountain goats scrambling on the slopes. We hike through meadows ablaze with purple lupine.

"Lakes, sea: Haines has it all. Perhaps we should hang around Southeast," I suggest. "I heard that a cannery in Tenakee Springs needs a caretaker."

"Where's that?" Ed asks.

"I looked it up in the guidebook; it's on Chichagof Island forty-five miles southwest of Juneau. The town's famous for its 108-degree sulfur hot spring."

Ed finds a pay phone and calls the owner. "He already has someone, Jan."

"Okay," I sigh. "Maybe we should check out more of Alaska first. We can always come back." I stare dumbly at the map as Ed traces the route of the Haines Highway across British Columbia's tail, then into the body of the Yukon. He measures. "It's about eight hundred miles from Haines to Anchorage."

"Unreal. You drive two hundred miles north in New Hampshire and you're in French Quebec."

"Big country, Jan. Do you realize that if you superimposed Alaska on the Lower 48, it'd cover one-fifth of its landmass? The distance from Barrow to the southern Panhandle is like the span from Maine to Florida; and the Aleutian Islands would reach all the way to California."

"Never learned that in geography class. It's so different being here, seeing it firsthand."

"In the Yukon, all you've tasted is Whitehorse. The Yukon's as big as all the New England states combined. Its population is only 25,000, and half of that is in Whitehorse city."

"Amazing. I feel like I've lived my life in a cage, and am tasting the jungle. I wonder what else is in store."

North to Alaska Again ～

In the Yukon, the van's thirsty again. Throughout the trip, thirty bucks have topped the tank. Now the meter spins like a game wheel. Forty, fifty, sixty, sixty-five, seventy. "Holy cow."

"Holy wallet, Jan."

An hour later, we stall in construction. I grab a novel and read aloud.

"Hey, you." A stranger stands outside gesturing wildly.

Ed rolls down the window. "Gas," he points, "under your van."

Ed looks. Our dollars are pouring into the earth. He grabs the toolbox, "Pliers. Hammer. Nails. Wire. Damn. Ah, two-step putty." He stuffs the goop into the hole and stops the leak.

In the provincial park, travelers Jerry and Alice invite us for tea and talk. "We'd best get some shut-eye," yawns Ed later that evening. We're barely asleep when the van shakes.

"An earthquake, Ed?"

"Could be a bear," he whispers.

"But wait, the bear's yelling!"

Ed grabs his pants and opens to Alice, her face as pale as paper.

"Jerry. He's passed out."

We race to the camper. Jerry's pulse is thready, hardly palpable. "He needs a doc, pronto," says Ed.

I check the map. "Not good. Must be a hundred miles to nearest medical services."

Alice and I sit by Jerry while Ed drives the RV. The road's like corrugated roofing. The camper skids round the gravel turns.

At 2 A.M., we knock frantically on emergency service doors. The nurse tells us to bring in the patient. Jerry's like a beached whale. Ed half carries, half drags him into the clinic. The nurse returns two hours later, with a still-shaky Jerry. "Whitehorse," she says. "Tomorrow. He needs more tests."

We pack Jerry back into the motor-home bed and return to the campground. Alice drops us off and races to the hospital with the camper and Jerry. We grab sleep in our van, and then continue on our Yukon way.

More shock comes at the grocery. Food is triple British Columbia prices. "Let's get a bag of spuds, Ed; we'll eat spuds and catch fish. The Yukon must be teeming with fish." I point to the wall map. "Here's a lake perfect for tonight. We can launch the canoe, then fish and feast."

Ed forks out fistfuls of cash for nonresident fishing licenses. But as we ascend in altitude, spring rewinds. Two-story drifts surround our campsite. "No ice auger, Jan. Can't fish."

"Mashed spuds, okay?"

"It will have to be." Morning descent brings the return of spring. We sit riveted as a bald eagle swoops, skims the river, lifts off with a twenty-pound salmon locked in his talons.

Then Ed brakes for bear. A black sow roots by road's edge with twin cubs. I roll down my window and shoot with my telephoto: Bear by the willow shrub. Click. Bear stares at us. Click. Cubs climb tree. Click. Bear hair in the air. Click. Bear eyes fill the viewfinder. What? I duck as the bear stands and swipes. Ed mats the pedal.

"What the hell was that?"

"She must have felt threatened."

"But we parked way back."

"Think we'd better master bear lingo; she was one mad mama."

Our next cranky bear is at milepost 1221. In the customs officer's sunglasses I see reflected a bearded man, long-haired woman, Doberman.

"Everybody out, including that dog."

The van is like a well-fitted ship with countless cubbyholes. The officer pokes through dishes, food, clothes, and cameras. He opens the upper cabinet and smiles: leafy green aromatic plants.

"Dry mint for tea," I explain. "That one is pizza seasoning. Echinacea for colds and flu. Soup spice. Rosemary." He sniffs like a bloodhound, then surrenders grumpily. "You can go."

We high five. We're back to Alaska again.

Zig or Zag ⌁

From Tok, Alaska, we've options... paved Highway 1 toward Anchorage, or Gravel 5 through the eastern Interior.

"Which way, Jan?"

"The bird towns. Let's check out Chicken and Eagle."

The autobiography *Tisha* has been our nightly reading. It's the true story of nineteen-year-old Oregon teacher Anne Hobbs who, in 1927, accepted a job in the remote Native village of Chicken, Alaska. The town's odd name, we read, honors Alaska's "wild chicken," the feather-footed ptarmigan. And "Tisha" is the students' pronunciation of "teacher." We're fascinated by Anne's challenges, and by her developing love story with the kids, the land, and with Eagle local Fred Purdy. We're keen to see Tisha's home turf. As we drive, the van is blanketed in dust. "This is one of Alaska's main highways?" I ask.

"Yes, and open summer only. I read that Alaska has over half a million square miles and only around two thousand miles of road. So much space you could be lost forever."

A truck is parked on a curve. Two women haul water from a creek. Ed stops and rolls down the window. "Need help?"

"Oh no," says the elder. "My daughter Lynn and I are well used to this. But thanks. I'm Tisha," she says, extending her hand.

"Tisha from Chicken?" Alaska's not so big after all.

Tisha quizzes us on our plans. "Alaska's a great place," she says. "But get out of the Interior in winter unless you like fifty below."

We say good-byes, then look at each other, questioning.

"Hell," I mutter. "Fifty below."

"Hell's hot, Janzie. Maybe we're getting too far north."

"Let's check Eagle, Ed. We've come this far. It's only," I pause, while glancing at the map, "another sixty miles or so. This Taylor highway ends there by the mighty Yukon River."

Signs in Eagle, Alaska, glare: "Park Service employees not welcome here." On Main Street, a drunk staggers. "Doesn't feel homey, Ed. But I'm knackered. It's only 4 P.M. but let's camp. Make it an early night."

We camp at Fort Egbert, an old army post established in 1899 to keep the peace during the Klondike gold rush. Over campfire supper, Ed toasts. "June first, Janzie. Welcome to summer in Alaska."

"What's that white?"

"Must be down from those cottonwood trees, Jan."

"But it's cold white."

"Crap. Snowflakes. Ouch. Something bit me."

"Me too. Look at the size of this. Bloody mosquito is big enough to carve steaks from."

"Let's go, Jan."

"Bed, already?"

"No. Pack it up. Going south."

"But I'm tired."

"Me too. Of this. Taking you to Shangri-la."

"The islands?"

"No," Ed laughs. "Homer. The Shangri-la of Alaska. Where the road ends and the sea begins."

"But it's over five hundred miles from here."

"I know. So we'd best get moving."

End of the Road ⁓

Throughout May, we've crept at a turtle's pace; now Ed's a mad hare. He mats the pedal and blazes south, toward Anchorage. Alaska's largest city brings traffic lights, the first we've seen in the state. I glance at my watch. "Midnight? It's still broad daylight. How much further, Ed?"

"Another five hours to Homer."

As we drive Alaska Highway 1, I flatten my nose to the window, and gaze at Turnagain Arm, the northeastern end of Cook Inlet. "So beautiful."

"This, Jan, is where Captain Cook looked for a Northwest Passage. He had to 'turn again.'"

"Wonder if we'll turn again, or if this is the end of the road for us?"

Two hundred twenty miles later, we reach Baycrest hill; Ed swerves into the Homer overlook and turns off the van. Below us spread pastures wild with flowers, spruce-green islands, snowcapped ranges punctuated by ice-blue glaciers and the vistas of Kachemak Bay. "See that that skinny finger poking into the bay?" Ed points. "The guidebook calls that Homer Spit; and writes that it's the longest road into ocean waters in the world. On that four-and-a-half-mile sand spit sits the harbor, shops, and most important, a beachfront campground. Let's head there."

We drive to the campground and park at water's edge. Gulls squawk. Eagles scream. Seals splash in the surf. Our need for sleep wrestles with euphoria. We're high on Homer.

Morning brings exploration of town. "Architecture's not like New England," Ed complains. "No dormers, cupolas, or class."

"I expected Alaskan houses to be mainly log, or at least Western like Skagway. Not a mess of plywood, metal, and *that*." *That* is the Last Chance junkyard piled with debris in central downtown.

We cruise East Road in Homer, struggling to see beyond broken bulldozers, rusty barrels, and derelict boats to the glaciers and mountain backdrop. Occasional log homes bring smiles from Ed. After Fritz Creek, pavement gives ways to gravel, which deteriorates mile by mile. Nature gains ground. Human impacts lessen. Twin glaciers rivet our attention.

At road's end, Ed stops by parked cars. "Turn again time, Jan." A ponytailed person leans over the fenders of an ancient Volkswagen. "Looks like that gal needs help."

"Need a jump?" asks Ed. The person stands and spins, revealing a warm grin and wispy beard.

"Fritz's battery is a dead duck. I'm Dave, spelled D-E-I-V."

Ed jump-starts Fritz and conversation.

"Awesome land around here. Any for sale?"

Deiv points to a hayfield with a glacier backdrop. "Jones has that up for grabs. Pretty cheap I think; about nine an acre."

"Nine hundred, that'd do us."

"You dreaming? Nine thousand of course."

"My land in New Hampshire was seven hundred an acre when I bought it. And it's a heap closer to services."

"This is Alaska."

"Exactly; there's so much land here. Should be cheap."

"Only 2 percent is privately owned; everything else is state, federal or Native."

"Those books we read by survivalist Bradford Angier about dirt cheap land in the wilderness must be a bit outdated."

"No kidding. Hey, you folks sound like you're from back East. There's a singer, think he's from New Hampshire, a Bill Staines, he'll be playing at Mossy Kilcher's barn at Seaside Farm."

"Bill Staines? He's in Homer? We kept trying to see him before leaving New Hampshire."

"You can meet him tomorrow at the potluck. Drive to 5 Mile East Road. Look for the green mailbox with the horses on it."

"Couldn't bust the party."

"Everyone's welcome. Bring a dish or something to drink. There'll be lots of music, and a short meeting about the subsistence fishery."

"What's that?"

"The personal use fishery; folks set out a net each year to harvest their winter salmon. Fish and Game's trying to change the rules. Marty, the local lawyer, will explain all about it, what we can do."

"Great meeting you, Deiv. See you tomorrow at Kilcher's."

The potluck brings luck. We hear Bill's folksy music, and meet Mairiis Kilcher, better known as Mossy. "Where are you folks staying?" Mossy asks.

"Our van. We'd like to spend time in Homer, but land here's too expensive for us."

"What about caretaking? I've a place at the head of Kachemak Bay, three miles beyond road's end at the school bus turnaround. I'd like to have somebody watch over it."

"What's the rent?"

"No rent; help with a few chores. The fence needs mending; the outhouse needs a new hole. I'd like to send a few horses out there to graze, but need someone to keep an eye on them. I'll jot you a map. You can take a hike out tomorrow to see the place."

Beyond the Skull Gate ⌇

We drive to the school bus turnaround, and hike a narrow gravel track to Rainwater cattle ranch. Ed studies Mossy's map and motions ahead. "This must be the trail." We step through a creek and scramble up a bank. Plants tower above us, bearing gargantuan leaves. "Is that rhubarb?" Ed asks. "It's tall as a horse."

I peer closely. "Can't be rhubarb. The stems are hairy. Wonder what it is."

"The map says the Skull Gate is next," reads Ed. We walk forward in mystery, until we finally spot a gate; on it hang skulls of long-dead cattle. "Didn't know Alaska was cowboy country, Jan." The death gate opens to fields of life—broccoli, barley, cabbage, potatoes. An army-style wall tent sits at the garden's edge; smoke pours from its chimney. We halloo loudly. Deiv pokes his head out and waves us inside.

A potpourri of smells hit my nose; pine, poultry, pancakes. My eyes rake the room. A kettle on the wood stove emits smells like Pine-Sol cleaner. A chicken in the corner nests on hay. Hotcakes fry on the griddle.

Deiv grabs stacks of *Mother Earth News* from upended stumps and clears three seats. "Hungry? Got plenty." He lifts plates from the plywood shelf and fills them with flapjacks. He fills three mugs.

I sniff suspiciously; floor cleaner in a cup?

Ed takes a sip and puckers his lips. "Turpentine."

Deiv laughs. "Spruce tip tea. Good for ya. Plenty of vitamin C."

My eyes fix on the sleeping bag lying across the back wall. "Is this where you live?"

"For now. I was caretaking Bennett's cabin here on Wind Point. Lost it last year in a chimney fire. I'm cutting logs for a new one. I'll put it up this winter."

"Where will you live while you build?" asks Ed.

"Here" says Deiv. "This is home."

"Will this be the first cabin you've built?"

"Yes, but I've been reading . . . "

"*Mother Earth News* . . . " I pipe in.

Deiv nods.

"Ed built a log home," I tell him.

"Cool. Maybe I can get some tips sometimes."

Ed nods. "I'd be happy to help."

After tea, Deiv guides us to the bluff. "The track you want goes there," he points.

There drops into space. Deiv strides to the eroding edge. "You can see Mossy's cabin from here." Ed steps forward gingerly.

"That red roof?"

"Yep, that's the cabin. I've got a garden going down there too; you guys can have it. I'll be down in a bit to show you what's what. Follow the hogback track; can't miss it."

We plummet off the cliff edge and wind down the narrow track with steep sloping sides. My knees brake and ache with each step. Our bodies vanish in roses.

"Wonder what that is?" I muse. A white-flowered shrub is at eye level. Its lower leaf edges are smooth; the middle to top have teeth. "If only I knew what it was."

Lower down, a cottonwood grove fills with flutelike trills, the song of the hermit thrush. In the meadow sits a log home by the sea, with snowcapped views. We step through the unlocked door into an arctic entry, a small anteroom off the main cabin. In it is a bin for wood, another for coal. Boxes on the wall bear air vents screened to the outside: the cabin refrigerator? We park our butts on a slab bench under the window and obey the sign tacked on the inner door: "Please remove shoes before entering."

The main room is a rectangle. A table parks by the picture window; the view is a postcard: meadows, mountains, beach, bay, glaciers. Inside are red cabinet doors and a couch, a black propane cooktop, and a white coal range. Adjacent the kitchen is a room with a double bed and a cold storage closet.

Outside are an old shop, decaying barn, and tilted outhouse facing the trees.

We sit in the field, heads on swivel. Red-roofed cabin, cottonwoods, bluff, beach: all this to caretake free of charge. We've endless water fresh from Swift Creek, more money than ever before in our lives. And more time too.

Deiv appears, and interrupts our reverie. He takes us to a six-foot fence. "Moose fence," he says. "Moose love cabbage." He points to cabbages, cauliflowers, potatoes, and peas. "You can have all this except these fava beans I'm trying out."

"Don't see any tomatoes," I say.

"You need a greenhouse to grow them. Problem here is cool soil, cool summers. Tomatoes like hot."

"If it's so cold in summer, winter must be horrid."

"Nah, Japan currents warm things up. Average winter temps are teens to twenty."

"Below? That's what we had in New Hampshire last winter."

"No," Deiv laughs, "above zero. Once in a blue moon we go below."

"And snow?"

"Might be three or four feet on Wind Point, up where I'm at, maybe a dusting down here."

"But they're only a ten minute walk apart."

"Elevation. Eight hundred feet makes a world of difference."

Deiv departs. We sit at the window and watch our world of difference. "Feels like entering a time warp," says Ed. "Everything's speeded up and slowed down. Yankees take forever to accept strangers; here we're new kids in town and all we get are open doors. People have time for each other." Ed lights his pipe. "So Jan, what do you think?"

"It's a no-brainer, Ed. This is everything we hoped for. Let's get back to town, tell Mossy yes, we'll definitely caretake the cabin."

Swift Creek Creations 〜

Moving day arrives. We tuck the van in the overgrown grass by the school bus turnaround. Deiv meets us with Sam and Toklat, draft-style horses who bear wooden frames shaped like an X. We load our life on the horses: typewriter, chain saw, books, tools, clothes, food, and kitchenware. The equines clang their way along the track, vanish into space over the cliff, and plod surefooted down the hogback to the beach.

Mossy's horse Gretchen arrives a week later. My head reels at the weird workings of fate. In place of Vibes, my half-Morgan, is a full-blooded Morgan imported from New Hampshire. With Gretchen comes stablemate Leila. "Get weight off Leila," Mossy warns. "She's far too fat. Ride her as much as you possibly can."

We're keen to oblige. On horseback we explore our new surroundings. From our cabin at the head of Kachemak Bay we discover twenty miles of beach between us and town. The horses love their low-tide explorations and virtually endless exposed beach. As we ride, my eyes flit from north-shore sandstone bluffs towering eight stories above us to the startling contrast a mere seven miles across the bay. The Kenai Mountain backdrop dazzles us with its lush spruce understory and 3,500-foot snowcapped mountains cut by icy, blue-tongued glaciers. We ride, gawking, until Ed notices that our football field–wide beach is rapidly vanishing. And the bluffs, poking nosily into the bay, are lapped by waves. We gallop frantically for home.

East of us lies yet more vast land, and more lessons. The Fox River flats—the flood plain where the Fox and Bradley rivers and Sheep Creek converge—is simple going at low tide, but its gullies fill swiftly as the tide turns, requiring swimming or jumping our steeds. We quickly learn regard for the Kachemak Bay tides, with their dramatic rise of up to twenty-eight feet in six hours.

Our Swift Creek cabin nestles a hundred feet back from the sea, flanked by bluffs, and fronted by fenced meadows. Feeding our hard-working horses is easy. Feed is free: the abundant summer pasture outside the door.

Chores are easy. Each morning we walk across the meadow with two five-gallon buckets, weave between shrubs to the creek, plunge the buckets in a deep hole, and scramble up the bank with eighty pounds of fluid. Ten gallons are sufficient for the day's cooking, dishwashing, and solar showers.

Breakfast is porridge or crunchy muesli with grated apple. Afterward we weed the garden, beach-walk with Max, and explore with the horses. Then Leila gets locked in her barren prison pen while Gretchen gets free-range grazing rights. We pick fresh greens from the garden and dig clams from the beach.

I journal daily and help Ed with projects. He shifts the outhouse to a new hole and orients it to the glaciers. With its half-door, the view is unimpeded. "Great place to sit," says Ed. "Love the morning constitutional."

Another project is weatherization for winter. "Homesteaders were in a hurry to get a roof over their heads," Ed notes. He thrusts his knuckles through a gap between the logs. "She'd be might nippy like this. But we'll set her right." He chinks the gaps with wads of insulation, then nestles thick rope to aesthetically hide the fix.

Alder trees become legs for a long kitchen bench. Ed cleans the old shed, retrofits an abandoned barrel stove he found there, and installs it. "We'll be snug as bunnies in a den."

Outside we explore beach and bluffs and wonder more what these strange plants are. "Where can I get a book on Alaska's plants?" I ask Deiv.

"Cooperative Extension Service," he says, and pulls a small book from his shelf. The Extension Service pocket guide is a fine start, but I keep getting stumped. Is that line drawing the same plant I've been looking at? My specimen is young and lacks flowers. Will it look like the line drawing in the book when it's older? Or is this something else? I chomp for more facts other than "can be cooked as a green vegetable." How do I do that? Do I use only leaves or are the stems okay too? Is there any part of the plant I should avoid?

Smelling the plants triggers memories—me as a kid playing in nature, catching squirrels by the tail, releasing snakes painted with mom's lipstick to see if I could find them again, and my questions to Dad, as I'd bring plants home from the vacant lot next door: "What's this red berry? What's this smelly leaf?"

And always and forever, Dad would answer: "I don't know. Don't put it in your mouth."

And now at Swift Creek, there are gaggles of green friends to know, and blessed time to explore. If only I had answers to my twenty thousand questions.

Lost in the Jungle ⁓

Swift Creek routines include fortnightly shopping sprees in Homer. We buy grains at Homer Natural, then hit the bookshop. "I'd like a book on Alaskan plants," I tell owner Joy Post.

"The Cooperative Extension Service booklet."

"Already have it. I need something with more depth."

"Have you read Michael Moore's *Medicinal Plants of the Mountain West?*"

"I wanted something on Alaskan edibles."

"I don't know of any books purely for Alaska," Joy says. "There are Canadian books and they have some Alaskan plants in them."

I check the library and borrow the Canadian publications. I hunt and peck to decipher Alaskan species. At Swift Creek, I weed Mossy's flowerbed while Deiv chats. "Ouch," I wince. "What the heck bit me?"

"Nettles," Deiv chortles. "Cook them up like spinach. They're great."

"Sure. And what else do you eat, nails for breakfast?"

"Cooking tames the sting," insists Deiv. "Nettles are great as a veg or dried as tea. Chuck 'em in your soup. Eat them when they're young like this, under a foot high. Later you can find young ones hiding in the shady areas. Come on up to my tent tonight; I'll treat you to gingered nettles and a Thai stir-fry."

The meal is awesome. The next day, I bravely pile nettles into my basket, pick eggs from the Swift Creek hens, and make a nettle quiche. Ed tastes and smiles. Max wails into his bowl and wags.

Mossy shows me elder flowers and tells me they make a fine tea for colds. "And you can chop the flowers and add them to pancakes, or dip the cluster in egg, roll it in seasoned flour, and deep fry." I whip up a batch of elder tempura. "Not certain if I liked them," says Ed. "Why don't you do them again."

I do. He repeats the request.

I repeat the recipe. Ed repeats.

"What's that wild rhubarblike plant?" I ask Mossy.

"Pushki. Some folks call it cow parsnip or wild parsley. My parents made soups with the peeled stem and unopened buds."

The fragrant, white-flowered shrub I wondered about on my first day at Swift Creek now has a name: serviceberry. Deiv invites us for a Wind Point brunch of serviceberry crepes.

"I canned these fruits last season; you'll be able to pick heaps on the hogback. They make great pie too." Ed's eyes light up.

Mossy visits and tells us she's launching horse treks. She'll trial the first overnight next week at Swift Creek and take folks on an eighteen-mile beach ride on her herd of Morgans. We announce we'll vacate for the weekend.

"Not necessary."

"But we've been wanting to go check out Seldovia across the bay," says Ed. "This will be a perfect time, and give you your space. We'll take a holiday."

The Land Beyond ～·

We book passage on the Tustemena, an Alaska state ferry similar to the Skagway boat. This ship's weekly route services Valdez, Kodiak Island, Homer, Seward, and Seldovia. The *Tustemena,* locals tell us, was once hauled out, cut in half, extended in size, and remolded together. She's now a solid "Trusty Tusty" but in bad seas she rocks and rolls, earning her less-flattering nickname, "The Dramamine Express."

Seldovia, our destination, is a town of five hundred, accessible only by air or sea. "When I was a kid," says Mossy, "ocean was highway and Seldovia was city; it had the hospital where I was born and all the major services and shops. When Sterling Highway was built, linking Homer with Anchorage, Homer boomed and Seldovia lost ground."

Events in 1964 further undermined Seldovia's position. The Good Friday quake that year crucified communities with forces equivalent to twelve thousand Hiroshima-sized bombs. Downtown Anchorage schools, business, homes, and roads crumpled to rubble. A seven-story tsunami washed away the Valdez pier, killing thirty-five people. In five seconds, Kodiak waters rose fifteen feet. The quake registered as the world's second largest. Only its timing on a holiday weekend, with folks being at home and away from the hardest-hit business districts, saved countless lives.

Immediately after the quake, Seldovia appeared to have been lucky; its coastal buildings stood tall on their pilings along the boardwalk Main Street. But fall tides brought angst. Waters that had previously lapped below canneries and homes now poured into them. Waves laughed at sandbags piled by the doors. Studies revealed that Seldovia's ground level had been lowered six feet by the quake.

Residents who wanted to raise buildings and maintain the town's character battled with the Corps of Engineers–funded razers. As hills were blasted and historic buildings fell, nearly half the residents fled in protest. Seldovia of yesteryear, we hear, exists only along lower Main Street, with residues of boardwalk and old-style homes perched atop piers. We're eager to see this community beyond road's end.

Weather delays the *Tusty* and we arrive in Seldovia in the wee hours. Ferry locals direct us to Outside Beach to camp. We cram into the van bed and fall asleep to a foggy backdrop and the crash of surf.

We waken to clear, blue skies. I sit up to face a snowcapped peak towering above a white range. "Mount McKinley, Ed. Mount McKinley!" I bob like a jumping bean, rapt to see Alaska's biggest mountain.

Fishing Seldovians correct my geography. "Nah. Only Mount Iliamna, a piddling twelve thousand feet." It's one of the active volcanoes across Cook Inlet, part of the Ring of Fire that rims the Pacific Ocean.

Ed quizzes locals catching sea-run Dollies. "The secret is pink pixies," he tells me. He runs to buy lures inset with plastic replicas of salmon eggs. Soon fresh fish sizzles next to eggs over easy.

Along the dump road, Ed frowns at roadside clear-cuts. "Aren't those blueberry shrubs?" I ask, pointing at the underbrush. "We'll have to come back later this summer."

The road dead-ends; we motor back through town, and out the other fork. We track Jakolof Bay Road, past MacDonald Spit, to an old logging mill; a sign proclaims "end of state maintained road." A drivable track continues. We motor up a switchback, along a cliff-face. Waterfalls cascade into culverts. We cross log bridges; the valley widens. We pass lakes and meadows blazing flowers. Ed pulls into a roadside clearing. We camp, lulled by river song.

Morning brings more driving and meanders. "Look at that, Janzie. Let's check out that waterfall." We squeeze through snarls of alders, and step into a meadow purple with lupine. Ancient spruce line the river's edge.

"Nothing like this back East, Jan. Except for alpine areas, our meadows are manmade."

"And if you don't keep critters grazing them, they revert back to woods. This is God's work, Ed. A natural field, full of flowers."

"With that waterfall in front of us . . . "

"And mountains around us," I add.

"Home." says Ed. "Let's buy this."

"I wonder who owns it. Do you think they might want to sell?"

"Let's find out."

Townies tell us the land along Rocky River is owned by Seldovia Native Association. The entire valley is Native land; title switches to Port Graham Natives at Boundary Creek, a few miles beyond our selection.

"The land's not for sale," says Fred Elvsaas, the Native Chief and corporation president. Our lips curve in disappointment. "But we have a leasing program," continues Fred.

Lease land? We've so much to learn about Alaskan land programs. There are state land disposal sales, land lotteries, and Native leases. Buying private land is but one of many options.

"Go to the dump," Fred tells us.

"The dump?"

"Yes, find a few metal rods. Then go to the valley and pick out the land you want. Stake the corners. Make a map. Then come back and we'll sign the papers."

Ed glances at me then nods to Fred.

We return to Rocky River and walk the land. "How much do we stake, Ed? How much can we afford?"

"It's all wild around us, Jan. Thousands of acres of Kachemak Bay State Wilderness Park behind us. All we need is a footprint, enough land for our cabin logs and firewood."

"Rocky River is the obvious east boundary; the road the west. That old skid road makes a good driveway and marker."

"Could end this line here," says Ed as he leans against a grandfather spruce, draped with moss.

"How old would you say he is?"

"Three hundred years at least."

"Imagine standing here by the waterfall, listening to river music, for over three centuries. Makes us feel like young pups, doesn't it?"

We walk and diagram. Ed includes the high meadow with waterfall view; a river-hugging low meadow, and a third wildflower meadow abutting the drive.

Back in town, Fred studies and calculates: "Two point five acres; remote parcels are valued at $3,000 per acre. There are different options, depending on how much you want to put down and how much you're willing to pay yearly."

We choose the high down, low annual lease. Ed hands the chief a check: $2,200. Fred hands us a lease, with terms to pay $235 each year to the tribe. The lease is valid for fifty-five years and is renewable, sellable, and transferable.

"What about property taxes?" I inquire, worried. The memory of our annual $3,000 Maples tax bill for Blueberry Hill triggers my anxiety.

"Property tax? Should run about twenty-five."

"Hundred?"

"What?" exclaims Fred. "Twenty-five dollars." I exhale. Ed asks about stipulations.

"You must survey the land within a year," Fred tells him.

"What about firewood and building materials?"

"Cut what you need."

"What about building codes?" Fred replies with a blank look. "Build what you want as you want."

"No permits?"

Fred shakes his head.

"What about septic systems?" persists Ed.

"Build an outhouse."

Ed clams up. We do a fifty-mile roundtrip to Stampers Market for a celebratory bottle of wine. Back at Rocky River, we walk around the property, and note relationship to sun and windbreaks. We stand and feel locations. We return again and again to the high meadow with the waterfall view.

Ed analyzes trees for potential cabin logs. "Check this tree, Janzie; place your eye here. See?"

"Look's pretty good."

"Nah. That's one's crooked. Look like this." He demonstrates again.

"Compare it to this; this one's good enough for the king's arrow." Ed explains how in New Hampshire, Yankee settlers carved marks on the straightest, clearest trees, saving them for masts for the king's navy.

I sight his chosen spruce and whistle in appreciation. Then my nose drops to the ground. "Smell this, Ed; wild roses. And look, here's a few unopened fiddlehead ferns. We can eat these for dinner."

We search the river pools, peering for fish. "River this clear back East would be loaded with trout. Too bad it's empty."

Ed scoops the water to his lips. "Look at the bright side, Jan. No fish poo to worry about."

We simmer fiddleheads, steep spruce tip tea, boil water for pasta, and chat round the campfire. In the spring, we'll return to Rocky River and build a cabin.

"How much do you think it will cost for our house, Eddy? Will we need a mortgage?"

"Nah, Janzie. There are enough trees for all the walls and rafters. Should take about three to finish her off."

"Three thousand; our own home free and clear? We'll have money to tide us over while we develop other streams of income."

"We'll return later this summer, Jan. We'll bring the chain saw and fell the trees. Have to season the logs before building, or window and door openings will get hung up as logs shrink and walls settle. But right now we'd best get our butts back to Seldovia. Ferry's due in three hours."

"Already? The week flew by. And what a week."

Return to Swift Creek ~

Weather and tides are the true ferry timetable; the ship comes when she comes. Ed passes time, wets his line on Outside Beach. I kill hours wandering in the tide pools. Ed cleans a Dolly and adds it to the ice chest. I scout seaweeds, observe crabs decked with algae. I then walk the shore, Cooperative Extension book in one hand, open bag in the other. I study the illustrations, comparing carefully to what's on the beach. From what I'm reading, Alaska's seaside plants tend to be quite safe. I slowly pick a salad of vivid green beach greens *(Hockenya peploides)* and bluish-gray oyster leaf *(Mertensia maritima).*

With yet another fish flapping on the line, Ed reels in as the *Tustemena* appears. We load up, head to Seldovia proper, and queue up for the ferry. The *Tusty's* gate clangs down, along with a realization: the ferry, too, is part of the Rocky River routine-to-be. Foot passengers in backpacks meander off, then trucks, cars, and cargo stream off. Hands finally wave us on, and point to the lane where we're to park.

Ignition off, we climb stairs after stairs to the solarium; a horn blast signals departure. We stand at the rail, binoculars in hand, watching the dance of life as rafts of sea otters float in the kelp by Yukon Island. At Homer we wait again as *Tusty* docks, anchors lines, and the intercom cries:

"Will all drivers please descend to the car deck." We squash in the sea of bodies surging into the ship's hold. Ferry staff point and wave, direct exiting vehicles. We join the parade exiting onto the Spit dock. Tourists swarm like wasps. Congestion stings and shatters the repose of Rocky River.

We blast through Homer, grabbing petrol and grub. At Homer Natural, Ed bags nuts and chocolate-covered apricots. At the bus turnaround, we strap on our backpacks and hike homeward.

The trailside greenery grows more familiar. The jumbled jungle of plants now has some distinct names and faces. I recognize red elder, the shrubs locals call "Alaskan lilacs" and botanists dub *Sambucus racemosa.* I spot the Hercules-sized cow parsnip *(Heracleum lanatum)* and am now aware it's edible if handled with tender loving care, but vengeful in sunlight, its juices punishing the culprit with hard-to-heal burns.

Past the Skull Gate, Deiv works his gardens. He sets down the hoe, invites us for tea and tidbits; then we head down the hogback to our sweet Swift Creek routines.

All's well except for Leila. She's a balloon. "We'd best get serious about her diet, Ed. I'll pen her by day, and pasture her out late when the sugars in the grasses are less intense."

Despite my diligence, Leila grows fatter still. When I go to fetch her from nightly pasture, Gretchen's at the gate, but no Leila.

"Someone's stolen Leila!"

"Oh Jan, a thief would have taken both. Check out this loose wire and these tracks." Prints lead to the beach. Galloping hooves head townward. "Do you think she went back to Seaside Farm?"

"Don't know. Must have been sick of our diet program."

An eagle grabs our attention as it plummets from a cottonwood and dive bombs a bird. Ed looks up. "Is that a pigeon?"

The bird swerves, reorients, beelines toward the cabin, and lands on the railing.

"Weird."

The pigeon coos as we walk up. Its leg looks odd, like it has a fortune cookie wrapped around it. The bird is docile and allows us to pick it up. Ed unwraps the paper around its leg and reads: "Leila home. Had foal. Surprise."

The next day, we drive to Mossy's to return the pigeon and see the miracle baby. "High Tide must have had a secret liaison with Leila while I was away last year," Mossy says. She gives us Enchantress as new company for Gretchen. I ride Enchantress to Swift Creek while Ed drives the van back.

Our days swell with beach rides, bluff explorations, and a wedding at Rainwater Ranch. A Canadian gal marries a local cowboy at an outdoor potluck; the bridal couple gallop away on horseback.

Deiv invites us to a Mexican dinner at the home of Homer local Sue Christiansen. We walk out to the bus turnaround with Deiv, and hop in Fritz for a ten-mile drive to Sue's rental near Bald Mountain. "You'll get on with Sue like a house afire," Deiv promises. Deiv's spot on; friendship with Sue is easy, instant, and full of promise. Sue spins tales of her travels in Tibet. We all swap stories about how we made it to Alaska, and our dreams of having cabins of our own. We feast on dreams and nachos and Deiv's classic handmade chile rellenos.

A week later, Ed and I are townward again to post letters, check mail, and shop for supplies. We pass Deiv in his gardens. "Don't you folks ever stay home?" he moans. "Must be your third trip to town this month. You're so decadent."

"Oh Deiv," Ed counters. "Don't be such a curmudgeon."

Our next curmudgeon is Ed's mom. As Ed deposits piles of coins into the pay phone, Ellen shrieks: "Eddie. I don't want you paying for this call."

"I've already paid, Mom."

"Well, you take them out. Call that operator; have her give them back."

"She can't do that, Mom."

"How's Mom?" I ask afterward.

"Never found out. All she did was yell at me for paying for the call. If I don't, she harps about that. Damned if I do, damned if I don't. If I ever get old and cranky like that, shoot me, Jan. What's the matter with older people?"

The Hitchhiker ~

Along East Road, on the way back from town, Ed brakes for a hitchhiker. I open the door to a braided backpacker. Lines etch deeply in her cheeks and laugh lines carve her eyes.

"Name's Helen Broomell," she says. "from Minocqua, Wisconsin. I'm fresh off the Yukon; I spent the past month paddling it solo."

"Solo?" I pump for details, but we're already at the home of her friend, Ed Berg. The pair insist we stay for supper. Over heaping bowls of pasta, we swap tales. Like us, Berg loaded everything in his van and headed north for better life.

"This trip to Alaska," says Helen, "is my dream come true. As a kid, I canoed Wisconsin lakes. And my Dad had a pal, Slim Williams, who came to the boy's camp my parents ran and raved about Alaska's mighty rivers. Got me fired up to canoe the Yukon someday."

"So, you've spent your life doing things like this?"

"Heavens no! I was a Chicago housewife."

"How old are you?" I ask.

"Sixty-five."

Helen quizzes us about our lives and why we left New Hampshire. As evening fades, I'm frustrated. I want to know more about this woman.

"Would you like to visit us at Swift Creek? You could stay over."

She arrives a few days later. We set up the couch as her bedroom and escort her around our beach and hillside. "I'd love to write an article about your Yukon River adventures," I tell her. Helen hesitates. "I think your life could inspire other folks; give a whole new perspective of what aging can be like. Would you be willing? Is it okay if I take notes of our talks?"

Helen shrugs. I dive in. "You said you were a housewife?"

"Oh yes, with six kids, spaced two per decade. My husband was alcoholic, and always telling me I couldn't do anything. And for a long time I believed him. My life revolved totally around my kids, and my chain-smoking."

"So how did you break out? What happened?"

"His abuse kept getting worse. It wasn't until I was fifty-six and had only two girls at home that I had the courage to leave. I started yoga, aerobic dance, cross-country skiing. Last year, I signed up for a two-week Outward Bound canoe course. Afterward, I remembered . . . Alaska. I can canoe the Yukon. When I finally felt ready, I got an aluminum canoe, gear, and supplies, and headed to Dawson City. Spent three and a half weeks on the river, and paddled around twenty-eight miles a day. Six hundred miles later, I pulled out at the Alaska Haul Road."

"But weren't you scared? Being solo? What about men? Bears?"

"Oh, no problem with men. Being older's an asset. Men only see me as a grandmother, and bring me home to their villages to chat with the elders. And bears, oh . . . lots of funny stories. One night I was tired and couldn't find a good campsite, and tied my canoe to a fallen tree at river's edge. I got a strange sensation, like I was being looked at. I opened my eyes and above me stood a black bear, ears perked, trying to figure out what the heck he was seeing. I laughed and he turned tail."

"And what about after you came off the river?"

"Sold the canoe, loaded my stuff into my pack, and took off to see the state. But it's so vast, I'll have to come back again sometime."

I ask her what she recommends to those dreaming of adventure from the comfort of their armchair. "Open up your mind; read about places that interest you. Pick a small-scale venture first, put all your preconceived notions behind you, and just go."

"Anything else?"

"Non-planning," says Helen. "That's an absolute essential."

"What's that?"

"Well, Jan, before this trip I read extensively about Alaska, its climate, history, animals, people. I set out a list of things I'd like to experience. And then I arrived in Alaska, and realized there was no way I was going to see all of this state. And that bush time has its own pace. Planes fly when they fly. Boats go when they go. Weather and winds interrupt paddling. So I threw away the plan, and changed track.

"All I keep is an open mind and an open schedule. And now I have more amazing experiences than the ones I anticipated. So tell others about non-planning, about not having rigid schedules, only general ideas of interest and flexible time. Tell them to show a willingness to accept people on their own merits wherever they are in a friendly way."

For Helen, it's time to continue on her quest. "I feel like a kid," I tell Ed. "I can't wait to be old enough to do things like Helen. There are so many retirement options other than death by television."

Buried Treasure ~

Swift Creek beach delivers treats daily: coal for the range, driftwood for the fire. On a morning walk, a patch of red grabs my attention. I mosey closer to the bluff and claw in the sand; a plastic buoy connects to yet another buoy. I scoop away debris and reveal more buoys and netting.

"I'll grab a shovel," Ed shouts. He returns with tools, and digs while I yank. Layer by layer we unearth a tangled mass—a mess of netting, coal, sticks, and fishing floats. We drag the beached-whale-of-a-net homeward.

The next days are net days: we pick out sticks and sew strands. "Looks like she'll come back to life, Jan. She'll be perfect for the subsistence opener." Deiv tells us the subsistence fishing period is summertime Christmas; allowable catch is twenty-five salmon per head of household; ten extra per family member.

Deiv admires our lucky find and offers to coach. "A good catch will be eight to ten salmon per tide, usually pinks, but if you're lucky you'll nail silvers."

Pinks, the canned salmon I grew up on, is Alaskan dog food. Kings (Chinook), silvers (Cohos), and reds (Sockeye) are the local favorites.

"Now a sea-run pink is good eating too," says Deiv, "but they turn to custard when they hit the rivers."

"Huh?"

"Salmon are prime when they're in the ocean, but when they hit fresh-water to spawn they fast forward toward death in a fortnight. Their bodies distort and their flesh turns to mush. Pinks get humped backs; sockeyes turn bright red with green faces, silvers get hooked jaws and rose-colored bellies. But don't worry, with the net set in the sea, we'll only get the best sea-run fish."

The next day, Deiv meets us on the beach, Sam and Toklat in tow. The scene is surreal, like an old movie. Sam wears the fishing net; Toklat carries a pack frame with empty wooden boxes. Behind the horses are glaciers, snowcaps, forests.

Deiv drops the net and departs with Toklat to collect wood for the smoker. We set the net.

The next morning I race to the beach, bouncing like a pogo stick. Then I spy the net. Nada. Not a single fish.

Deiv arrives with Sam to check our success. He laughs and whips the tide book from his jeans. "High tide was a thirteen footer; your net never kissed water. Tomorrow's tide is fifteen feet. Shift the net there," Deiv points, "and you're sure to catch something."

A four-wheeler drives up. Bearded men in pink shirts gesture excitedly. "Ours!" They point at our net. "Ours."

"Buried," points out Ed, "by the bluff."

"Ours," says the spokesman, with a heavy Russian accent.

"Buried." says Ed. "Broken."

The Russian shakes his head. "Ours."

"Ruined," I say, "all broken." I point to where we mended it. "We spent days fixing it."

The Russian men jabber to each other and point. "Ours."

"Yours," I finally concede. I rub my stomach. "Hungry."

The men babble more Russian, touch my arm, and nod my way. "Too skinny." They chat more and decide.

"Use net," says the elder. "Catch fish. Then we catch fish. We keep net."

We smile, shake hands, and wave farewell.

"Thought you were going to have a Russian war on your hands," says Deiv.

"Good blokes," says Ed. "Figured we could work something out. You'll have to tell us more about the Russian settlement sometime. Except for you on Wind Point, they're our closest neighbors."

"The Old Believers keep to themselves," Deiv says. "They work together as a community. The men are awesome fishermen; they build all their own boats."

We shift the net, wait for the tide to flood, then wait for slack water. Finally we return. "Look Janzie. The net's jumping. We've got one!" As the water drops, we start to count. "One silver salmon. A flounder. Seaweed. Sticks. Chunk of coal." A second silver, then three silvers. We're on a roll and feel like we did counting piles of money on the Blueberry Hill floor.

"Eight salmon. Nine. Ten." With each pause, we free gills from gillnet and admire shiny silver bodies.

"Eighteen salmon. Nineteen." We run our eyes down the net. Silver still gleams.

The net empties at thirty-three. Every single salmon is a silver, between twelve to fifteen pounds in weight. We limit out in a single tide.

Deiv returns with Sam and Toklat and does a high five. We stuff the horses' pack boxes full with fish. Sam carries the load to the cleaning and processing area. The catch is the first, easy step. We've no refrigerator, no freezer. What do we do with thirty-three fish on a warm summer day?

With Deiv, we gut and fillet fish after fish, and cut fillets in strips. "Keep that skin on," says Deiv, "It keeps them from falling to bits when smoking." Deiv grabs a five-gallon bucket, pours in water, salt, sugar, and seasonings. "Soak the fillets in this brine overnight, then dry the fish on a clothesline."

"What?" I ask.

"You've gotta firm them up for smoking."

In the morning we drape fillets on a line strung between trees. Ed preps a tall wooden box, and digs a tunnel for a stovepipe to enter. I chip green alder for a smoky fire. We transfer the line-dried fillets to smoke-house rods, light chips in the metal box, and babysit; every few hours we replenish chips.

"Smoking flavors the fish and helps preserve it to some degree," Mossy has told us. "But it won't last the winter. I vacuum-seal and freeze my smoked fish. But at Swift Creek you will have to sun-dry some as jerky, and can the rest."

We do as directed. We buy boxes of glass canning jars, and an extra bottle of propane gas. We clean and boil jars, pack the smoked strips vertically, cap the jars, and process at ten pounds pressure for two hours.

Cases stack in the pantry. Smoked salmon jerky, canned smoked salmon, and . . . Ed's third creation.

Ed places salmon fillets in a five-gallon bucket of water, along with one medium potato.

"What are you doing Ed?"

"You'll see, Jan. This is a Yankee specialty."

Ed dumps in heaps of salt.

"Gross, Ed. You'll ruin all that good salmon."

"Nah. You can only eat so much smoked fish. They do this all the time down East. Lots of time with cod; don't see why salmon won't work."

Ed empties the carton of salt and grabs another.

"Yuk. What are you making?"

"Salt fish."

"Well, yeah. But how much salt are you going to use? You'll ruin it."

"Nah. You've got to add salt 'til the spud floats. That's how you do it when you don't have a salinity meter."

Ed leaves the salt fish overnight in the brine; in the morning he hangs it on the clothesline covered with cheesecloth. He brings it in at night, puts it out by day. When rain threatens, he shifts operations to the old shed. Finally, he takes his salted dry fish and piles it in a box in the cool room. "All we've got to do this winter is soak it in changes of water to freshen, and use it in casseroles."

"My mom used to make a great pie with canned salmon and mashed potatoes," I remember. "I wonder if it'd work with salt fish?"

"Pie," says Ed as he licks his lips.

I laugh. Ed's fixated on pie. But the next day, I worry. In the shed is a new wooden box the length of my body. And there is a hole in the front yard, the perfect size for a coffin.

The Coffin ～

"What's with the grave and the coffin?" I ask Ed.

"See the powder on the mountains? Termination snow; summer's ending."

"So you're going to kill yourself?"

"Have to get our potatoes in. This will keep them from freezing. "

Ed sets the coffin in the hole. We head to the garden and dig potatoes, parsnips, and carrots. Ed layers plastic over the filled box and heads to the meadow with a handheld scythe. "We'll dry hay and pile it two feet high on top of the box as insulation."

Deiv tells us about Hungrybodies, an organic food co-op. We flip through its catalogue; there are pages and pages of choices.

"We need oats for porridge," says Ed.

"Okay, oats. There are whole oats, oat groats, steel-cut oats, rolled oats number five, rolled oats number three."

"Rolled oats," suggests Ed, "number three?"

"I suppose, no clue what they mean. Okay, what size? Twenty-five pounds, fifty pounds?"

"We'd better get a fifty-pound sack. We'll use oats for muesli and bread and oatmeal. In fact, make that two."

"Okay. One hundred pounds. How about a tin of maple syrup to top our porridge and sunflower seeds and nuts and raisins to add to it?"

"Great. And we need beans, cooking oil, and honey." We fill out the form, wince at the total, and get ready for the next trip to town.

On the beach we forage for driftwood and collect wave-washed coal for the kitchen stove. We cram the wood and coal bins to the rafters. "Swift Creek's ready for the changing season," says Ed. "Now we need to get back . . ."

"To Rocky River," I pipe in.

"Let's get our cabin logs cut and drying."

Felling Times ∼

We hop the next ferry and repeat the now-familiar sea waltz across Kachemak Bay. Along Jakolof Bay Road, cottonwoods gleam gold. Deep in the valley, goosebumps prickle as we spy the waterfall. We park the van and step through the grassy opening between the spruce: Home Sweet Home.

Along the river, Ed selects forty trees, the number he estimates we need to construct our fourteen-by-eighteen-foot cabin.

We bask in Indian summer days and crisp fall nights. Ed fells, limbs, and bucks trees to proper length. I haul brush to piles. We join forces to roll logs onto blocks for air circulation. Everything flows; the log pile grows.

Ed selects a spruce a foot and a half in diameter. "This one's for foundation posts." He trims it to six foot lengths, then lights his pipe and ponders.

"We've still three days 'til the *Tusty* returns. Let's buzz to town and buy some creosote. We'll get pier holes dug and a foundation in."

We head to Stampers Market, the shop with everything from nachos to nails.

"Sorry," says the shopkeeper. "No wood preservative."

Ed frowns; we can't proceed with the cabin project without it. Homer shops feel the moon's distance away.

I hunt on the shelves and shift tins of paint and varnishes.

"Give it up Janzie. He says he doesn't have any."

I ignore Ed and pile tins in the aisle. An army of cans marches across the floor.

The shopkeeper comes over.

"What are you doing?"

"Looking for creosote."

"Told ya there isn't any."

I ignore him. I grab more cans off the shelves.

The clerk stomps to the register. "Damn women, worse than mules."

A final dusty can is tucked in the far corner. I spin it so that the label's visible. "Creosote," I say triumphantly.

"How'd you do that, Janzie?" says Ed.

"Women's intuition. Come on, Eddie. Let's get back at it."

Home again, I dig foundation holes. "Not like Yankee digging, Ed; not a single rock, only pure gravel."

"Doing a great job, honey. I'll go creosote the pilings."

With each shovelful, I fret. How will we move the green monster logs to our upper meadow? We've no draft horses. The van can't get to them. What does Ed always say? Brains not brawn?

"Jan, need you." Ed calls. Ed has laid two round poles like railroad tracks in front of a massive log. We muscle the spruce onto the rollers. Then, with light pressure, it trundles along the track. We leapfrog tracks, glide across the meadows, and slide the foundation post into the hole. Ed levels as I backfill and tamp. "One done, seven to go."

We dig and set, then roll two full-length logs to the site. Ed restarts the chain saw, halves the logs, and lays the sill course.

I stand back and admire the handiwork. "Hate to stop now."

"Have to let the logs season, Jan. We'll be in a world of hurt if we don't." Ed glances at his watch. "Better hustle; *Tusty's* due in."

Changing Season ⌒⟋

Hungrybodies airs a radio announcement: bulk provisions are in. Their arrival coincides with the first light snows. In Homer, we cram seven hundred pounds of sacks, tins, and boxes into the van. Ed stops at the toy store and emerges with a red plastic sled. At the bus turnaround we bungee two fifty-pound sacks of oats onto the sled and stuff miscellaneous extras into our backpacks.

Three miles later, we perch atop the glaciated hogback, the rim of a radical toboggan shoot. "I don't have a good feeling about this, Ed; maybe we should take the switchback."

We backtrack to the junction, to where Deiv lives at Wind Point, and choose the longer winding trail. Ed secures a safety rope to the rear of the sled. He pulls, I brake; I do my best to keep the load from banging his heels.

We unload at the cabin and relax with a cup of tea and then strap on ice crampons, scramble up the hogback, and traipse the miles to the van. We reload, and head to the switchback. Back and forth, to and fro, up the hill we go; out with empty sled and packs, back again, laden like Sherpas. Eighteen miles later, our pantry is stocked, fat for the coming cold season.

Atop Wind Point, Deiv gears for the white season in his wall tent. Veggies stack in his earth-covered root cellar next to jars of canned salmon. For the horses, he has harvested hay with the scythe, skidded it on sleds, and stockpiled it in his pole barn.

Deiv is now focused on rebuilding his cabin. Ed volunteers to help. The men are the odd couple of construction: Mr. Precision versus Mr. Mother Earth. I stand aside, and stick to meals, music, and social engagements with Deiv.

But today, Deiv and Ed are horse-logging, skidding Deiv's house logs to his site. I grab my Nikon and join the men. Sam stands patiently in the traces while Ed and Deiv struggle to free a tree snagged on branches. "Here, Janzie, grab the reins. Hold Sam while we get this free."

I nonchalantly loop reins on my arm as I fiddle with my camera settings. I look at Sam and giggle. His eyes droop; he looks ready to start snoring. This definitely merits a photo. I lift my camera as Deiv frees the snagged tree. Thwack; its branch springs forward and slams Sam's butt.

The scene is a cartoon. Sam leaps upward and forward. What's not funny is that I'm in his path. I'm bowled flat like a tenpin, and kiss the snow. I feel an imprint, sized like a dinner plate, pressed on my tailbone. Now, there's intense pressure in my lumbar region, and searing weight in my mid and upper back. I'm helpless, limp. My mind detaches from my body. I see the horror scene below: a 1,300-pound beast walking across a woman's back.

I hear something. It sounds like Ed's voice, but different, anxious.

"Janzie, Janzie, don't move, I'll get help."

Move? I can't move. I can barely squeak a whisper. "Wait. Ed, wait. Don't leave me."

"I'll go." says Deiv. "Ed, you stay here with Jan."

"Wait," I mumble. "Hang on."

Ed kneels by my prostrate body. "Can you move your fingers, Jan?"

Fingers. What are fingers?

"Janzie, can you move your fingers?"

I send a signal to my brain: "Fingers, move." Things at the end of one hand wiggle.

"Good, Jan. Can you do the other?"

I pause. Think again. The other does a slight wave.

"Good. What about your toes?"

I will my brain to think "toes." I tighten toes on one side. Then the other.

"Oh, thank God," murmurs Ed.

"Camera?" I mumble. "Where's my camera?"

Ed finds my Nikon lying in the snow. "Your camera's fine, honey."

"I want to get up," I tell Ed.

"You shouldn't move."

"I think I'm okay. I want to see if I can sit."

Ed argues with me, but I insist. Ed and Deiv help. I slowly sit. Ed carefully rubs my back. "How are you doing, Jan?"

My body shakes like an aspen. "Take deep breaths, Jan; take your time." My body calms and starts to feel solid.

"Help me stand." Ed and Deiv grab my arms and lift me to my feet. We stare at each other in disbelief. A horse walked on my spine. I'm sore and achy, but intact.

"You must have a guardian angel," says Ed. "Lots to be thankful for."

"Speaking of which," adds Deiv. "Thanksgiving dinner next week in my tent; I'm making a special meal. You'll have to join me."

"We'll be up."

Thanksgiving ～

On Thursday we drool up the hogback. "Been ages since we had turkey."

"And stuffing. Bet Deiv makes a great stuffing."

"Hope it's dripping with gravy."

"And pie; hope he makes pumpkin, and pecan, and apple."

We pass expectantly through the flap of Deiv's tent and reverently sniff the air. The aroma is musty, different.

We pour wine. Deiv heaps plates with roast, gravy, boiled potatoes, peas.

We fork in a strip of roast, and chew. The meat's like shoe leather. I heap on extra gravy, and chew more. Ed's brow furrows like a plowed field. Deiv's a kitchen whiz with Thai, Mexican, breads, and pies. How'd he kill this roast?

"What's this meat?" I ask.

"What do you think?"

"Not turkey," says Ed.

"Doesn't taste like beef or lamb or moose."

"Val," Deiv says.

"What? The only Val I know is your old . . . no . . . not her?"

"Yep, went to goat heaven. She's past milking."

"And past the expiry date," Ed whispers to me. Deiv rises to fetch condiments. Ed surreptitiously slides his goat roast to the floor for Max. Max wolfs it. I ditto Ed's trick. Max grabs my meat and spits out by my feet. I prod Max with my toe and nudge him to eat. He spins and retreats. Crap. Deiv's walking to the table. I cover the food with my shoe.

Ed rises and piles his plate with succulent salmon and a fat wedge of Deiv's pie.

My foot's still stuck on my roast. I drop my napkin, bend to retrieve it, and slide the scraps into the cloth. Finally, I'm able to rise for smoked fish.

Ed's chewing the pie with a strange look. "Looks like pumpkin, but tastes different. What this?"

"Guess," says Deiv.

"No clue. Good though," says Ed.

"Rutabaga," says Deiv, grinning.

"Those big turnips?"

"Had heaps of them."

"Never heard of anyone making turnip pie, but good though."

"That reminds me," says Deiv. "Alaskan logging camps have a policy where new guys on the job get assigned as cook. And they work as cook until someone complains of the cooking. Fred, this pal of mine hated cooking. But no matter what he made no one would complain.

So he decided the only way he was going to get out of the job was to make a pie."

"Is that where you got the rutabaga recipe?"

"No," Deiv laughs. "Fred decided he'd make a pie they'd never forget. Went out to the forest, found himself a great big pile of moose turds. Baked them in a pie shell, and topped it with whipped cream."

We sit enthralled. "And?"

"This big burly logger took a big bite. Stood up and yelled, "My Gawd, it's moose-turd pie! It's good though."

We laugh. Ed rises and refills his plate with a second wedge of rutabaga. "This really is good, grows on you."

"You'll have to come to Christmas at our place," I tell Deiv.

"I'll bring some canned goat."

"What if you make another pie? We'll treat you to a New England style turkey," says Ed.

Readying for Santa ⌒

With Christmas coming, we ponder which presents we can mail to family back East. "They'd love some canned salmon," suggests Ed.

"Great idea for the adults, but what about the nephews and nieces?"

At Homer's toy shop, Ed hands me an Alaskana coloring book.

"Good idea," I say, as I flip through it. "It's the Alaska we see every day: moose, mountains, fishing boats, sea otters." Then I freeze. "See the Eskimos build the igloo," I read disgustedly. "Alaskan Eskimos never lived in igloos except as emergency shelters. I could do better than this."

"Why don't you?" challenges Ed.

"Well maybe I will." Back at Swift Creek, my head dances with ideas, my mouth babbles rhymes.

Hop aboard a plane and we'll take a flight
to the Arctic, where there's endless summer light.
Eskimos once lived in sod homes—made from the ground.
Today, wooden structures are typically found.

"Something's not right," I complain. "I need to add more detail. How can I do that and not bore the kids?"

"What about having a character explain things? He could pop in here and there with fun facts. You could have some Sourdough . . ."

"Sourdough says," I exclaim. Let's see: "Sourdough says . . ." I write frantically, sip another tea, cross out lines, write anew. "Listen, Ed." Ed lights his pipe and sits back as I recite.

"Sourdough says: 'Igloos (ice houses) were built by Natives in Canada and Greenland. Alaskan Eskimos used them rarely, only when on extended hunting trips. They lived in houses made of sod. Today they commonly live in wooden homes heated with oil.'"

Ed nods. I add Sourdough, a longtime Alaskan wise in the ways of the North, to pertinent pages. The book includes animals, fish, geography, and glaciers. I draw images of our Alaska and staple finished pages into booklets for my brother's children.

We mail them to New Hampshire, pick up a family box of goodies at the post office, stick them in the cabin corner, and wait for the Twenty-fifth.

Temperatures plummet; fat flakes fall. "If this keeps up, it's going to be a white Christmas," I predict.

"This weather puts me in the mood for a good hot . . ."

"Pie?"

"How'd you guess, Jan? How about one of these salmon pies you talked about? Like your mom used to make?"

"Our canned salmon's already running low, especially since we gave away a case of it to family."

"We've got all the salt fish. All we have to do is freshen it."

"Great. You freshen it. I'll make pie."

A Tale of Pie ⁓

Ed ambles to the creek for five gallons of water and returns empty-handed. "Need an ax, Jan, she's froze solid." He returns a half hour later, carrying a bucket of ice chunks. I light the propane to melt a pan of water. Ed puts the remaining ice in a bucket on the wood stove. We stare at the small puddles in the pot. Ed heads back to chip more.

I pour meltwater on the fish, wait an hour, drain the salty fluid, and take a bite. "Yuck, this salmon tastes like the inside of a salt shaker," I grimace. I pour the remaining fresh water on the fish. Ed heads to the creek for more ice.

We melt, drain, taste, shake our heads, refreshen the fish, wait again, repeat again. Our stomachs rumble. "Looks like we'd better sacrifice some canned fish for tonight's pie, Jan. We'll soak the salt fish overnight; maybe make some creamed salmon on sourdough toast tomorrow."

"Surely the salmon will be fine by morning. But we'd best freshen it again. I'll go for ice this time." I grab my white air-insulated boots, the kind Alaskans call Bunny Boots. I struggle to pull a boot on. It's got something inside. I tip it and brown flakes fall like snow.

Ed peers at the pile: "Oats, sunflower seeds, raisins, almonds, black bits." He heads to the bedroom. I hear the pantry door open and shut. "Voles. They've chewed holes in all our grain bags. They blended their own granola in your boots."

"We'll have to buy plastic buckets on our next town trip; do some rodent-proofing."

Morning brings bad news; our salted fish is still too salty to eat.

"Schofield's folly," laughs Ed.

"We'll have to be patient. In spring there'll be endless water again. We can set it in the creek to rinse thoroughly. We won't go hungry; there are still heaps of veggies in the coffin, and rice."

"And oats," says Ed. Max groans. Max eats the same diet we do, and loves all food (as well as items we insist aren't in that category), but he's starting to strike on oatmeal. When I set down his morning porridge, he glares and stomps to the corner.

"Maybe we overdid it with two fifty-pound sacks of oats. I need a change of pace too; can't wait for Christmas dinner." I tell Ed. "I'm even dreaming of roast turkey."

We head to Homer to shop for the big day and stare at the freezer case. "You need a college degree to read the turkey labels; they're injected full of chemicals."

"Let's check out the ones at the natural food shop, Jan."

Ed hefts a medium turkey; pure, simple, organic. "Must be a misprint; sticker says seventy-five dollars."

I take it to the cash register and come back frowning. "It is seventy-five dollars," I exclaim. I set it back in the freezer.

"But look Janzie, it's got a pedigree." Ed holds up the leaflet that details the free-range lifestyle the turkey has had, the farm's certification, its organic feed.

"You could shoot a spruce hen," I tell Ed. "They're good, and free, though a tad tough."

"Oh come on Janzie . . . remember the goat . . . we promised a turkey."

"Okay Ed . . . it is Christmas. We're all due for a treat."

Winter Holidays

We hoe into our Christmas feast with Deiv, surfeit on pie, and bask in friendship and fortune. Deiv nestles on the corner couch and strums guitar while Ed and I clean up the kitchen. Deiv takes a break and asks if we heard our bush line: "Mossy sent Christmas cheer to the Swift Creekers and wants you to drop by Seaside Farm, ASAP."

It's our first bush line; there's nothing like this back East. In Alaska, folks dictate a message to public radio, which broadcasts over the air at set times each day to the phoneless.

We head over to Seaside Farm the next day. Mossy wants to know if we'll caretake her town ranch while she spends a month in Hawaii. "Chores are easy. Grain the horses. Toss hay to the cows. Feed the chickens. Watch over the tenants in the rental cabins." In exchange, we'll have free use of the spacious oil-heated house, a fully equipped kitchen, and unlimited television and video watching.

"Who do we call for plowing?" Ed asks Mossy.

"I've not had the driveway plowed in twenty years. It doesn't get that deep."

"Really?" Perhaps the Alaskan winter is another myth, something designed to keep Alaska for Alaskans.

We tell Mossy we'll do it. "Easy duty," Ed whispers. "It will be fun to be at the Ritz for a bit."

Mossy departs; we shift to Seaside Farm. She leaves us with one ominous directive: to keep a close watch on Leila's foal, Surprise, who has started eating poorly and losing balance. Mossy is awaiting test results from the vet.

Our room is upstairs; its double bed presses against the picture window, overlooking Kachemak Bay, the Kenai Mountains, and Grewingk

Glacier. We watch as a moose trots through the yard, hopping fences like a show-jumper. "What a great life we have," I tell Ed. "Room with a view, wildlife by the window, no stress." We snuggle to sleep.

Sounds wake us.

"Bang. Bang, bang bang bang. Bang."

Ed groggily peers at his watch. "It's only 6 A.M. Who's here at this hour?" He grabs his trousers and hauls himself downstairs.

A tenant is on the doorstep. "I'm trying to shower for work; there's no water."

Ed turns on the kitchen tap; no water. He finds his flashlight; we bundle up and head out to track the problem. There's nothing obvious by the house. In the paddock, Mossy's Morgans are skating on ice. The barn latch is broken; inside, the Shetland gorges on grain next to a ruptured water pipe. The Seaside Farm storage tank is bone dry; all tenants are waterless.

We head back to the house. "How about a coffee, Jan, while we sort this out?"

"No water, Eddie, remember. How about a cold juice?"

Ed scans the phone book. "I wonder who Mossy uses for a plumber?" She's still in transit; there's no way to call her.

The door resounds like a kettle drum. "Bangbangbang."

"Go tell them I'm working on getting the water fixed."

I come back and report, "It's heat. There's no heat."

Ed grumbles. He bundles into his down parka and scouts the new problem. The propane tank's empty. "I wonder who Mossy calls for liquid propane? How does she pay?"

Next Max sniffs Mossy's old cat. She slams his nose and leaves a claw sticking out like a porcupine quill.

"Gads, Janzie, why'd we ever leave Swift Creek?"

"Easy, Ed. Easy as pie."

Chalk and Cheese ⌣

Not all Seaside Farm tenants are equally affected by the lack of water and heat. Mike and Randy, renters in the red cottage at the top of the drive, have a wood-heated hut and haul water from the grocery store spigot.

"What's that on your shirt?" I ask Randy, pointing to lettering I can't quite decipher.

He unbuttons, reveals the full text on his tee: "There is nothing, absolutely nothing, half so much worth doing as simply messing about in boats."

"*The Wind in the Willows?*" I ask.

"Yep, said to Mole by the Water Rat," says Randy.

"The *Water Rat* is the name of the boat we're building," adds Mike. He leads us to a twenty-four-foot sloop under a tarp. "When it's done, we'll sail the *Rat* around the world."

We invite the duo for silver salmon dinner, where I ask, "Why Alaska?"

"Why not? Great country. Good place to start a new life." The Minnesota men are recovering from divorces, and Mike from being a medic in Vietnam. Ed and Randy swap metaphysical ramblings and talk about how thoughts become physical reality. The evening gallops. As we part, I share the classic Alaskan hug. Mike returns a relaxed squeeze. Randy stiffens like a fish in rigor mortis. "I don't like to hug."

Afterward I say, "Mike's definitely the optimist, as mellow as a marshmallow, but Randy was an ice block when I hugged him."

"They're as different as chalk and cheese; what characters."

"And sailing around the world. In New England, I didn't know anyone who lived like this. It was a huge deal going sixty miles to camp. Once, Dad tried to take the family to Boston museums. Mom was a whiz with numbers but a basket case with maps. All I remember is being lost in an endless tunnel with crabby parents and no more trips to Boston ever, and it was only forty miles away."

"In Alaska, Jan, the sense of distance and what's possible is so different. Folks here so commonly go 'outside' each winter, and it's not outside the house, but 'outside' into the world, like Mossy's trip to Hawaii. Alaskans think nothing of building a boat, sailing the world, scaling mountains. Their lives are like meteors hurtling through space."

"Makes me wonder what I've been doing my whole life, until you, until Alaska. I'm so glad we're together."

Ed folds me into his arms and pulls me close.

"I'm glad too, honey."

Surprises ⁓

Mossy calls for farm updates, relieved all is again on an even keel. The only exception is the filly, Surprise, who wobbles like a drunken sailor. The vets want to put her down. "There's one more thing we can try: Jack Epperson," says Mossy.

"Another vet?" I ask, "I don't remember seeing him in the yellow pages."

"Jack's no vet; he's a retired marine dispatcher and does hands-on healing. He usually works with people, but maybe he'd be willing." Mossy gives me the number; I call Jack. He agrees to see Surprise.

"How'd you get into this?" I ask Jack when he arrives.

"Watching television. I leaned back on my hands and found they were hot. I placed them by accident on someone's injured back. They told me how much better they felt. That started it."

We head out to the barn. I hold Surprise while Jack places one hand on her withers and another near the top of her tail. As soon as Jack begins to run energy (as he calls it), the filly yanks back and wobbles away. I catch Surprise again and bring her back to Jack. We yo-yo back and forth; Surprise bolts each time she receives electric-like currents from Jack's hands. After the fourth recapture, though, she sighs deeply and stands still. Jack keeps his hands in place for twenty minutes.

During the week, Jack returns for more treatments. Surprise gets steadier on her feet and begins feeding enthusiastically.

"Strange," I say to Ed. "Do you think it's a coincidence?"

"Jack certainly turned the tide. I don't know what it is about Alaska, but bizarre things happen here constantly."

Mossy returns from Hawaii, and we head back to Swift Creek. The next oddity occurs in the outhouse.

Strange Skies ~

Our Swift Creek routines include my nightly toilet. While I perch on the outhouse seat, I stargaze. The panorama of blue-tongue glaciers emerging from Harding Icefield is a world-class shithouse view. Deiv says this icefield, including its thirty-eight glaciers, spans 1,100 square miles, nearly the size of Switzerland. Switzerland has seven million people; Harding Icefield has zero.

But tonight, one star looms above the barren icefields, strangely bright and pulsating. I'm mesmerized. I make a mental note to check our star-gazing guide. The star shoots vertically, and stops. In less than a blink, the same star shifts horizontally and halts above Grewingk Glacier. This is too strange. I grab my drawers and run to the cabin.

"Ed, you've got to see this star."

"Oh honey, it's snug in here. I'll see it tomorrow."

"Ed. You've got to see it." Ed gets his coat. "Look. Look!"

The star still hovers over Grewingk Glacier. "Kinda bright, maybe a satellite," says Ed.

"Keep watching," I insist.

Ed watches and yawns. "Oh honey, think I'll go back . . ." Before he can finish, the star rockets north to Dixon Glacier, directly across Kachemak Bay from us. It pauses, then shoots vertically until it vanishes from view. Ed's jaw gapes. "Weird."

"Yeah, that's what I thought. No airplane moves like that. And besides, what would one be doing over the glaciers at this time of night? It reminds me how Dad would tell me about objects appearing on the radar screen when he was in the Air Force; things that moved beyond the speed of all known aircraft. Unidentified flying objects."

"Well it certainly is unidentified, and flying."

We talk until the wee hours, then sleep dreaming of skies, flying objects, time travel, cows jumping over the moon, jets hurtling through space, satellites beaming messages. The dreams are jumbled, chaotic. Noise intrudes. Whap, whap, whap. I must be dreaming. Whap, whap, whap. The noise escalates, and screams: WHAPWHAPWHAP.

Ed races to the window butt naked. "A helicopter, Jan. Out front. Wonder what it's doing here?" Ed glances at his watch. "8:30 A.M. Barely getting light."

We toss on clothes and dash outdoors. "Oh, sorry to disturb you," the pilot apologizes. "I didn't realize anyone was living here. Have to check that survey point on the beach. I'm surveying for the Bradley Lake Hydroelectric Project. Over there." He points east across Kachemak Bay. "In that valley north of Dixon Glacier is a glacial lake. They're going to dam it and cut a swath through Fox River valley to Anchorage for transmission lines."

My gut wrenches. That amazing wilderness, changed forever?

Deiv arrives as the copter lifts off. "A surveyor," we tell him. "For the hydro project."

"Bradley? That's been going to start any day now for the past two decades. Maybe it's finally getting serious."

After breakfast, we lighten the mood with reading, and sip herbal tea. I sit back, and stare at the view. I rub my eyes. There, framed in the picture window is Hoss Cartwright, straight out of a Bonanza episode.

Bonanza ～

Hoss Cartwright? I blink again. Wrong, it's only a Hoss stand-in. The big man's on a big bay, with a rifle in the scabbard. A gray horse heaped with gear trails behind.

"Hi neighbors. I'm Big Mike," says the burly stranger. "Pleased to meet you."

"Have a cuppa," invites Ed. "There's hay in the barn for the horses."

Mike unbridles and shares his story over tea and cookies. The tale is growing familiar: another educated, Lower-48 escapee gone north to find peace back of beyond. His beyond is a log hut ten miles up the Fox River. Big Mike scribbles a map. "Come on up, I'll show you my valley."

"When we get enough snow," Ed says," we'll do a winter ski trip and drop on by."

A fortnight later, fat flakes fall to sea level. The snow builds and entices us from our cozy cabin to the white world. We load packs with sleeping bags and food. I pause before our sourdough, a pot of wild yeast bubbling by the woodstove. "What do we do with our starter, Ed? If we leave it here it'll freeze to death."

"It's darn near like a pet with all the daily feeding and care you do. Can't let her kick the bucket, though; you've been carting her around since New Hampshire."

"My parting gift when I quit my job. Genuine sourdough culture, from potato water and airborne yeast. I was told this starter came from the Klondike gold rush. After a hundred years of growing, we can't let it croak. I read that prospectors added extra flour to the starter when on the trail and made a sourdough ball; they hung it in a pouch inside their shirt to keep it warm. We could try that."

"What if we dry it instead?" counters Ed. "And reconstitute the sourdough when we get back. That'd be a lot easier."

"Hate to take a chance."

"It'll work, Jan. Trust me." Ed tears a sheet of waxed paper and spreads a thin film of starter on it; he places it on a rack above the barrel stove to dry.

"Hope you're right. Your way beats sleeping with a sourdough necklace."

We exit Swift Creek after sunrise and ski across the Fox River flats. Max trots alongside, bearing ten pounds of our goods in his dog pack.

Hours later, the valley narrows; a whisper of a track leads onward. We stop and rewax, then continue the rhythmic shuffle shuffle of the skis. We break for a thermos of cocoa and a smoked salmon sandwich. "How much further?" I ask.

Ed stares at the scribble. "Not far."

Two hours later, I wonder, "Could we have missed it?"

"Smoke," says Ed. "Through those trees."

A curl of smoke rises from a small log building. We halloo. Big Mike flings the door open and crushes me in a welcome hug. His sleeves are rolled up, his shirt dusted with flour. "Making sourdough bread for supper, and moose stew's on the stove. There's plenty to go around," he insists. "Besides," he adds looking at me, "you're so little. You can't eat more than a gnat."

The cabin's even smaller than Swift Creek. A roaring fire has it nearly sauna temperature. We sip tea and await the evening feast, when we hear knocking. Mike grabs carrots from a bin and throws open the door.

Horse heads reach inside, muzzles extended for treats.

After hearty dining and late night chats, I unfurl our sleeping bags on the plywood floor and drift deeply into dreamland. I hear stirring and crack an eyelid. It's still dark outside the windows. But there are tantalizing smells . . . fresh coffee and a familiar sour tang.

"Come and get it," says Big Mike. "Breakfast is on."

He heaps our plates with mounds of sourdough hotcakes smothered with butter and serviceberry jam. I protest the amount. "You'll need it," he insists. "I'm taking you skiing to Clearwater Slough."

We wax up and head northeast. Mike pauses at a snow patch little different from the past six hours of snow patches. "Isn't Clearwater a beaut?" Mike beams at the hollow. "You have to come fishing here next summer; this place boils with salmon." Today, the slough is colder than a commercial freezer, and the January light is already fading.

"I think we'd best stay here tonight; we can camp in that trapper's hut."

That? One wall is collapsed, and the other three shakily form a walk-in room. A rusted woodstove gapes holes.

"Not much choice," whispers Ed. "The hobbit hovel or the shelterless outdoors."

We sweep away rotted wood, rusty tins, and wire to make room for our down bags. I find a balding broom and sweep rodent droppings. Big Mike lights the stove and heats water. We wrap mittened hands around tin cups of cocoa and huddle by the fire.

My eyes burn. I nudge Ed. "I feel like a salmon in a smokehouse."

"Would you rather smoke or freeze?"

"Could be snug at Swift Creek," I pout.

Ed digs in his pack and grabs granola bars, salmon strips, crackers, fruit, and chocolate. "Chocolate; my hero." But even that tastes smoky. It's only 6 P.M. and already dark as a cave. We've little else to do but sleep. Ed and I zip our sleeping bags together and snuggle in. Max stands, shivering.

"Okay Max," says Ed, "in you go." He nosedives into the bag and wiggles like a caterpillar to the very bottom, where he curls into a ball and groans: his happiness sound. We sigh; our feet are toasty.

Two days later, back at Swift Creek, we relish tales of the Fox River expedition, our time with Mike, and our extra night with bush dwellers Dennis and Susie Wade and their daughter Laralei, where we slept under their kitchen table in their tiny cabin.

"But it's great to be home," Ed says.

"I wonder how the sourdough fared?"

Ed checks the tray of dried wafers. "They look like Holy Communion hosts," I tell him.

He breaks a few into a bowl, adds warm water and stirs. "It's bubbling, Jan. It worked."

"Our cash reserves aren't going to last forever, Ed. Perhaps our sourdough could be a feeder stream of income."

"Good idea, Jan. Remember when we were looking for a gift for my sister? And we checked out those sourdough packets in the shops? Their ingredients list was only flour and regular bread yeast. This is the real thing. Let's do it, Jan. I'll dry the culture and grind it to powder. We'll package it up. You can write up a flier."

"We could include recipes for sourdough breads and waffles and hotcakes."

"And sourdough history, too."

We get to work; Ed adds flour and water daily to the pot, then waits until it expands and bubbles. He spreads it thinly on plastic wrap and lays it on racks above the wood stove to dry. Meanwhile, I recipe-test and write.

"Mossy says that when she was a kid, she always loved visiting here, back when it was the Russell homestead. Ma Russell always had a sourdough pot bubbling. I wonder what creative things Ma Russell did with it."

"If only these walls could talk, Jan. Wonder what else went on here at Swift Creek."

"We could ask around; might be some folks who still remember life here in the forties and fifties. Wonder how far back its history goes. Mossy seems to think this is one of the oldest cabins in the bay. Maybe we can find out. Might even get to the root of that rumor about a ghost."

Guns and Ghosts ⌁

Answers arrive on horseback. Local resident Sara drops by on her ride to the Fox River. "Have you seen her yet?" she asks.

"Who?"

"Ma Russell's ghost?"

My eyes roll back like a cowpony. Oops, won't get to the bottom of things unless I listen. "No, have you?"

"As a matter of fact, yes. I stayed overnight at Swift Creek a year ago," she tells me. "I looked out the kitchen window and saw a buxom woman in a big apron. I went outside to say hello but no one was there. It was very strange."

"The Russian gals are big and buxom."

"Ma's dress was plain, not like their dresses. Besides, I would have seen them walking back to their village. They couldn't vanish in thin air, unless they were a ghost."

On my next town run, I stop at Mossy's. Mossy made countless childhood visits to the Russell cabin. "What did Ma look like?" I ask her.

"About your height, Jan. Only big and bosomy. Always wore a full apron."

I tell her about Sara's vision.

"Exactly as she describes."

"But come on, Mossy. Be real. A ghost?"

"Lots of folks have seen her."

"Ya, ya" I say, dismissing the subject.

Then it happens. Ed and I have our first spat. It grows nuclear in seconds.

I march out of our bedroom, towing blankets.

"I'm sleeping on the couch," I holler.

"Good."

A while later he creeps to the couch. "I'm sorry Jan. I don't know what got into me. Let's kiss and make up."

"I don't want to kiss."

He reaches for my hand.

"Don't touch me. I don't want your cooties."

Cooties. I've not used that word since I was ten, when boys were slimy creatures from the deep lagoon. Cooties. The word makes me laugh. The spell breaks. Anger evaporates like steam. I return to our bedroom. Ed and I snuggle, kiss, make up.

But the incident leaves me puzzled. It is so untypical of our relationship. It feels, almost . . . ghostly.

When Mossy drops by a few days later, I mention the tiff.

"Sounds like Ma Russell's been around," she says. "Ma was famous for blowing things out of proportion. She'd fling frying pans at Pa. That bullet hole in the picture window is from when she shot at him. She had a whale of a temper."

"My experience with Ed was strange, Mossy, almost like a phantom taking over. I couldn't help myself. And it was over the littlest thing. I can't even remember what set it off."

"With Ma, alcohol got her cranked up like a wind-up toy."

"We had a brandy before bed. But it was only a sip."

"With Ma, all it took was a sniff."

I dismiss the ghostly mystery, but begin to research Swift Creek history in earnest. Homer News is keen to publish local history, adding even more incentive to my project.

I interview Seldovia homesteader Steve Zawistowski who knew the Russells well. He tells me how Pa (Oris) spirited Ma (Hazel) away to Swift Creek from town, to get her far away from the maddening grog. "Ma was a good-time gal," Steve says, "who drank, smoked, danced, and cussed."

Ma discovered the disgusting, fermenting fluid of a neglected sourdough pot had a kick. She would slurp it, and then go off like a cannon. Pa would shake his head and retreat to his shop. Steve paints a picture of Pa as a mellow country man, slim as a bean, and adept with ax and saw. He was cannery carpenter and, later, supervisor of the crew that built the Log Cabin Visitor Information Center in Anchorage in the mid-1950s.

"Pa's penchant" adds Steve, "was character analysis. He could tell if folks were going to make it in Alaska or not. His favorite visitors were the cheechakos, tenderfoots full of pie-in-the-sky dreams of settling the Fox River valley. Pa would take them under his wing. He'd write them lists, complete with brand names of exactly which tools and which food to buy. 'Store it in my loft,' he'd insist. 'Lots of room there. It'll give you a halfway point for shifting things to your site.' They'd rush out and buy all Pa's favorite guns and gear. Then they'd slam into the reality of life beyond the road system: vagaries of weather, boot-sucking mud flats, bears raiding their cabin. They'd quit, abandoning their stockpile snug in the rafters of Pa's barn. 'Angels are here again, Ma,' Pa would say, smiling."

I chuckle, imagining life with the Russells and their ongoing angelic parade. We take a break from the interview. I brew Steve another cup of coffee, which wets his lips once again.

"Now one of Ma's weaknesses was romance. She loved love stories. She must have plum run out of novels. She told Pa about this deejay on the radio with a voice sweet as honey. 'He's in love with me, Pa,' she claimed. Pa wouldn't bite. Then a low-flying plane buzzed the cabin. 'It's him. It's him. He's coming for me, Pa. Taking me to town. Taking me away from this place.'"

We have another chortle. I check my list of questions. "Were the Russells the ones who built this place?" I ask.

"Nope. The cabin dates to 1927, Prohibition time. Charles Dennison put up the main structure. Federal marshals raided here time and again but could never find his still. He hid it across Kachemak Bay. Ma and Pa homesteaded at Swift Creek throughout the forties; they're the ones that added the bedroom, pantry, workshop, barns, and sheds."

Later, Homer pioneer Lee Cole fills in more of the background for my story. "The Russell place," he tells me, "is the first place in this country I ever had to take my shoes off. It was an immaculate cabin with sparkling red-print linoleum, a spacious picture window, and fresh-painted Dutch door. The old kitchen stove used to shine like a mirror on top. And you always had to remove your shoes. Ma used to say she'd be damned if she'd spend all her time scrubbing a dirty floor."

When Ma got ill in the fifties, the Russells moved into town. But I'm starting to wonder if some part of Ma isn't still here, keeping shoes off and sniffing for grog. But it can't be. Folks don't really believe in ghosts, do they?

More Russian Dealings ⌒

With the horses back at Mossy's for the winter, we now hike everywhere. The sea-level snow has been short-lived, and skis are useless except atop Wind Point.

Our favorite day hike scouts the Kachemak Bay shoreline with its ever-changing amusements: leaf fossils, petrified wood, eagle feathers, weird rocks, red clay, volcanic lava, fishing buoys, and coal chunks. The name "Kachemak," we've learned, means "smoky bay" and is believed to be of Aleut derivation. The name refers to coal seams in the bluffs that would smolder and make the bay area smoky. We've not yet seen this phenomenon but we celebrate each time we find coal eroding from the bluffs as it's more fuel to keep our home fires burning.

The newest amusement is a garden of ice sculptures. A blast of sub-zero temps flash-freezes the harbor mouth and cove edges; the bay's tides shift as much as twenty-eight vertical feet in six hours and pulverize ice sheets into dinosaur cubes. The shapes tickle our fancy. "Bear," I say pointing.

"Centaur," answers Ed.

"Stegosaurus," I retort, nodding at a massive spiky chunk.

"Boat," he replies.

"Don't see a boat in that one. What are you looking at?"

"Over there. Listen," he says, holding his finger to his lips.

Shouts carry across the water. Men in a dinghy no bigger than a bathtub strain at the oars and scream.

"Must need help." We dash toward the boaters and stop, sides heaving, to catch our breath and get a better look. "Russians," says Ed. "Looks like they're chasing something."

"That fishing boat looks like it's drifting."

"Must be one they moor on their mudflats; ice must have snapped the anchor. They're okay, Jan, only chasing the escapee."

Back in the cabin, the picture window reels in *Doctor Zhivago* scenes: Russian cowboys gallop the beach, panniers flying, beards tossing in the wind. "What colorful neighbors," I tell Ed, "tough as nails. Yesterday I met a pregnant Russian woman on the switchback pulling a sled, heading to the new village ten miles up the Fox River Valley. She crashed on the ice, but before I could lend a hand she bounced up, laughing. Wish we could get to know our neighbors more but those 'keep out' signs at the entrance to their village beyond Swift Creek make it clear."

"We're not welcome there. No outsiders are."

"Can't blame them for wanting to be left alone in peace to raise their veggies, critters, and kids. They've no desire to have folks butting in, snapping photos, and interrupting their secluded life."

The turning point to friendship occurs on a breath of wind. Ed finds a kite in a dusty corner of the old shed. It flies. A flock of kids from the Kachemak Selo village shyly gather to watch. Ed offers the little ones the line; they beam, take turns. The next breezy day, we find seven Russian noses pressed against the picture window, waiting to see if we'll play kite.

Now we have a Russian adult visitor, Troy, in the Swift Creek kitchen. He wants to know if we'll sell him the cabin. We give him Mossy's contact details, but warn it's quite unlikely she'll want to part with Swift Creek. Troy is curious about our life; he coaxes us to visit him at his home in the main Russian Old Believer settlement, Nikolaevsk, near Anchor Point. We're honored by the invitation. On our next town run, we detour to the village, but get lost within. "I'll ask directions," I tell Ed. I walk up to a home where I can hear voices, and knock. Silence. I knock louder.

I scratch my head. Perhaps I'm hearing things.

I go to the next house. I knock. I wait. I knock louder. I wait again.

I go to the next house. There's no answer again. I could swear I'd heard voices.

"Let's look at our map again, Ed. Hmmm. Could it be that house?"

I go to the door. Troy answers and welcomes us in. Helen, his wife, greets us with a smile, and their infant straddles her hip. Helen brews us tea. The house is tidy and American-looking, except for one corner. A shrine with Russian icons dominates the area. Helen potters about the kitchen and emerges with ravioli-like pasta with tender moose meat centers, accompanied by slices of her homemade whole grain bread.

Our chats meander from natural food cooking (which Helen practices) to tales of their honeymoon in Hawaii and descriptions of Russian wedding customs. "You should come to my brother's wedding next month," exclaims Troy.

Ed and I glance at each other. "We'd be delighted to attend, if it would be all right with everyone."

Troy insists. He laughs when we describe how no one would answer the door. "Knocking meant you were strangers. It's customary in our village to walk into each others homes."

We depart, arms crammed with loaves of bread and jars of homemade preserves. We try to refuse, but it's futile. We have new friends.

With the wedding coming, we decide we'd best be culturally prepared. We've long been curious about the Old Believers, who remind us of Amish rolled in rainbow paint. Men sport beards and bright tunic shirts (*rubashkas*) with high-necked, embroidered collars. Women have long hair and ankle-length dresses.

I search the Homer library. "The Old Believer faith, Ed, traces to seventeenth-century Russia, to when Patriarch Nikon launched reforms: everyone had to make the sign of the cross with three fingers instead of two, had to spell the name Jesus differently, had to walk the opposite direction in processions. If they didn't they'd be tortured and killed. So the Old Believers fled to China, Australia, Brazil, and Canada, wherever they could live free."

"Didn't most of the Homer area group come from Oregon?"

"Yes, near Woodburn, Oregon. But the Old Believers thought their kids were getting too much exposure to nasty American habits. So they migrated to Alaska in the sixties."

"The culture's such an interesting mix of old religion and new technology, Jan. Their fishing fleet has all the hottest techno-gadgets. They helicopter washing machines and generators to even their most remote sites. But they wear traditional clothes and believe exactly the way they did in the sixteen hundreds."

For the celebration, I wear a long skirt, and Ed his best shirt and pants. According to Troy, the wedding will last all week, and the couple will accrue substantial finances for beginning wedded life. Our attendance is for a single afternoon of the outdoor feast.

At the wedding, our arrival brings stares. We're bland as Pilgrims next to the Russians' gaily colored finery, and very obviously the only non-Russians present. Troy greets us enthusiastically and introduces us to his family. Plates of food are thrust into our hands. Another Russian hands us glasses, and reaches into a fifty-five gallon trash bucket with a ladle. *"Braga,"* he says as he fills the glass.

"Braga," I repeat. Is this a toast? Or the drink itself? The drink is sweet, obviously some type of homemade wine. My glass refills instantly, my plate too.

"We'll be flat as road kill," Ed whispers, "unless we take it slowly." I inhale the aromas of the spiced dishes and gawk at the fantastic clothing in more hues than a paint store. My fingers ache to click images but dare not; cameras are noticeably absent. I sit on my Nikon and imprint images on my mental screen. As we nibble pirogis, my mind backslides. "Remember elementary school, Ed, and being crammed under desks during bomb raid practice?"

"Big difference," he whispers, "between the big bad Russians that teachers warned us about, and the warmth of these people."

More food hits our plates. How, I wonder, do we depart gracefully? And how too will I ever describe today with my war veteran Dad?

Books and Beyond 〜

The post office brings heaps of letters. Ed grabs one, flicks it in the fire.

"Who was that from," I ask.

"Nothing important. INLAND Revenue. Doesn't apply to us, Jan. We live coastal."

"Don't you think you should have opened it?"

"Nah," he says, sorting through the mail. "Now THIS is important. Something from your family."

The letter is from my brother John. It's chock full of thanks for the Christmas presents: "The kid's loved their Alaskan coloring books. You should publish them."

"We need more income," seconds Ed. "More feeder streams. We spend money in dribs and drabs; every time we buy a stamp, develop film, fill the van with gas. We need a return flow. Maybe John's publishing idea is right on target. We could publish your book."

"My drawings are too childish, Ed. Fine for a personal present, but not for general distribution."

"Do you know any artists?

"My other brother, Jim, but let's check first to see if publication is financially feasible."

On our next town run, we stop at Fritz Creek Printers. Owner Jim Clymer raves about our proposed projects and advises we can save money by having everything camera-ready. His wife Al shows us examples. We then ask for an estimate. To do a costing, she needs to know which paper we desire. White? Beige? Colored? Which weight? Glossy or matte? Which color ink? Which paper for the cover? How many colors on the cover? Photographs or artwork or both? Our heads bog in details; I had no clue there were so many decisions. "What kind of binding do you want?" she continues. I examine samples. "Staple bind."

"While we're here, Ed," I add, "let's enquire about costs for publishing the sourdough. I like the idea you had of doing a flier with recipes that would accompany the dried culture." We begin the game of twenty questions again with Al. This time we decide quickly: beige card stock, trifold, brown ink. Umpteen answers later, the Clymers' calculator spits numbers. "Twenty-five hundred dollars for one thousand copies of the children's book." This includes the twelve-hundred-dollar surcharge for printing plates, which we can reuse time and again.

Are there a thousand people who'll want this book? Will it ever go to press again? Then there's another thousand for the sourdough flier. "It's such an investment, Ed."

"It's what you've wanted to do, Jan, be a writer. Here's your chance. Call your brother. Use the pay phone at the gas station. I have to stop and fill up anyways."

I dial Jim. "Alaska," I bait him. "Free air tickets and all the food you can eat, just do illustrations for *The Alaska Story*."

"I'll be up in spring," he assures me, "with my girlfriend Linda; she's an artist too."

In readiness for our marketing venture, Ed buys a sheet of plywood, handsaws it in sections, and carries the pieces to Swift Creek to assemble. "Your books and the sourdough will get lost on store shelves, Jan. We need them to stand up and be seen. I'm making you display boxes to hold them." Ed builds wooden stands, then uses a wood burner to produce rustic dark streaks through the lighter wood, and then seals the display boxes with varnish.

Jim and Linda arrive in late April, as Swift Creek bursts from its wintry glaciated siege. The couple's packs are overloaded and they're parched and panting by the time we reach the cabin. "I'd love a cold one, Jan," Jim tells me.

"No beer here, Jim, but I can give you some cold water."

"That'd do. My tongue's like cotton-wool. I'll drink anything cold."

I dash to the creek for fresh water, and return carrying five gallons of septic brown fluid.

"Why are you hauling that wash water inside?" asks Jim.

"It's the creek. Swift Creek broke free of ice and it's a tad muddy. We have to let the silt settle a while."

I try to divert Jim's attention as two inches of sediment collect in his glass. I pour off the clearer portion and fill his cup. Jim grimaces as he sips. "Tastes like you rinsed your socks in it."

"What do you have for supper?" he continues. "I'm as hungry as a grizzly."

"Silver salmon."

"Wow. Awesome." I go back to the creek to collect the salted salmon I've had freshening in the rapids for twenty-four hours. I taste: fishy salted mud.

In the cabin, I pull Ed aside and tell him about our salt salmon boondoggle. "We'll have to break out the last of our smoked salmon. Tomorrow we'll buy some frozen fillets and a six-pack of beer."

Days pass. Our drinking water situation is growing desperate. I'm now in a bad way. As the creek silted, my bowels grew goose-loose. My stomach's gurgling and abdomen's bloated. Even my fingertips ache.

"Must be runoff from the ranch upstream contaminating the water," says Ed. We now boil water, but my intestinal condition, giardiasis, amplifies. I dig through first aid supplies and study my homeopathy book. There's nothing specific to my situation. On our next town trip, I ring an East Coast homeopath. He asks strange questions. Do I feel better in hot or cold? Morning or evening? What foods do I crave?

"Take two tablets of homeopathic arsenic in a cup of water," he advises.

"How many times a day?"

"One time only."

Twenty-four hours later, my symptoms are gone.

But our boiled mud water is awful. Hauling water from town is impossible. It's hasn't rained in two weeks. Whatever will we do for water?

Nectar of the Gods ⌒

Atop Wind Point, Deiv's busy drilling birch trees, inserting spigots, and collecting sap in five gallon buckets. "Going to make syrup," he tells me. "Now back in Russia, they bottle and export birch sap as herbal tonic to tone and strengthen the whole body. Sap's loaded with vitamins and minerals. Russians drink pure sap like water."

"Bingo!" I shout. I skid down the hogback and head to an elderberry shrub. I cut a stem, push out the soft stem pith with a small stick, then boil the stem to remove any toxic pith residue. Ed drills a two inch hole on the sunny side of a birch. We empty our five gallon bucket of its dreadful silt, attach it by the handle to the notched spile, and wait. Morning triggers a rush to the birch: five gallons of sweet water. I dip a glass in the bucket. "No silt," I say triumphantly. "No giardia."

"Tastes slightly sweet, Jan."

"Good though," adds Jim. We drink sap straight, make tea with it, cook pasta in it, brush our teeth with it. "Nectar of the gods!" I exclaim.

Jim and Linda launch a full-fledged drawing marathon. I backpack library books so Jim and Linda can see Alaska's diverse regions. I watch as Jim draws kids tide-pooling on a beach; he passes the illustration to Linda. She sketches facial expressions and hands it back to Jim. Their art is like a tango.

I hand-print lettering to mount below their finished drawings and keep reworking rhymes. My main task is keeping the couple happily drawing. I bake oatmeal cookies, steam beach clams and spring nettles, sauté salmon and halibut purchased from town. I serve sourdough hotcakes drizzled with the last of our maple syrup.

"Birch syrup's even better," insists Deiv.

"Can't be better than maple," protests Ed.

"Betcha. Come on up and see the process."

After breakfast, while our guests glue their butts to the bench by the picture window, we scramble to Wind Point to witness. Deiv chainsaws a three-foot-diameter spruce into sections and hands Ed an ax. Ed splits gnarly rounds; I haul the chunks.

"Stack them there," Deiv directs. I stockpile the wood by a rusted outdoor wood stove. "Deiv must be doing his entire winter wood supply," I whine to Ed. "But, no matter, we're learning birch secrets."

Deiv quits cutting at 10 A.M. and gets the fire roaring. He strains sap through cheesecloth to remove twigs and insects and fills a kettle. Deiv adds another armload of wood to the stove, and sets the pot to simmer. As levels drop, Deiv adds more sap. We monitor constantly, adding more wood, more sap, and stirring occasionally.

I break to feed Jim and Linda, and grab goodies for the Wind Point crew. When I return, Deiv's still adding wood to the stove and sap to the pot. It appears little is happening, except for sap and the woodpile evaporating. Perhaps this isn't winter wood, only today's sap-making supply.

"How much longer, Deiv?"

"Syrup should be done by late tonight."

"That long? You must get a heap of syrup."

"Well, I've got fifty gallons sap . . . should yield about two quarts birch syrup."

"With maple you'd have a gallon of Grade A."

"Ratio's a hundred to one for birch."

"Must be fantastic to merit this work."

I go for snacks, take turns stirring sap, traipse below again to check art progress. After supper, I return with Jim and Linda, who are eager for the tasting party.

"Stir constantly at the very end," Deiv warns, "or the syrup will burn." We carefully babysit the fussy child.

Finally, we dive in with spoons. Deiv slurps a spoonful, licks his lips in bliss. I taste; it's like blackstrap molasses tinged with maple. Ed tastes and whispers. "Don't know how often we'll chop down the forest for firewood to brew this."

But sap straight from the tree gets unanimous approval. A single birch, tapped at the height of the season, streams three to ten gallons sap daily for the thirsty artists. Jim and Linda sketch page after endless page of Alaskan scenes, while savoring cool birch spiked with wild mint. The only fish they see is what's on their plate. The only bears are in a can and spelled with a double *e*. For them, Alaska is a pretty view, a mud creek, and an art marathon.

Twelve days after their arrival, we converge at the printers. The Clymers make camera-ready plates and print the book. We stack the pages on banquet tables. Like factory workers we walk the line, collate, and staple book after book. We bang the final staple at 2 A.M., and cram cartons into the van next to the stack of display boxes. We drive to road's end, park, walk home, and collapse.

Morning brings a drive up the Sterling Highway to drop Jim and Linda off at the Anchorage International Airport. "Come back when we're living at Rocky River," we console Jim. "Crystal water. And awesome fishing in Seldovia. You must see Alaska in high summer."

Ed parades me to bookstores, museums, and the Alaska Zoo. I march into shops wearing a broad smile and plunk down a display filled with twenty books. Some storekeepers buy on the spot, some on consignment, with only an occasional "no thanks." Two days later, the van is bereft of books and our address book rich in contacts for our coming sourdough marketing venture. We race back to Homer, and stop at Fritz Creek printers to commission a second book printing and to pay for Sourdough fliers. We head back to Swift Creek to celebrate.

A Tale of Two Mays 〰

May Day brings visitors. Mossy arrives on horseback to check the state of her pastures; with her is brother Atz, a fellow songwriter and performer. The siblings grab guitars from the cabin, lounge in the beachfront meadow, and strum and sing. A hermit thrush plays flute, while the white-crowned sparrow cheerily sounds his three note rendition: "Spring is here."

I nibble a dandelion blossom. Ed puffs his pipe, a dead giveaway he's contemplating something. "Mossy," he drawls, during a break between songs, "what do you think about lending me Jezebelle?"

"My farm truck?"

"Yep. Only for a couple days. I'll plop her on the *Tusty* with a load of rough-cut from Small Potatoes Sawmill, zip up to Rocky River, and dump things off. I'll have Jezebelle back at Seaside Farm on the Wednesday ferry. Need to stockpile supplies for the cabin."

"No problem. By the way, why don't you come to town tonight? Atz and his family are performing."

We head to Homer for an evening concert; the school auditorium swells with bodies. "I loved them all," I tell Ed afterward, "but Atz's daughter Jewel blew my socks off with her yodeling solo. What a voice. What presence that little girl had."

"Bet Jewel will be a household word someday, Jan."

"Wouldn't be surprised. Our friends back East think we're in the boondocks and yet we're far more cosmopolitan than before: Russian weddings, live music on the lawn, local and international concerts."

In the audience are our friends from Seaside Farm, Mike and Randy, builders of the *Water Rat*. Ed mentions his lumber-moving plans, and has an instant volunteer crew. "I'm up for an adventure," exclaims Mike.

"This trip should be pretty boring," Ed warns, "only driving to Rocky River to drop materials." With three bodies on line for the work trip, there's no room for extras. Max and I settle into our solitude at Swift Creek. Ed and company depart in blue skies for Seldovia, and return on the next Homer ferry.

"How'd it go, Ed?"

"Ferry crossing was the usual. But Randy kept groaning it was too damn hot; got his wish for air-conditioning out at Jakolof Bay. Scattered snow patches became snow hills; by the time we hit the mill there were drifts four feet high."

"Crap. Did you bring the wood back to Homer?"

"Didn't have to. You know that sign at the head of Jakolof Bay by the mill: 'end of the town-maintained road'? Someone plowed past it. Figured we'd get a half mile or so and then have to drop the wood, but the plow kept going. But where the switchback climbs hard by the cliff, it was all glaciated. Jezebelle spun like a cartoon, then slid backwards. Randy and Mike bailed out the door. I tried to too, but my sleeve snagged in the handle. Kept pumping the brakes and finally got her stopped at the edge of the drop-off. The guys had to chip exposed patches of gravel with their camp hatchets, and spread it like chicken scratch on the icy bits so I could get Jezebelle up the hill."

"So how far did you get with the wood?"

"Bizarre, Jan. All the way to our driveway. Had us head-scratching the whole time."

"Who in their right mind would plow the valley?"

"Well, while we were in the ferry queue, Sheriff Andy marched up to

Jezebelle, bent down as best he could with his big belly, and glared at the turned down edges of the license plate. Told me her registration's so old, she should be in a museum. And I told Andy, 'I'm taking her right over to Homer to be in one.' He said if I come back to his town, it'd better be with a rig with papers."

"So who plowed the road?"

"I asked Andy about that. He told me one of the locals got himself a brand new truck and plow. Rocky River was the only place to try it out."

"So when do I get to go to Rocky River, Ed? I'm aching to see it again."

"Next week, Jan. Randy volunteered to join us with his old Land Cruiser. Said he can get into all the lower meadows with his four-wheel drive and skid all our logs right to the building site easy as pie."

Easy as Pie 〜

The next Tuesday we load up the Land Cruiser with come-along (a hand-operated ratchet lever winch), tents, gear, and food (including homemade pie) and head to Rocky River. As we depart, Homer bakes in a sixty-degree May heat wave, and the roads are lined with flamboyant dandelions.

Rocky River is a different scene. Fiddlehead ferns peek timidly from cold earth, dressed in papery shields. Our battery radio ballyhoos more blue skies for Homer. The only blue we see is Ed's raincoat. We soggily sit in a Gulf Coast downpour. Rain changes to hail, slows to a drizzle, then escalates to driven sheets.

"Look, guys," I say, pointing, "horizontal rain. I've never seen sideways rain before."

Ed explains how winds funnel from Windy Bay, gather steam across the wide clear-cut region, then bellow into the narrow waist of our valley.

I zip my rain hood tighter. We need to keep working in order to catch the return ferry tomorrow.

Randy turns the key on the Land Cruiser. Silence.

Ed pulls the chain saw cord. Silence.

"I'm cold," I grumble. "Going to start a fire to brew us some hot tea." I walk to the Visqueen-covered shelter Ed erected when we did the pilings. The plastic has been shattered by winter winds. The wood is as wet as a baby's diaper.

My eyes alight on the stack of rough-cut lumber, hauled last week from Homer, snug and dry under a new blue tarp. Ed walks up, finds me rummaging in the pile. "That's for the cabin, Jan."

"We need firewood, Ed. Otherwise it's peanut butter sandwiches and cold water."

Ed grabs an ax. "A couple boards won't do any harm."

I get a fire going while the guys tinker with the machines. They pause for hot drinks and warmed pie.

"Still sounds quiet out there," I comment.

"The Land Cruiser won't go; it doesn't like the damp. Neither does the saw."

"And this was supposed to be easy as . . ." I finish the sentence, taking another bite of dessert.

The guys fiddle with the machines. I'm wet, cold, cranky. I burn more of the woodpile to stay warm. Max crawls under a spruce; he shivers and looks miserable, and noses me with his "home" look.

"Sorry Max, we are home. But I know how you feel buddy, I'm miserable too. Can't wait to crawl into a warm bag."

At dusk, I pull off boots and raingear and dive inside my bag. "Gross, Ed. The bag's soaked."

Ed steps out into the torrent. "The fly's dripping water onto the tent corner, puddling water inside. No way to fix it; design flaw."

"What'll we do? We can't sleep in these bags."

"Get dressed."

"Where we going?"

"To bed."

We pull on rain pants and coats, socks and rubber boots, and slide back inside our bags.

"Better?" asks Ed.

"I feel ridiculous but at least we're dry. Listen: the weather's changing. The rain's stopped drumming."

"But there's a funny sound, like whispering." Ed unzips the fly and peeks out. "Snow; fat flakes."

"And this is May? Think we made a mistake?"

"I think we could use an angel."

Morning brings overcast skies and gray faces around the campfire. Randy still can't get the Land Cruiser running. The battery radio forecasts finer weather is en route. We string lines through the trees and hang our bedding and the tent to dry. We burn more milled lumber to heat water. Breakfast is hot coffee and cold pie. We hear a strange rumbling. Earthquake?

The rumbling intensifies.

"A vehicle! A vehicle," I shout. I sprint to the road, and flag down the truck. It's the mill's mechanic. He tinkers with the damp Cruiser and tows it to the road. The men push; the Cruiser springs to action. The mechanic tinkers with Ed's saw; it starts.

Four hours later, our forty cabin logs are stacked in place at our building site. We gasp as we glance at our watches. The ferry's due in.

We pile into the Land Cruiser and drive the twenty-five miles back to town. A queue of cars waits for the late-again *Tusty*. Two hours later, we board and head to its cafeteria for steaming coffees. We clink our cups with Randy. "To a successful mission," says Ed.

"To the angel," I add. We smile; the building logs of our home are ready and waiting. All that remains is our final week at Swift Creek and packing. We stop at Seaside Farm to update Mossy of our imminent departure. "How will you get back to Swift Creek?" she asks us.

"The same way we always do."

"But East Road is closed beyond fourteen mile. Mud's so bad, even the school buses can't operate. You'll have to hike home."

We drop Greenie in Mossy's field and walk the fifteen beach miles back to Swift Creek. Worries ease as we walk. "Funny how I always used to stare at the glaciers but now it's this that fascinates me." I point left, to the pastel bluffs, punctuated by sandstone boulders. "That one looks like a spaceship," I tell Ed. "Reminds me of the UFO we saw."

"Alaska, Jan. Never know what will turn up next."

Baby on the Doorstep ⌁

Back at Swift Creek, our minds feel split. "Swift Creek's been magic, Ed. I hate having it end."

"But our own place, Jan, Rocky River."

"I'm happy and sad at the same time; what a special first year."

A knock interrupts; it's game biologist Dave Holderman, en route to the Fox River valley for an overnight campout. We ply him with tea and welcome him to stop longer on his return.

"It's the camaraderie of this place, Ed, that I'll miss so much; always something happening. Rocky River is so isolated; our nearest neighbor is seven miles away."

On our morning beach walk, colors are brighter, smells more acute, time trancelike. "I wonder if it feels like this," I muse, "when one has a terminal illness, and every breath could be one's last."

We skip along the shoreline; Max's keen nose pries and prods everywhere. "Looks like he's reading a newspaper," laughs Ed, "the Tidal Telegraph."

Max stops at a gray log, raises his hackles, and barks. He circles, sniffs, and woofs again. We sprint to the log. I crouch down and gape: a silky creature mews softly.

"A seal pup, Janzie, still dangling its umbilical cord. That eagle," he points to a cottonwood, "is waiting for us to move to peck its eyes. They always go for the eyes first."

"Gross, Ed. We can't let that happen. But where's mom? Why isn't she here?"

"Must be dead. Wouldn't leave her pup here exposed like this. Besides, seals haul out on the rocks across the bay, not here on the mud flats."

"Dave Holderman will know what to do; he's supposed to stop by later today. Maybe we can keep it safe 'til he returns."

We carry our mewing package into the cabin, as Max dances at our heels. We set the seal on the floor while I search the pantry. There's powdered cow's milk, canned condensed milk, soy milk. "What do you feed a seal? And how will we get it into the pup?"

The door rattles. Max woofs. "Yay! Dave Holderman is back."

Ed glances out the window. "Nope, strangers, a couple with a baby." Deb and Harvey are potential caretakers of the cabin, sent by Mossy to check out the scene. We show them the Swift Creek attractions, including the seal. They donate their baby's bottle for our strange pet. I fill the bottle with warm reconstituted milk, wedge the seal's mouth open, and slide the nipple in. "She's not sucking, Ed."

"Squeeze the bottle, Jan. Pump it."

I do, and milk dribbles out. My hand becomes a bellows, squeeze, pause, squeeze, pause.

"Is she getting any?"

"Hard to say. I'm soaked."

Dave Holderman finally arrives. I answer the door, cradling the seal. His eyes widen. He listens to our tale. "You did the right thing; that pup would have been eagle bait if you'd left it. Would you like to raise her?"

My eyes light up.

"Jan," says Ed.

"I know. Next week we move mid-valley, not a good place to raise a sea-dwelling mammal."

"How about caring for her this week," asks Dave, "until I locate a suitable home?"

"Oh yes," I exclaim. Ed seconds the vote.

"But you'll have to bring the pup to town to get her on a proper formula. She'll die if she's kept on cow's milk."

We load the seal, now dubbed Harriet, in my backpack and hike the fifteen miles back to Seaside Farm to retrieve Greenie. We encounter one other person on the beach, who stares in amazement at the strange gray head sticking from my pack.

At Mossy's, we call the vet, Dr. Ralph Broshes, and schedule an appointment. Ralph examines the pup and frowns. "She's quite dehydrated. You'll have to puree herring, add these vitamins to it, and feed her every four hours."

We buy herring, return to Mossy's, and explain our dilemma: it's impossible to make seal smoothies without electricity. Mossy hands us her blender and invites us to move into the upstairs bedroom.

I'm now mom; life revolves around four-hour feeds. Harriet slurps fish smoothies with as little enthusiasm as she did milk. She dribbles me with fishy inflow, douses me with unsavory outflow. My clothes reek and I dump them into Mossy's washer after each feed. Rising twice each night gets old quickly; my eyes get puffy. If only I had a nanny.

A Nanny for Harriet ～

Dusty, one of Mossy's tenants, hears about Harriet and wants to hold her and feed her. I hand over the pup and head for the shower. Dusty is intrigued with the seal. I'm intrigued with Dusty, an artist who specializes in animal portraits. "I hitchhiked to Alaska," Dusty says.

"Alone? Isn't hitching alone dangerous for women?"

"I wasn't alone. I had June and Joy with me."

"Good pals of yours?"

"June's my Aussie shepherd and Joy is my pet bantam hen."

"You hitched with a dog and a chicken?"

"They helped get me lots of rides."

Dusty describes crossing the Yukon, and how the driver fell asleep at the wheel and rolled the motorhome. "We were both banged up. At the hospital I was ordered to stay overnight for observation. Told the doc I couldn't; I had my dog to take care of."

"I'll take your dog home with me," he volunteered. "You have to stay."

"Well, what about my chicken?" I asked him. He looked puzzled and told me to keep my chicken with me. All the nurses were fascinated with Joy and sat around my bed feeding her tidbits. In the morning when the doc walked in to check me, he stopped in his tracks. "I thought you meant a cooked chicken!"

Dusty promises to take over one of the pup's nightly feedings. I take Harriet to the bath and plunge her into cool salted water. She fusses, trying to escape. When I remove her from the water, she shivers.

"Wonder if she's sick, Ed?"

"You wouldn't think a seal would shiver from water."

Harriet flops across the hall following me, mewing loudly. "She's more like a dog than a seal," I laugh. I pick her up and she settles, nuzzles her mouth close to my chin, and sniffs my breath. "Now I know why women like to have babies."

The phone rings. Mossy answers. "Jan, for you."

"Good news," says Dave Holderman. "I've found a home for the pup. Marian Beck at Halibut Cove will take her. Marian's a fisherwoman, with a steady supply of herring. She even has the federal permits needed; she's experienced with raising seals."

My eyes blur.

Halibut Cove ᐧᐧᐧᐧᐧ

Marian runs a thirty-four-passenger ferry, the Danny J, between Homer and Halibut Cove on Ismailof Island. The Cove, in the early twentieth century, was home to herring saltries. It now houses reclusive painters, potters, and fishermen, as well as tourist galleries, bed and breakfasts, and seafood restaurants. Marian, like her mom Diana Tillion, is an artist; and like her dad Clem, a fisherman.

Marian cradles Harriet to her chest. "I'll take good care of her," she consoles me.

"I know, but it's hard."

"First seals, like first children, are always hard. There's so much you fret about. When Scrape, my first seal, would exit water and shiver, I'd be positive he had pneumonia. Later I learned that those hypothermic shivers are the way seals adapt from wet to warm."

"Oh, that explains it. Harriet acted like she hated water."

"Oh, that's typical, Jan. Seals need swimming lessons."

"A seal can't naturally swim? They don't take to water like ducks?"

"I stand by when I first put pups in the water," Marian says. "Some get stuck under logs, or swamped in the wakes of fast boats, or dive when they're not properly prepared. They can drown when they're first in the ocean."

"She's hard to feed," I warn, "really fussy, and hardly sucks at all."

"That's because seal mothers have slits rather than teats. For primary feeding, I use a stomach tube. And for bottle feeds, which are important for emotional rapport with the pup, I use the back of a slit rubber glove, which is more similar to the mom's anatomy. The right formula took me quite a while to evolve."

I beg her recipe in case I ever raise a pup again.

Marian's Sealshake

40 unsalted herring
1 cup vegetable oil
1 tsp. liquid vitamins
Puree in blender. Strain. Heat to lukewarm.

"And after feeding, pups love to rest in your lap," Marian says.

"That bit I noticed; there's so much more to being a surrogate seal mom than I thought."

The other part of mothering, which I'm now experiencing, is the letting go. "It's important to avoid turning a seal into a trained and dependent pet," Marian tells me. "They're meant to be wild and free. It's always wonderful when they return to visit, but you have to encourage their independence."

Ed and I abandon our babe to Marian's loving arms. We return the van to Mossy's, hike back to Swift Creek, and pack up our final belongings. Due to the road closure, Mossy will collect us in her boat. At high tide, she appears in her Boston Whaler, and bobs in the surf as we ferry our goods to water's edge. We hand box by box over the bow. We lift Max in, clamber aboard, and wave good-bye to the cabin. Our life is turning, and so is the tide.

PART THREE

Prickly rose
(Rosa acicularis)

"*The scream resounds again.*
My head tilts, trying to get a bearing
on where it's coming from.
It sounds like someone or something
desperately needs help."

Once Upon a Valley

At Rocky River, June swells with golden days, clear skies, and endless light. My only squawk is the state of the river. "What a shame there's no fish."

"No silt," chimes Ed.

"Ya, ya, and no fish poo, but still I only wish . . ."

"If wishes were horses . . ."

"I'd have a stableful."

Our stable these days is our green van, parked between the young spruce trees lining our gravel drive. Behind Greenie sits our latest addition, Randy's battered Land Cruiser, which is an ideal runabout for the Gulf Coast network of old logging roads south of our cabin.

House construction flows in the sublime weather. Each day I straddle a spruce, armed with a drawknife, a single narrow blade set between wooden handles. I tilt the drawknife blade and pull; it digs. Outer bark strips slide from the knife; spruce perfumes the air.

"Too deep, Jan," Ed corrects. He demonstrates how to slant "just so." He strips bark from the log as easily as peeling a banana. "Make certain you leave some of that red-brown cambium. See how it contrasts so nicely with the blond wood." Ed makes using a drawknife look so easy. I try again. This time I manage to strip three feet of outer bark before I smack a knot.

"Trim rough bits like that with the hatchet."

Soon I have the rhythm and the technique. Peeling logs is like dancing: the clumsy first steps and then, ah, the body knows the pattern, and shifts effortlessly to the beat.

Meanwhile Max plays, paws under the trees, sniffs voles, and suns in the meadow. Periodically I pause, brew cups of tea, and call Ed for a smoko. As the roar of his chain saw subsides, we bask in riversong, the trill of the thrush, the sewing-machine whir of the warblers. We admire our progress.

The spruce logs are backbreakers. Ed moves the unmovable with ropes and come-along. Our Rocky River cabin is Ed's first experience using full round logs. In New Hampshire, Ed milled pine logs flat, top and bottom, using a portable "Alaskan" mill bolted onto each pine. This "Scandinavian style" method for our Alaska cabin uses round logs; it requires a chain saw (or adze) to cup the bottom of the whole log so that it nestles over the log below.

Ed cables a log, slides it up skids onto the wall with his come-along, and temporarily secures it in place with a metal U-shaped spike he calls a log-dog. With calipers and pencil, he traces along the wall and marks the irregularities of the log. He rolls the log onto its back, supported by the connecting walls, while he cuts along his guideline. Then he rolls the log back into place on the wall for a test fit. He fine-tunes his measurements, then upends the log again .

"Reminds me of a turtle flipped on its back," I tell him. Ed laughs, resaws, retests, redoes cuts as necessary. When the log is just right, Ed staples yellow sill insulation into the hollow that he has cut, then rolls the log back into its permanent place on the wall. With a hand drill he bores holes, then inserts steel rebar to hold the log walls in alignment.

"Everything has to be free-moving," he tells me, "or the house will hang up as it dries, and let weather in."

Max, meanwhile, digs voles, sleeps, catches bees, sleeps. Finally he noses me. "Max is bored again."

"Let me finish this log," insists Ed.

Max nudges again. "Oh come on," I beg Ed. "Let's go exploring."

Ed sighs and lays down his chisels and hand-drills. Max bounds across the meadow like a bunny. We walk along the river, smelling the latest blooms. I pinch the leaves of an irregularly lobed plant. They're aromatic. I remind myself to determine its identity.

"There are so many new plants to learn here in the Rocky River valley," I tell Ed, "and hardly any nettles. And we're miles away from all the coastal edibles. We'd best start a garden like at Swift Creek." In our spare time from building, we till a small garden. I hike through the forests, returning home with buckets of bear scat and moose nuggets to fertilize our patch. From town we haul seedlings. "Fresh greens soon," I promise.

But morning brings gloom. The prolific residents of Rocky River, the red-backed voles, have delighted in the new additions to their diet. Our patch bears few survivors.

Our construction ticks along, like a clock with a sluggish battery. We average one wall log a day, most days. Town runs gobble bites from the building window. Two months after we start, four walls stand tall. Ed sets cross-ties to support the loft floor, plus an extra for roof support. The rafter raising begins in early August. Max, bored again, lures us on walk-about. We wander downriver, stand on a high rock by a clear pool, and bask in our solitude.

"Look, Janzie" shouts Ed.

I glance about. Moose? Black bear? Eagle? I follow Ed's finger to the river and peer deeply. A wavy steel gray shape waggles. "A fish! Our river has a fish." We look again. More wavy shapes. And larger wavy shapes. Dolly Varden? And salmon? We hoot over our naïveté. We hadn't seen fish before, simply because it was before the salmon run. On our next trip to Seldovia, we check out books on salmon and their life cycles.

"Wow, Ed. The salmon we saw were definitely Coho, or silvers. Says here that they've come back from the ocean to spawn. The eggs they're laying now in their gravel nests will hatch in the early spring, and then they'll become inch-long alevin, and they'll stay in the nest living off a yolk sack for the next month. This is a critical stage; if there's sediment from logging or pollution they won't survive. But in pristine conditions like Rocky River, the alevins will become fry and they'll live in the river for a couple years, hiding under rocks and vegetation to keep away from predators. At a year or two old, as five-inch smolt, they'll head to sea. They'll live in the ocean a couple years, growing into ten- to twenty-pound fish. Now our salmon are finding their way back to their home river. Biologists think salmon recognize home by the taste and smell of the water."

By mid-August, we hit a series of firsts: first snow on the peaks, first fall rain, and first frost. The few lettuce plants that survived the vole predation are limp. "Only a sixty day growing season, Ed. I doubt we'll ever be able to have a successful garden."

But our afternoon walk brings promise. Creekside greens that I recognize as Siberian spring beauty *(Claytonia siberica)* defy the cold. "Looks like this will be our salad from now on. I'd best learn what else we can eat here in the valley."

We step up the construction pace, but the weather throws tantrums. We sit in the van in the wet evenings and I strum playfully on the guitar.

It's a drippy dreary day in Seldovia,
and I'm wishing that I'd built an ark.
I'm trying to look on the bright side of things,
But the skies are dreary, gray, and dark.

I pen more lighthearted verses, all gross exaggeration, about raining for forty days, washing bridges to the sea, and similar artistic nonsense. A fortnight later, we worry. I scan the amphitheater of mountains and hand the binoculars to Ed.

"Count the waterfalls."

"Thirteen. Why?"

"There have never been more than six before. They're dumping tons of water into Rocky River."

"We're high in the meadow, Jan; nothing can bother us here."

The intensifying rains make it impossible to work. We sit in the van, read, and write letters. Ed's frustrated. He wants to get the roof secure before winter bites. That night, we huddle in the van, encamped inside a drum. I step out for nightly business. "Bloody sideways rain," I squawk to the horizontal, driving sheets. They saturate my sleeve.

"Come on Ed, we need air," I tell him when I return. "Grab your storm gear, let's go." Ed protests. I insist. "We're turning into slugs; we need exercise." We hike three-tenths of a mile south to the log bridge over the Rocky River. The waters tear furiously at the bridge pilings. Boulders bounce in the rapids.

Back at the van, we play cards, and listen to the rain drum. Is it getting more thunderous or only our imagination? In the morning, I hop outdoors for my walk with Max, relieved that the rain has finally hit the pause button. As we hike, butterflies flutter in my stomach. The dry section of the road has a gully ripped through it. A crazed army of bulldozers has been on a rampage. I feel like Dorothy in Oz. "We're not in Kansas anymore," I tell Max. Talking to him anchors me. Things around us are different. I rub my eyes, disbelieving. The south bridge is gone.

Flood ⌇

Ed's still in bed. I race in breathless. "Gone, Ed. The bridge is gone!"

"Don't be ridiculous, Jan; it's a brand new bridge. They rebuilt it last week."

"It's gone, I tell you."

We run to the river crossing, and gawk at the roiling waters. "Good thing we head north, Jan. We'd best get the vehicles out." My stomach knots; I pray we're not too late. Half a mile later, we stop. The Wolverine Creek culvert dangles in the limbs of a fallen tree. "Looks like Godzilla has been here," says Ed. "No way to get the van across that gully."

We return to start and embark again, this time with the Land Cruiser. The four-wheel-drive Toyota scrambles through the ditch, claws around the curve, and stops at a flood-felled tree.

"It's like Monopoly, Ed. Back to start. Don't pass 'Go.' Don't collect two hundred dollars."

"Only this game is: back to start; do collect the chain saw."

We load the Land Cruiser with tools and go again. Ed winches the roadblock aside. My gut gurgles as we approach Windy River. The other log bridge is . . . is . . .

Intact.

"Almost done now, Jan. Just a sweet slide down the switchback." The switchback's snaky track is a critical link between valley and town. Only now it's gone; the entire hillside is gone. All has slithered nine hundred feet downward, cliff top stockpiled into cliff bottom.

We abandon the Land Cruiser and struggle ahead on foot. Alder branches become safety lines on bare rock edges. We struggle to dent the earth for footholds. Ed perches above the precipice. "Big honking motorhomes drove this last week, heading to the lower Rocky River to fish. Now all is gone in a flash."

"Flood," I add, "the power of water, power of Alaska. How will we ever get our vehicles out of here?"

"Let's ask at the logging camp." Ed knocks at the manager's trailer, at the head of Jakolof Bay. We're ushered inside. As we chat, the manager, Floyd, leans back and hurls a gob of spit. The wad flies across the room and lands smack in the corner spittoon.

"Got a dozer that might open the road?" Ed asks.

"Nope. Sold it. Done cutting in the valley. Shipped the rig to Homer yesterday."

"We're in a world of hurt," says Ed. "Our two vehicles are stuck in the valley."

"Yep. That's a problem." Floyd pauses, spits again. "Now if I were you, I'd call Anchorage, hire one of those Hercules helicopters."

"Doesn't look like we've got a choice."

"Good luck to you; wish we could help."

We hike from the mill toward Seldovia and intercept a vehicle exiting the Jakolof Bay dock, which gets us a lift to town. We stop at the harbor pay phone and search the phone book. Ed dials, I eavesdrop. "Do you have a Hercules helicopter that can airlift vehicles? And what's the estimated price?" After a moment, he hangs up.

"That was short and sweet," I comment.

"Short, not sweet," corrects Ed. "Yes; five thousand each."

"That's more than either vehicle's worth."

"Let's have a bite before we hitch back, Jan. There's got to be an answer."

We munch hamburger and drink beer at the Linwood Bar and dredge our minds for solutions.

"Why don't we practice that creative visualization we've been reading about, Ed. Let's picture our vehicles on the town side of the switchback."

"How much will this cost us?"

"Don't worry about a price," I say. "Picture the vehicles there; picture yourself happy." I take a final bite of my burger and wipe my lips with the napkin and say, "Let's go back to the mill."

"Floyd already said he can't help."

"I feel we should go back there," I insist.

We hike along Jakolof Bay Road and flag down the first vehicle. At the mill, Floyd is still in his seat, doing his spittoon act.

"Don't you own any other equipment?" I ask Floyd.

"Derelict; my other dozer's broken. It needs welding and a lot of work."

I persist. "Isn't there anyone around here who could weld?"

In response, Floyd leans back, reaches for his back pocket, and grabs more chew from the round tin.

Our angel spits again.

Good Neighbors ~

"Best welder I know," says Floyd, "is Herb, out Red Mountain Valley. Herb worked part-time for us for years. Until now, with us moving out and all. Herb's darn clever with machines. Can fix anything."

"Even broken bulldozers?"

Floyd nods.

"Herb must be in a pickle too with the switchback out," I continue. "Haven't met him yet but we've seen heaps of rigs out by his place. What's he got, four vehicles?"

"Five," pronounces Floyd as he shoots another wad. "Herb's quite a guy, the hermit of Red Mountain. Except when he needs money to feed those beefalos. Now one winter, he didn't get enough hay put up, and brought some in on the ferry. He'd pick up a hay bale in each of those banana hands of his, and carry them up that snowed-in switchback and out the seven miles to his place. Tough as guts, that boy is."

"Now, what if Herb could weld up your machine, get it running?" I ask.

"Well then I'd be happy to put a man on the dozer and get the switch-back open for you folks. But only so you can all get out. You drive back in and it happens again, you're up the creek."

Cuppas complete, we traipse to the Land Cruiser atop the switchback. We clamber in, and scramble in four-wheel drive through washouts. In Red Mountain valley, Herb hears the rig and pokes his head out from his trailer. "Hey neighbor," Ed calls out. We introduce ourselves and blare the good news: Floyd can get all of our vehicles out. "But," Ed continues, "you'll have to get the dozer running." Herb scuttles to the mill while we head homeward.

"I'm knackered," I tell Ed, yawning. "It'll be early to bed tonight."

"We'd best hit the feathers as soon we get home, Jan. Have to move into the cabin in the morning."

"But it's got no roof."

"And we've got no choice."

New Life ⌁

Dreams of an angry God haunt my dreams: wrath, waters, sliding cliffs, falling bridges, floating arks. I wake, adrenalin pumping. Morning oatmeal grounds me and coffee buzzes me to action. Ed directs operations. "Gut out the van. Pitch the tent in that corner."

"Tent in the cabin?"

"Sure. Flat wood floor. The wooden walls will keep out driving rain."

"What will we cook on?"

"I'll dismantle the van's stove. I'll do cabinets later; meanwhile it can sit on a stump. And with the oven hitched up we can even make pie."

"We? Got a mouse in your pocket?"

"Right, you can make pie. Speaking of which, as soon as we get the van unloaded let's drive to Seldovia, get some hamburger for a shepherd pie, and apples for an apple . . ."

"Pie," I finish.

Ed beams. "A day without pie is a day without sunshine."

The day teems with moving tasks. Ed chainsaws waist-high stumps for holding rough-cut boards for a temporary kitchen countertop. I erect the tent, and lay out the mattress, down bed, and pillows. Ed slams together wooden boxes to hold clothes; I fill them and stuff them in a corner under a tarp.

"Luxury camping," I quip. "And lots more walkabout room; the van was becoming a sardine tin." I fold an old blanket and tuck it by the tent for Max. Ed anchors a tarp to walls and rafters. "Just in case," he says. "Don't want any more soggy nights."

In late afternoon we hop into the Land Cruiser. "Can't wait to see if the mill has started road repair," Ed says. At Wolverine Creek, we stop, amazed; the culvert's back in place, water flowing through, gravel tamped above.

"Looks like yesterday was but a dream," I marvel. At the switchback, rusted vehicles line the cliff edge, forming a foundation for rock and gravel clawed from the mountain. The Land Cruiser roars down with ease. At the mill, we pump Floyd's hand. Ed reaches in his wallet, grabs bills, and slides them to Floyd. "No way," he refuses, "only being a good neighbor."

We park the Land Cruiser and hike the seven miles back to the cabin. We reload into the van, drive past the mill, and onward to town for supplies.

"Celebration night," says Ed as we depart Stampers Market. "Our first night in our very own home."

"Heaps to be thankful for," I reply, "but it looks like another big squall is coming. We'd best do as Floyd suggests: get supplies in and then drive the van back out. The river is still at peak. That means another seven-miler."

"A seven-mile hike to the cabin every time, Jan; we won't get fat."

"Or lazy."

"And Max will be thrilled with all his walks."

"And we won't be bugged by salesmen."

"Ever."

"What a difference a day makes."

"One small day, one big flood."

First Company ～

Floyd's good deed turns the tide to bluer skies, crisp days, and construction production. Ed raises the rafters; I pound nails in the loft floorboards. Our kitchen's rough but functional, our corner tent cramped but dry. "Reminds me of Deiv living in his wall tent," I tell Ed.

"But no chicken nesting in the corner."

As we speak, we startle to the public radio broadcast. "To the Rocky River ramblers: coming out on next ferry to help pound nails. From Deiv on the Point."

"That's spooky. Must hear us thinking about him."

"Or vice versa."

I'm ecstatic Deiv's coming; the roof job is next. It's now two on the roof, me on terra firma. I hand boards and fetch nails. Volleys of banging drown birdsong. Inside, the cabin darkens. Boards blot the sun like a solar eclipse.

I go for tools, brew tea, bake cookies, hand up more boards. The pile on the floor dwindles. The men proceed to rolled roofing. We celebrate the roof's completion with barbecued salmon, blueberry pie, and herbal tea.

"To the good life," says Deiv.

"And good friends," I add. "We really appreciated the help, and the company."

The next day, Deiv catches the air taxi back to Homer. We disassemble the tent, sit on stumps, and clink our teacups: "To a dry roof overhead."

Later, we snuggle by firelight on the down piled in the corner. "Soon we'll have our own bedroom, Jan."

"Soon, Ed. Right now I'm thrilled to have a dry roof, dry bed, and warm arms. The rest will come in good time." Ed blows out the candle.

Let There be Light ~

With roof up and tent down, our living standards escalate. In the loft, Ed nails two-by-twelves to the floor. He tops the frame with removable boards, forming a storage compartment for out-of-season clothes. I hand up the foam pad, feather mattress, and down duvet. I comb through boxes for the new sheets saved for this occasion. I scale the ladder, make the bed, and pounce on its freshness. Ed fusses with his tools. "Quit it, Jan. Gotta make a clothes pole, here under the eaves."

"Later. Check out what we've done." I bop Ed with a pillow. He jumps on the bed and play-wrestles.

"Bliss," I babble, as I nestle into the new bed.

"Want bliss?" he teases.

"Again? Thought we had bliss last night."

"Light-years ago, Jan."

After bliss, we lounge and admire wood knot patterns in the ceiling. We see shapes, another game like Swift Creek beach ice sculptures. "Eagle," I say.

Ed repeats, "Eagle." He looks to the right, not to my knothole.

"No, Ed, the ceiling knot; here."

"There," he points. "Eagle, in that spruce, welcoming us." The eagle lifts, flaps, drifts upward, circles.

"I'm so glad you framed this gable with huge openings." I extend my arm through the airy triangles. "Makes this room so bright and cheery. Room with a river view."

"Eventually we'll get glass, Jan. For now I'll staple clear plastic as windows."

"Let's have a tea and celebrate." We descend from sunny loft to gloomy downstairs. Log walls stand tall, interrupted only by the door opening. "Feels like a fort down here, Ed, like we're barricaded in to fend off enemies. And it's getting awful chilly leaving the door open all the time for light."

In response, Ed starts his chain saw and attacks the wall.

"Eddie, it's okay," I bellow. "I'm teasing." The chain saw drowns my voice. His answer is a volley of wood chips. Ed slashes the wall vertically then horizontally. A section of wall crashes outward. Ed stills the saw. "Better?"

Light bathes the cabin with golden rays. "More?" he asks. I beam. He carves a hole by the kitchen bench, and a final picture window midway down the long wall. He grabs the roll of clear plastic, scissors, and stapler. "Windows, Jan. Glass later, but for now we've light."

"What a difference a hole makes. The cabin's getting that homey feel."

"Almost. Grab your pack. Time for a town run."

In Seldovia Ed seeks and finds a fifty-five-gallon drum with a flat plate top, along with lengths of stovepipe. "We'll drive it home in the Land Cruiser; I can start the install while you take the rig back out."

"Might as well stockpile groceries too if we're doing a drive in; don't know how much longer we can, roads are already getting washouts from the last rains."

"Let's get a bottle of brandy, too, to warm the evenings. Already getting frosty enough to freeze teats off a sow."

I drop Ed at Rocky River with the supplies, then drive back to the mill, and hike home the seven miles. At meadow's edge, I stare at the golden cottage framed by frosted mountains. A blast of heat welcomes me inside. Candlelight flickers. Ed rushes with a hug and a snifter of brandy.

"Home, Jan. Welcome home."

"She's a real home now, Ed. Roof, windows, heat."

"Tomorrow we start a real kitchen."

"Tomorrow, Ed. Let's savor today." We sit on stumps, hug the fire, and sip brandy.

"And real chairs," adds Ed.

"Tomorrow; what's that Shakespeare quotation you and Stevie always used to recite doing concrete, the one about tomorrow?"

To-morrow and to-morrow and to-morrow,
Creeps in this petty pace from day to day,
To the last syllable of recorded time;
And all our yesterdays have lighted fools
The way to dusty death. Out, out, brief candle!
Life's but a walking shadow, a poor player
That struts and frets his hour upon the stage
And then is heard no more. It is a tale
Told by an idiot, full of sound and fury
Signifying nothing.

"This winter," continues Ed, "I want to memorize Robert Service."

"Tomorrow. Live now. To us." We clink glasses.

"To us, Jan. To light, to warmth, to home."

Valley Living ⌇

Each dawn brings changes, ticks time. Frost shifts priorities. Today's task is firewood. Ed scans the riverside forest and nods in the direction of a dead spruce.

"Spruce? You know better than that, Ed. Our friends back East would laugh at us burning spruce. It creosotes the chimney and doesn't leave coals. Now what about that dead tree over there?"

"Cottonwood, Jan; could burn it all day and barely boil water. Yeah, I know what Yanks say 'bout burning spruce. My old speech exactly, but back there we had hardwood. Here's we've spruce, spruce, or spruce. No birch like on Homer side. And it's far better than cottonwood."

Ed fells the spruce and cuts it into four-foot lengths. We flip sections on our shoulders, and head to our new Visqueen-covered wood shelter. To and fro we go, like pack llamas. While Ed splits rounds, I cart kindling.

Now, Ed's onto a new project. Before we can even brew a cuppa, he's on point. "Lift, Jan." I grab one end of the plywood kitchen bench. We play musical furniture and shift stumps, boards, and food into the opposite corner by the plastic picture window.

I sweep the cleared space. While soup brews on the relocated propane stove, Ed heads to the wood stash to salvage remains of last year's Jezebelle delivery.

With handsaw, chisels, and planes, Ed makes magic. Rough-cut two-by-fours shapeshift into smooth cabinet frames. Boards plane into uniform shelves. A four-inch spruce slab becomes a countertop. Day by day, board by board, a functional kitchen appears. The van sink nestles into a hole cut in the counter. "It'll drain into a five-gallon bucket, for now, Jan. But come spring, we'll dig a gray water system and filter sink waste through layers of rock."

I'm the gofer, and more: I go for nails and for boards. I brew tea and make pie. I plane, sand, and seal.

Winter now blankets the valley; darkness intensifies. Schofield's workshop operates by candlelight within warm log walls. Spruce slabs and alder branches become kitchen chairs. A bent spruce knee and boards become a corner couch.

Ice cakes grip the river, but rapids maintain open leads. As I scan and scoop, resident water ouzels fly beneath ice sheets, still hunting river bugs.

Winter fare features hearty soups, rice and beans, sprout salads, canned salmon, and spuds. But eating triggers an element of life little talked about. Inflow brings outflow, liquid and solid. Swift Creek had an outhouse for daily business. But at Rocky River, all we've had time to build is a four-foot-deep hole topped by a wooden box, with a seat made from a block of Styrofoam.

"No odor Jan; lots of fresh air," insists Ed.

"Yeah, yeah." To cope, I train my body to work in a wink, and to wait until after Ed's daily move. The first to go sticks bare bum to a frosty seat; the fact that Styrofoam warms and dissipates shock quickly keeps other projects pulling rank over a proper outhouse.

Baths are what Ed calls cat washes or "pits and pubes." My shoulder-length hair requires heating a kettle of water and hauling it outside where I do my daily shampoo, rain or snow.

Twice a month we hit town to restock. Today's tally is a bag of apples, frozen turkey legs, cheese, eggs, and nails. "Huh," I say. Ed follows my gaze. On the top shelf sits a round laundry tub. "Honey, could you reach that for me?"

"But why, Jan? We do our wash in a five-gallon bucket. Don't need it."

"I'd like to check something."

Ed reaches up and hands it to me. I clamber in and sit cross-legged. "Perfect, Ed. A bathtub. I bet you'd even fit."

"Nah, way too small for me."

"Try. I bet it'd work."

Ed shoehorns his six-foot frame; his knees bench-press to his chin. The storekeeper walks by, the same one who'd been cranky about the creosote. He stares and shakes his head.

"This can double as a laundry tub, too," I say. "All we need's an agitator." I scan the next aisle. "Voilà!" I hold a rubber toilet plunger.

"We're on a roll; bathtub and washing machine for twenty bucks. And no breakdowns ever."

Daily routines are simple: haul water, restock wood box, cook, clean, have recess with Max. As our white world deepens, we swap hiking boots for skis. Surrounding us are miles of closed roads and thousands of acres of wilderness. With our cross-country skis, we track routes of the resident wolverine and read dramas of owl and hare imprinted in the snow. My eyes sweep the landscape. "The snow's so pretty, Ed, and yet I feel trapped in a black and white world, with only shades of gray. Whatever happened to Technicolor?"

"There, Jan . . ." Ed points to cherry-red rounds peeking above the snow.

"Winter berries? I wonder what they are."

We ski closer. "Prickly stems. Hmmm, these must be the rose hips I was reading about."

Ed tastes one and spits it out. "Blah. Hairy."

"I think you're supposed to eat only the pulp. If I remember correctly, three of these hips have more vitamin C than a whole orange. I'll do some homework."

"Do you mean . . . ?"

"Yep, another trip to the mail shed."

To the Post ⁓

When we first inquired in Seldovia about renting a post office box, the postmistress suggested we use the much closer, and free, Kasitna Bay facility.

"Watch for the trail past MacDonald Spit; park in the pull-off; follow the track to the Bay. First time you go, bring a container."

"How big?"

"Depends on how much mail you expect. Mail arrives twice weekly by floatplane; whoever's there first sorts it into everyone's containers."

Her directions lead us to a mossy trail, descending to the water's edge.

High on stilts perches a tarpaper shack sized like a pony stall. Uneven stairs lead to a deck. Above the plywood door posts a rectangular sign: KASITNA BAY U.S. POST OFFICE AND AIRFIELD.

"Joke, right?" Ed scoffs.

"Let's check it out, Ed. It looks unlocked."

Inside the hut are shelves stuffed with cardboard boxes, glass gallon jars with paper labels, and standard mailboxes. Names are scrawled across each. Marsha Million. David Seaman. I study an envelope. "Looks like our address will simply be: via Red Mountain, Homer, Alaska 99603."

"But why Red Mountain, Jan? Red Mountain is out Windy River valley by Herb Stetler; this is Kasitna Bay."

"Another mystery, Ed; we'll have to ask."

What we do now know is that using the Red Mountain post office requires checking the tide table. Residents with skiffs arrive at high water and dock directly to the upper deck. Landlubbers like us need low tide, in order to access rickety postal stairs by the beach.

"This is so amazing, Jan, that this hovel is an official United States post office."

"And it works. Probably the best bargain in America. A twenty cent stamp carries this letter by floatplane across the bay, across the country, all the way to Dad's doorstep in New Hampshire. A simple stamp even gets me library books."

Today's mission is an interlibrary loan request for books to answer my rose hip question. I flip through our full mail box. "Ooh." I rip open the letter; a blue slip flutters to the ground. "Another rejection slip. Oh Ed, I keep writing and all I'm collecting is fire starter. These stupid apologies: 'I'm sorry but this doesn't suit our needs at this time.' I don't think they're sorry at all."

"But you sold that bannock story to *Field and Stream* for $250, Jan. Don't forget that."

"Beginner's luck. Figured this was an easy business, swap words for dollars. But there's a lot more to it. My last ten submissions have only brought rejection slips."

"Maybe you've not found your niche yet. What worked before?"

"Bannock was something I was learning about and enthused about."

"Well, what now?"

"Roses? I'm learning about roses. I'll write about them!"

We drive to the mill, ski onward, our hearts rosy with promise.

Holey Socks ⁓

Two weeks later, we return to the mail shed, pick up the interlibrary loan parcel, backpack books up the hill, and ski them home. I read about roses and spend the next week experimenting. I simmer hips in water until soft, pour the mush into my hand-cranked stainless steel sieve, and press the pulp into a pan. I taste and scout the cupboard and add honey, cinnamon, cloves, a touch of dry mint. I serve Ed a steaming bowl of hip soup, accompanied by a slice of rose-speckled bread with rose hip jam. "What do you think?"

"Yummy. Wonder what else you can do with roses? We have a meadowful."

"It's fun to research. Perhaps *Alaska* magazine would be interested in the results."

I park my butt daily in the loft, at my new Ed-built spruce desk. I read and take notes, field test, and write. Ed and Max are willing guinea pigs for all food dishes. I type up results and refine recipes. My determination to write now has added impetus. Ed's checked our money stash. "Eight hundred dollars, hon. That's all we've left."

"But we had twenty-five thousand."

"Two years ago, Jan. Add it up. Three grand for the cabin. Two and a half for the lease. Another three for publishing the book. Cost of our cross-country travel. Film. Postage. Groceries. Tools. The new raingear."

"Yeah, yeah . . . and our monthly bottle of propane, winter brandy, pipe tobacco, ferry tickets, toll calls to family. I guess twenty-five thou doesn't last forever. But I didn't realize what dire straits we're in."

"Our outflow's a river, Janzie, and inflow's a trickle. But I don't know what else we can do this winter but keep on keeping on. At least we're not in debt like in New Hampshire. We own our home free and clear. Let's count our blessings."

As winter continues, Ed counts blessings, and I count dwindling dollars. Each fortnightly town trip reduces our stash by another chunk. I write, mail submissions, and worry. I scratch for solutions. "The gold bar, Ed. That's still back East. Couldn't one of your buddies dig it up and cash it in for us?"

"Oh Jan, the bar's under three feet of snow and four feet of frost. No one could find it, or dig it. Plus the gold's worth so little these days."

"Plummeted from eight hundred an ounce to what, two?"

"Thereabouts. I think we need an alternative. That one's next to impossible."

In March, Ed digs again in the stash and comes downstairs sheepish. "Our last hundred, Jan." We click on our cross-country skis, strap on backpacks, tie on Max's saddlebag, and ski to the mill. The rhythmic cross-country stride triggers a mantra: "last hundred, last hundred." At the mill, we switch to the Land Cruiser and drive onward silently.

At Stampers Market we restrict ourselves to basics: rice, beans, pasta, sprouts, fruit. Ed holds up a bag of coffee. Ed treasures his morning cuppa, then switches to our free "Night on Rocky River" blend of spruce needles, rose petals, and goldenrod blossoms. I nod yes. A few coffee beans aren't going to make things worse than they already are.

We pile into the Land Cruiser with our boxes of groceries.

"Ten bucks left, Jan."

"Look at all this snow," I whine. "No sign of spring coming anytime soon."

"Cannery work doesn't start up in Homer for ages yet."

"Food might get mighty boring but we can still eat for a little while."

The Land Cruiser chugs along the skinny track. An oncoming vehicle interrupts our chatter and forces Ed to road's edge. Our passenger side front wheel breaks through the snow crust. The Land Cruiser angles strangely, slides down the precipice, tilts on two wheels, then rolls onto my side door.

"Janzie, Janzie, are you okay?"

"Think so. I feel like a soup sandwich . . . ooh, change that . . . egg sandwich. And Max is the spread. Can you drag him off? He's heavy."

Ed shifts the dog and unravels me from the mess. We slide out the doors, thankful they still operate. "I don't think anything's hurt too badly except the eggs," says Ed. "The snow cushioned the impact."

"You folks okay?" we hear loudly from above. The other driver has returned.

"Fine," hollers Ed. "Got anything that can pull us out?"

"Nah, this car will never do it."

"Can you call us a tow truck?"

"Nah, no tow trucks in Seldovia . . . You folks want a ride?"

"No, it's okay, we'll figure something out."

The driver departs.

"Oh Ed, what are we going to do?" I wail.

"Visualization," answers Ed. "I'm mighty impressed from our results after the flood. Picture the jeep back on the road, Jan."

"But this is different."

"Don't bring in doubt," he insists.

"Okay," I pout. "Our life's a mess."

"It worked before."

"What's it going to cost us? All we have is ten dollars."

"Don't worry about the money, picture us on the road, and happy."

"Okay, okay. Don't have a choice, do I?"

"Breathe deeply," Ed coaches. "Focus. See the jeep right side up. See ourselves smiling."

Noise intrudes. "I wish that racket would stop. I'm trying to concentrate."

The clanging grows louder. I open my eyes. The Seldovia road grader is high above us. The driver rolls down his window. "Are you folks okay? How about a tug up?" He throws down a chain; Ed secures the bumper. We stand aside as the Good Samaritan drags the Land Cruiser up the embankment. Then he pulls as we lean and get the rig upright. Ed reaches in his wallet and drags out our last ten-spot.

"No, no," insists the driver, "only being a neighbor. You folks were in a pickle; simply setting you right."

We thank him profusely, load into the Land Cruiser, and rebox our goods. I scout the floor, pick up coffee beans from the broken bag, and secure them in the pocket of my backpack. When we reach Kasitna Bay, we park, and trudge down the mile to the mail shed. We stuff mail into our packs. An envelope flutters to the floor. Ed retrieves it.

"It's from *Listen* magazine, Jan. Must be the article you sent about the twins who lead the outdoor program with wayward youth."

"Must be another rejection slip," I say glumly.

"Open it up," insists Ed.

"I'll wait, I don't want to be bummed for the ski back."

"Oh come on, Janzie, take a peek."

I rip open the envelope, unfold the letter, and hold up the insert. "A hundred-dollar check, Ed. We eat for another fortnight."

Ed whoops. We whirl around the shed. "See Jan, you'll fly home on your skis now. Good work, sweetie."

"I guess the angels haven't forgotten us after all!"

The Boot Maker ⌁

My success with Listen *fires me with enthusiasm,* as does our burning need for funds. "Check this out," says Ed, as he hands me a recent issue of the *Anchorage Daily News* that he'd lifted from a Seldovia dumpster for fire starter. "Their 'Letters from the Bush' column looks perfect for you."

I mail a vignette about our lifestyle to Anchorage, and receive a letter of acceptance. Small but steady checks fill our gas tank and buy bags of beans and rice. My confidence soars.

"How about a feature story," coaxes Ed. "The Sunday supplement *We Alaskans* does lots of profiles. How about a story on Marsha?" We've heard rumors about Marsha Million, a custom boot–maker living in Little Jakolof Bay.

"Wonder if she's colorful enough for a story?"

"One way to find out, Jan."

Marsha's mailbox sits, like ours, in the Red Mountain mail shed. "Hi Marsha," I scrawl on the back of an envelope. "We live up at Rocky River, and we'd love to meet. I'm interested in doing an article on you and your boot business for *Anchorage Daily News.* Send us a bush line if interested. Jan, Ed, and Max."

A few days later KBBI bush lines: "Jan, Ed, and Max. Meet me at the mail shed on Thursday at two. Prepare for an overnight. Marsha."

We wait by the mail shed and watch as a petite woman pilots a sixteen-foot wooden skiff to shore. Marsha wraps us in a hug of welcome and stares at Max. "From your message, I thought Max was your kid."

"He is, only furry."

"Hope he gets along with my cat Winthrop."

"He likes cats," I insist. I can tell Marsha's not convinced.

"Hop aboard, I'll grab my mail." Marsha double-steps the rickety stairs and emerges moments later with a bulging sack.

With one sleek pull, she restarts her motor and guides the skiff along the rocky shore and through the channel into Little Jakolof Bay. It's our first view of the cove; cottages nestle along the spruce-laden shore.

"Had no idea so many folks lived here," says Ed.

"They don't; they're summer places for Anchorage doctors and dentists. I'm the only year-round resident." She noses the bow to the floating wooden pier and tosses fenders over the side. Ed reaches to tie the skiff. "Leave the lines alone," she snaps. "I'll do them myself." Ed slides his hands back to his pockets.

We scramble onto the dock. The ramp to shore is near vertical. "Tides," says Marsha. "This is the lowest this month." Max looks uncertainly at the steep skinny ramp. I dig my toes into the wooden cleats, and clench the railing with my right hand as I grab his collar and tow him with my left. At the top I turn and gaze. The bay is placid, backed by volcanic snowcapped drama. "Another Alaskan paradise," I mutter to Ed.

Marsha strides into the moss-draped forest and disappears. We spring into a trot and follow her track. Devil's club stalks overhang the path; we dodge its hellish prickles and peer ahead for Marsha. She crosses planks over a creek and halts by a rough-sawn hut. "This is where I'm staying right now, while I build my house."

"Who's the builder?" I ask.

"I told you. I'm building it."

"By yourself?"

"Yes."

"Back East," I explain, "saying 'I'm building my house' usually means 'hiring a contractor.' Where'd you get all these skills? Was your dad a builder?"

Marsha hoots. "Nope, town lawyer."

"So where'd you learn construction?"

"Seat of the Pants School of Building."

I chuckle. "Where'd you go to school before that?"

"Chicago. Studied illustration art."

Marsha strides through the hut's plywood door. Her gear stacks in fuel crates along the wall. A barrel stove promises warmth. "Drop your packs, I'll take you next door; show you what I'm up to."

We dogtrot behind Marsha and stop at a structure towering on seven-foot pilings. We scramble up spruce stairs onto a mass of deck. "All local timber from the mill," says Marsha, "plus escaped logs I found in the bay and milled up. Walls are rough-cut two-by-six."

"I can hardly believe you're doing this alone; you must be Wonder Woman."

"Nah. Locals gave me a hand lifting the walls," Marsha says modestly.

"I'm not surprised; raising them must be like bench-pressing an elephant. Building alone is quite a mission; no one to hold the other end in place."

Marsha takes us on tour. "Over there," she says, "will be my kitchen and dining area. That," she points, "will be the bathroom."

"An indoor bathroom?" I ask, astonished. "Out here?"

She nods. "With bathtub, shower and flush toilet."

"Wow."

"And that'll be the guest room," she adds, indicating another framed room the same size as her spacious bath.

She leads through the living-room-to-be to her upstairs. Before us is a boot-making factory in full operation. Leather is stacked tidily adjacent to an industrial sewing machine.

"The boots are my only source of income," Marsha explains, "so I had to do this room first; have to keep up production even as I'm building. This is what I do every day, ten hours a day."

"How do your customers ever find you?"

"I go to them; each August I set up a booth at the Alaska State Fair. My booth's the only thing I ever built before tackling this house."

"Gutsy," I whisper to Ed, while Marsha makes us tea. "I was worried whether Marsha was colorful enough for a feature."

Cups in hand, Marsha continues. "I set out boot samples at the Fair and take custom orders. My customers often have foot problems and can't buy off-the-shelf shoes. Others seek unique styles."

Ed stands on a chair while Marsha demonstrates; she wraps a sewing tape around the ball of each foot, measuring instep and foot length. I shoot madly with my Nikon, recording her comments on tape as well as jotting back-up notes.

"How'd you get started into shoemaking?"

"We'll get into that one over supper. I have a silver salmon we can pan-fry with some hedgehogs."

"Hedgehogs? You're cooking salmon with porcupine?"

"What? Mushrooms! *Dentinum repandum. Dentinum* means teeth; their gills look like hedgehog quills, only they're soft. I can up a case of hedgehogs for all-season use."

"I'd love to learn how to recognize them."

"Come back later when they're in season. The guest room will be ready by then, too."

Back at the hut we introduce our furry children. Winthrop hisses and raises his hackles. Max wags his stump of a tail furiously. Winthrop bats his catnip to Max; Max races circles, drops it. Our kids will obviously be friends, and so too Marsha and I.

During supper, Marsha tells how she came north to Alaska with friends. "I wanted to experience real Alaska. I flew out to Toksook Bay."

Photographs

▲ The Canadian bighorn sheep that stopped traffic, froze cameras, and stove in cars.

◄ New Hampshire, the "Live Free or Die" state where this story began.

(photo—Washington, New Hampshire)

◄ Ed and "Greenie," en route through Yukon Territory to Alaska.

▶ Homer, Kachemak Bay, and
the land "beyond road's end."

(photo by Norma W. Dudiak)

▼ Cabin by the bay: the Swift
Creek cabin and the hogback to
Wind Point.

▲ View of Kachemak Bay and
glaciers as seen through the Swift
Creek cabin picture window.

◀ Janice shows off a cabbage from
the productive Swift Creek garden.

(photo by Edward E. Schofield)

▲ Deiv Rector and Ed gather coal near Swift Creek, with packhorses Sam and Toklat.

▲ Janice helping Deiv and Sam bring in the hay.
(photo by Edward E. Schofield)
▶ Chopping Swift Creek ice for drinking water.

◀ Relaxing at Swift Creek.

▲ Deiv Rector proudly displays his birch syrup; Ed (in background) chops wood.

▶ Mike Berger and Zip visit at Swift Creek.

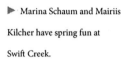 ▶ Marina Schaum and Mairiis Kilcher have spring fun at Swift Creek.

▼ Peeling logs for the Rocky River cabin.

(photo by Edward E. Schofield)

▲ Marian Beck holds Harriet, the seal pup orphan from Swift Creek.

◀ Digging the Rocky River outhouse hole.

(photo by Edward E. Schofield)

▼ Building the Rocky River
cabin using the Scandinavian
scribe method.

▼ Moving a log up the cabin wall with the help of ropes and come-along.

▲ Deiv Rector helps Ed with the Rocky River cabin roof.

◀ Cooking in the makeshift Rocky River kitchen after the flood.

▲ Daily ablutions, wilderness style (before the sauna was built).

◀ Rocky River and the cabin as seen from the hill.

◀ Maneuvering along the Rocky River road washouts after the flood.

▼ Marsha Million, the Little Jakolof Bay boot maker, displays her wares.

▶ The Red Mountain post office, on the shore of Kasitna Bay.

▼ Randy Neuschwander in the "plastic palace" he wintered in before building his cabin.

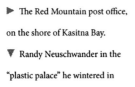

▲ The Rocky River cabin after its window surprise.

▶ The finished cabin interior.

▼ Brenda Foster and Anne Schofield wait for the Tustemena ferry from Homer to Seldovia.

▲ Helen Broomell, the "solo on the Yukon" grandmother, paddles her canoe.

◄ Steve Hughes builds his home on the lake; Ed lends a helping hand.

🌲 Yet another Rocky River silver!

(photo by Edward E. Schofield)

▷ On the trail, cooking salmon and wild greens.

▷ Ed at the Rocky River cabin prepares silver salmon for the smoker.

◀ Ray Fournier and Jean B.
Desclos in front of the old Seldovia
boardwalk.

▲ Ginny DeVries at Red
Mountain.
▶ At Red Mountain with the
Toyota Land Cruiser.

▶ Mary Anne Walker with
bull kelp.

▶ ▶ The Port Dick sauna.

▲ In New Zealand Ed is visited
by Inca, an inquisitive yellow-eyed
penguin being rehabilitated at
the Moeraki penguin hospital
and sanctuary.

◀ Dan Unsworth holding volcanic
lava at Katmai.

▲ Nelda Osgood and Ed, by the Rocky River sauna.

▶ Jim Desclos delivers pizza to the Steve Hughes cabin.

▲ Homer artists spread public awareness of impending clear-cuts.

◀ Jean B. Desclos and the Rocky River "grandfather spruce."

▼ Willie Condon with an oil-injured loon, awaiting transport to the Homer bird recovery center.

▲ Gore Point, before the *Exxon Valdez* oil spill.

▶ A moose and her calf in the front yard at Gardensong.

▶ Janice with a bowl of fireweed.

(photo by Norma W. Dudiak)

▼ The Gardensong cabin dining nook.

"Where? Never heard of it."

"It's a village on Nelson Island, off Alaska's southwest coast. I worked for the Adult Literacy Laboratory program teaching English to Yup'ik elders. None of the A.L.L. materials were suited for Eskimo life, so I worked with the ladies to record their own tales." Marsha drops her voice. "But then I nearly got run out of town."

"What'd you write?"

"It's what I did. One night after we were done with our studies, I took out my tarot cards. All the women were keen for readings. But the town fathers thought I must be a witch. My Anchorage boss, Gretchen, pulled strings so I could stay; she was totally taken by the Toksook Tales we were recording, and the word bingo and illustrated curriculum I'd developed. Only place I could find to rent there was a shanty made from flattened oil drums attached to a driftwood frame. It makes this hut look like a palace."

"Any insulation?"

"Tundra moss."

"Heat?"

"A whisper of an oil stove. It got to forty below zero that winter, cold enough to freeze mercury."

"How'd you survive?"

"Got married," she laughs. "My hubby helped in that department. But cold feet launched me into boot-making. I had an agonizing bout of borderline frostbite. The ladies felt sorry for me and gave me an old pair of mukluks. They hadn't been used in ages and were falling apart. I decided that if I was going to repair boots, I might as well learn to make them. My adopted auntie, Frances, took me to her home, and sat me down. For days I watched her make mukluks for every kid and his family. She'd look at someone's feet, do a visual measure, then chew hide, cut, and sew. Not a word was spoken. She gave me looks, like 'do you see?'"

"So I stared at my feet, chewed, cut, and sewed. When I put my mukluks on, the ladies laughed so hard they nearly wet themselves. They'd point and burst into hysterics all over again. I wore that pair as long as I could, then gave it another try. I used my first as a pattern, but with alterations. My second pair was a bit better; the women still laughed but I could tell they had a twinkle of approval in their eyes."

"So where's your husband now?" I ask. A male presence is obviously absent.

"Still in the village," Marsha replied. "He was always doing the Eskimo thing of going out hunting, and when he'd return, he expected me to gut and skin the animals plus do all the cooking and cleaning while he sat and watched. Finally I had enough; I grabbed the bed sheets, slashed them in half with a butcher knife, handed him his share, and left."

"And then?"

"Homer. Lived in the Homer hills. That changed after a bar trade at the Salty Dawg Saloon. Some drunken Texans swapped me their skiff for two cases of canned pink salmon and an eiderdown quilt I'd hand-plucked from Toksook ducks. That skiff changed my life. I fell in love with the Kachemak's coves and finally found this place I could rent in Little Jakolof Bay. The local doctors love having someone here full-time; it's great security for their summer homes. So one of them is letting me build my house on some extra land he has."

"So that's when you started making boots?" I ask.

"No, next I hand-seined salmon with my A.L.L. boss, Gretchen, over on Yukon Island. Her family, the Abbatts, are some of the oldest homesteaders in this district. Her Uncle Chuck was a history buff and learned that Civil War soldiers were paid in scrip that could be exchanged for federal land. So he went down South, bought up heaps of 'junk scrip' for next to nothing, then went to the Feds with a fistful. The law was still on the books, so they had to give him title to Alaskan federal land, including prime land on Homer Spit. So Chuck started the Salty Dawg Saloon there back in the forties."

I decide I'd better get the interview back on track. "So after hand-seining you started boot-making?"

"Nope. I commercial fished on the Gulf of Alaska in that wooden bathtub I got in the bar trade. Hard going; got me thinking about how I could make a different living out here. A Homer gal saw me in my muk-luks and asked me to make a pair. That did it. I built a booth, went to the Alaska State Fair with the prototype 'custom-made Mukluks,' took orders, and came home. They sold okay, but eventually I wanted more variety. So I added my Mary Jane's," she says, holding up a pair of women's flat-heeled shoes with a hard sole and a small strap. "And then the Rocky River Boot. It's impervious to salt water and can even be worn pushing a boat in and out of the water."

Like a magician, Marsha produces boots from her bottomless box. "The Red Mountain boot is made of chrome-tanned, then oil-tanned leather. The difference results in breathability. In cold weather you need something that lets the sweat evaporate from your feet as you're moving. The moisture escapes and keeps your feet warmer."

She explains her fitting process. "I run through a whole series of questions with people before they buy boots, so that I know where they're going, if it's wet or dry, hot or cold, if they'll be walking city streets or saltwater beaches, if they have special foot problems."

"Basically I'm a craftsperson, an artist, Jan. And this is a rotating art form. As I introduce a new edition, an edition being three to five new styles, I remove old ones. Except for my classics. Now," continues Marsha, holding up yet more styles, "I have an entire line."

We sip tea, and chat late into the night.

Two weeks later, I'm ecstatic. Marsha's tale appears in the Sunday *We Alaskans* as a cover feature. We eat again.

Tides of Change ⁓

Another check, from Alaska *magazine* for my wild rose article, shoots us over the moon. "It's been such fun researching roses, chatting with plant people, and testing recipes," I say to Ed. "What do you think about us doing a book on Alaskan wild plants?"

In response, Ed lights his pipe. "It's the book we've been trying to buy," he puffs. "There's nothing like it on the market for Alaskans. Might be a lot of work."

"And a lot of fun." I draft a book outline, and add a sample chapter, cover letter, resume, and tear sheets of my rose article. I mail it to Robert Henning's Alaska Northwest Books, the same company that owns *Alaska* magazine.

The verdict arrives in our Red Mountain mail box. "Eddie, Eddie!" I shout. "It worked. Alaska Northwest Books wants to see a manuscript draft. I've got six months to do it; I'd best get to work."

I glue my butt to a stool and plunk madly on the keys of my forties-era typewriter. Plants sprout to life on the typed pages. The outside world still screams winter. In Homer, light is now a twelve-twelve split of night and day, but at Rocky River the clock ticks slower as eastern hills and western peaks abbreviate dawn and dusk. Trips to the mail shed for more interlibrary loan materials gobble more precious daylight. I type into candled hours.

To eliminate distractions and create a quiet environment for productive writing, we implement a radio news blackout. We hide our watches in the trinket box and trigger the battery radio only for daily bush lines. "Let's focus on our own life stage," insists Ed, "create our own reality, a world at peace."

Weeks later we waken to rifle-shots. "Mad gunman? Think you need to dig out your Magnum, Ed?"

"No, Jan," Ed laughs. "It's nature's cannons announcing spring. Let's go see." As we reach the bank, a thunderous crack erupts, ice sheets shatter, and the river runs free. We return to the cabin and step inside as the radio blurts Easter greetings, followed by a bush line for Ed to call a Homer number. We ski to the mill site, take the Land Cruiser to town, and use the pay phone at the harbor office.

Ed has a job, a few day's work laying concrete in the new fish ice-house on Homer Spit. We return to the head of the bay, ski the seven miles to the cabin and pack Ed's gear; Ed skis out again. "Be back in a few days," he tells me, "with groceries. Good chance for you to write with no distractions."

Writing Marathon 〜

I stride into solitude with ease. I devour the latest box of interlibrary loan references on plants. I study range maps, and narrow my flora selections to species specific to Alaska. Max ensures I break for fresh air and food.

Breakfast, to Max's dismay, is still hot oatmeal. Lunch is oat bread with fresh sprouts and the last of our cheese. Supper is rice, beans, sprouts, and canned salmon, or bean soup. "Eddie's home soon," I croon to Max as I wash our few dishes. "Maybe he'll bring us turkey."

The bush line brings updates: "To the Rocky River Retreaters, more work in Homer, another week at least."

"More oatmeal," I tell Max, as I dump rolled oats in water. "I promise I'll get eggs when we next get groceries." I click the propane striker; no response. "I'd better change the tank."

I lift the spare bottle under the cabin. It's empty. "Good for you Max. Guess we'll need to get your eggs after all. We need propane to cook."

Ed usually handles the propane. I stand with the wrench and wonder. "What's Ed's rhyme about taking off the bottle—'lefty loosey and righty-tighty'? Or was that for bolts? Opposite on LP gas?" I fiddle with the bottle, finally get it loose, and strap it onto the red sled. I cinch Max's packs around his belly, click on my skis, and stride off, sled rope hooked to my back.

The road is still wintered in, except in sunny spots, where snow has crusted to ice. I slide and struggle, unclick my skis, and rewax. Conditions change again. I scrape old wax, redress the boards, and clamber over hill and dale to the welcome flats. The pass is deep in white, and I make time all too quickly to Red Mountain junction where downhill begins. The sled chases my heels and chases Max. I crash in a heap of dog, skis, and sled. The bottle breaks free and rolls down the bank. I unclick and give chase. I notice strange prints in the snow, a flattened area like a moose bed, but on a steep slope?

Back on the road, I retie the bottle and continue down. Snow gives way to icy gravel. I park my skis underneath a spruce and head off on foot, dragging the sled. Bare patches alternate with deep drifts.

I sigh with pleasure as we reach the van. I turn the key; no response. "Hell's bells, Max. Looks like we're not going anywhere. No one at the mill anymore and no way to get a jump." I leave the propane bottle in the van, and retrace our grueling steps back to the cabin.

Home again, there's another bush line. "Still making bacon; you'd best take Greenie for groceries." "Ha, Eddie," I talk back to the radio, "Greenie's a no-go. Hope you bring some bacon home soon."

At the mention of bacon, Max salivates. "Okay, Max," I tell him. "Looks like it's a barrel stove-cooked supper tonight. How about hot oatmeal with peanut butter?" Max hangs his head.

"Okay," I relent, "How about potatoes with sprouts? Or sprouted potatoes?" Our potatoes are now end-of-winter soft with growths that need to be removed before peeling.

"You know," I babble, happy to have a live being to talk to, "what we really need to do is practice visualization. What I really could go for is a juicy steak."

The Other Side of the Story ⁓

Ed arrives a week later as I'm sitting down to my evening meal. I rise, do hearty hugs, and grab another place setting.

"Only home for an overnight, Jan; told my boss I had to get home with groceries for you. But from the look of things you restocked in Seldovia."

"Nope, honey. Van's dead as a doornail. I haven't been out."

"Then how'd you get steak and wine?"

"Angels, Ed; door to door delivery. Max and I were getting desperate, down to sprouted taters and sprouted alfalfa seeds, and oats of course. But we couldn't even use the stove because the propane died."

"So how'd you cook?"

"Baked these spuds inside the barrel stove on the coals. And managed to fry the steak in the cast iron pan on top in a few dribbles of oil."

"So who were the angels?"

"A couple from Anchorage. They were hunting in the valley and got sopping wet. They spotted the smoke and came up to investigate. I gave them a dry roof and warm fire and let them stay the night. They emptied their packs before leaving."

"So what's this? Doesn't taste like beef."

"Mountain goat."

"A heap better than old Val."

"So, tell me, how'd Homer go?"

"Started out with a bang. En route out, I was making good time on the skis so I stopped for a smoko at the top of the switchback. Packed my pipe and tamped the tobacco, and struck a match, which pitched me forward. I was like Norheim, the Norwegian who invented ski jumping, Jan. Went off the rock, skis spread in V formation, body planed forward. Only I plowed face first into the snow. Thought my pack was going to bury me. Laid there flopping like a hare in a snare, snagged in pack and poles and skis."

"See, Ed, that proves my point. Smoking is hazardous to health."

"Nothing compared to living in the plastic palace; thought I was going to die of hypothermia during the cold snap."

"Plastic palace?"

"Where I was bunking. Mike and Randy invited me to stay with them. They bought five acres out East Road on Wilderness Lane and didn't have time to get cabins built before winter, so they bought rolls of black plastic and wrapped it around some spruce. They covered the top with rafters and more plastic. And they've lived in it all winter long. Heat is from an oversized tin can, one of those fifty-buck-special wood-burners from Spenard Builders. We'd hug it, thawing our hands on mugs of boiled cowboy coffee, eating cold canned beans. Dining seats were stumps, which kept turning into firewood as they dried, and getting replaced with new logs. Thank God my sleeping bag is down; these nights have been mighty nippy."

"And the job? It was supposed to be only a couple days work."

"The concrete curbs were piss-poor, so I redid a sample right out front. Hit you in the eyeballs whenever you drove up. So the boss had me do the rest of them. That's what I've been working on. They're honking to get the icehouse done before fishing season, so I'm back again tomorrow. Told my boss I had to get you some food before you starved to death."

Summer High ~

Spring sprints to summer. Herbal research shifts from the blankness of the page to the bounty of outdoors. I sit immersed in Technicolor: soft pink roses, deep green shoots. My eye presses to the Nikon viewfinder, seeking definitive plant portraits. I harvest wild cucumber shoots for spring salad, salmonberry blossoms for tea, and fiddleheads for stir-fry. The plants are on solar steroids, crazed on endless light. I gallop to keep up. There are so many plants to learn, and so little time. The elder flowers blast from bud to blossom; green fruits form a week later. I mutter secret prayers for photographic success. There'll be no chance to try again this season.

"Here, taste this," I say to Ed. I slide a second sample to Max. Ed dives in, and Max sniffs and makes certain it's not oatmeal. Both finish with pleasure . . . most times.

Some days, it's back to the kitchen. "Maybe I picked it too late, or missed a step. Cow parsnip root, pushki, is supposed to taste like parsnip." "No parsnip flavor here, Jan. And cow pies smell better than this."

"Okay, boiled pushki root isn't the way to go. Maybe I need to roast it." Peeled stems earn a pass as cream of wild celery soup, but roots thwart my best attempts. Other conflicts in herbal literature also baffle me.

"This book says our red elderberries, *Sambucus racemosa,* are toxic, Ed. But I've seen red elderberry jelly for sale in Homer."

Ed scours the pile of plant books. "Here it is, Jan. It's the seeds that are toxic. So it's okay as jelly, toxic as jam."

Some mysteries resolve; others deepen. Mistaken identities expand the scope of my research. "Look how similar this edible geranium leaf is to poison monkshood; now I need a section on look-alike plants to beware of."

Days dart. August brings seed heads and termination snow on the peak.

Firewood duties call; the bow saw jumps and gashes me to the bone.

"You need stitches, Jan."

"Another hundred we can't afford. Let's see what we can do first."

"Keep pressure on it."

"I am, but it's doing little good."

"Didn't you read about a plant for stopping bleeding?"

"Yarrow. *Achillea millefolium.* Crusaders carried it in their saddlebags to staunch wounds. We've some outside by the porch."

We pick leaves and flower heads. "Now what?" asks Ed.

"The book says to use a poultice, from *pultes* for paste. For an emergency field poultice, we're supposed to do this." I pop the ferny leaves and bitter blossoms in my mouth and chew to a mash, then plop the goop on my bleeding wound and hold. "Look, it stopped."

"Nearly instantly," Ed marvels. "But won't that mush make the wound dirty?"

"It's antibacterial."

"Maybe you need a section in the book, Jan, on medicinal uses and herbal first aid. It's so easy to get in a world of hurt here in the bush. And so many Alaskans hike and hunt and camp and live remote."

I agree. "It would certainly add another dimension. I'd better write Alaska Northwest and ask for an extension. This deadline's nearly up and I'm nowhere near ready to send them a manuscript. Besides, now I need to start researching medicinal properties. Makes me worry a bit, Ed."

"What about?"

"This started as a simple project, but the book is taking on a life of its own. This is becoming a quest. Wonder where it'll lead next."

Once Upon a Journey ‿

September equinox passes; days abbreviate quickly. Golden leaves blanket the river's shores. Termination snow deepens on the peaks. Cold triggers thoughts of Christmases past and wonders of Christmases future. "Remember Thankschristmas on Blueberry Hill?" I say to Ed. "Makes me long to see family again."

Mail from Ed's mom Ellen stirs the pot. "Her handwriting is really shaky; I'm worried how she's coping," he says as he hands me the letter.

I decipher her scrawl. "She's tired of long, cold winters, Ed. All she talks about is you building her a house in Florida."

"No way, Jan. Too many restrictions there. Don't want a career in the stifling South. But I do need to check on her."

"But can't your sis in Maine do that?"

"Mom and Anne haven't spoken in years." Ed leans back and lights his pipe. "Sure would be good to see Anne again, though.

"I would love to see my family too. My parents aren't getting any younger."

"Let's drive East, Jan. We'll visit everyone, see the country, and come back with the spring. We've got our Permanent Fund checks and savings from that dock job."

"Should we lock up the cabin, Ed? There are stories going around of bush homes being vandalized or bears breaking in."

"Locks only keep good folks out, Janzie. If someone wants in, they'll break in. Then we'll have a door to fix too. And bears can't get in because our door opens outward."

"You're right. And it's so easy for travelers to get soaked and hypothermic in this valley."

We leave a guest book and directions to turn on the valve on the propane tank under the cabin. We pen reminders: "Make certain the fire is out. Cut kindling and refill wood box. Sweep up. Latch door. Leave seeds, nuts, or bread for Marco the Steller's jay." We glue the notes into the first page of our book, and add a final note:

"Please enjoy your stay. Walk gently in this beautiful valley. Open your heart, listen to the river's voice, and be in peace."

We walk past the bog that swells in summer with irises. Max tests the frozen pools while we hug the road. As we gain elevation, ice becomes snow, reversing again as we descend the switchback. We do the now familiar drive to Seldovia and the ferry dance, then say farewell to Homer friends, and beam north.

Past Tok is the invisible line where the countries change; we camp nightly in Canada's free off-season provincial parks. In the Yukon, Ed is keen for salmon supper.

"The lake is frozen already, Ed. We're foiled again."

"Not this time. Ice fishing, Jan. We've got a hatchet. It's only autumn, how thick can the ice be?" Ed flails at the lake, chips flying. He runs out of arm length before he runs out of ice.

"Looks like plain mashed spuds again, Ed. We'd best get cooking; it'll be dark in a tick."

We huddle by Ed's fire, boil spuds, eat, and then dive under the down. Max crawls to base as foot warmer. Morning clouds of cold breath trigger hot debates as to who'll brew coffee and thaw the van. I lose and glance at the thermometer as I dress. "Twenty below, and only September. The sunny South is not sounding so bad after all."

We drive across the endless plains, then Ontario and on to the Montreal gauntlet. We head for Ed's sister's home in Maine. Anne, Ed tells me, has recently finished remodeling and selling two single-family homes in Portland, and bought a house in Steuben.

"Where?"

"Up north of Bar Harbor, past Acadia National Park. Anne says it's named after Inspector General Baron Frederick William Rudolph Gerald Augustus von Steuben. Big name for a postage stamp of a place."

"Do you know her address?"

"Only the rural route number. But how hard can she be to find?"

We stop at the Steuben post office.

"Ayuh, Anne Schofield. But you ain't Anne, can't give you her mail."

"I'm her brother. I don't want her mail. I only want to know where she lives."

"Ayuh. If you're her brother, oughta know where she lives."

"I know the post box, but need to know the physical address."

"You need a psychic, go to the carnival. You oughta know where your sister lives."

"Give it up, Ed," I whisper. "You'd get more info out of a stamp."

We exit, exasperated, and head to a shop. No one knows Anne.

"What do we do now, Ed? She's the new kid on the block and must keep a low profile."

Ed sits silently at the wheel and closes his eyes.

"Tired?"

"Shh. Give me a second."

He turns the key, drives, and pauses at a junction. "We'll turn left here, Janzie."

"I thought you didn't know where she lives."

"Yep."

"Then where?"

"Shh." Ed heads out of town and pulls into a gas station.

"But the tank's full."

"Yep."

Family ~

"Anne Schofield?" The attendant's face corkscrews in thought. "Ayuh. Pumps gas here; lives in that there apartment."

"How'd you do that Ed?"

"Later, Janzie. Let's see Anne."

The siblings hug. Anne plunks us on the couch with cold beers, and sets herself in a recliner with a cigarette and a Manhattan. "Gawd, I love this state," says Anne. "Wicked awesome. How about a heap of lobsters tomorrow?"

"Lobsters? Yum. But it'll be our treat."

"My treat; you have to help catch 'em. I work with Handy three mornings a week."

Some call 4 A.M. the godly hour when the veils are thin between the worlds. But we cuss like heretics as we pry ourselves from warm sheets. We grab coffees and dash in the pre-dawn to the lobsterman's home. Inside the rambling kitchen, lights and radio blare. A teen is ironing clothes. Handy's wife Celia is packing lunches; a baby crawls by her knees. The eldest son is geared to go. We head out, and leap in the skiff with Handy; teen Shaun takes the other boat.

Coastal fog rises as we cruise offshore islands. Sun crests the horizon. Our skiff boasts a motorized pulley to lift traps from the cold Atlantic. We watch as Shaun tediously hand-pulls each pot, measures lobsters to make certain they're regulation size, empties the pots, rebaits, and resets. Both Handy and Shaun are responsible for seventy-five traps.

By late morning our traps are complete. Handy motors up to his son. "Ain't you done yet?"

"Eight more pots to pull, Pop."

"Lazy sod. I swear you're number than a pounded thumb."

That night we feast on lobster tails and family tales.

"When I was a kid," I tell Anne, "Dad would take us down to the Lobster Pound at Salisbury Beach near my Aunt Claire's camp. Bags of bodies were seventy-five cents. We'd suck juice from the legs, scavenge meat scraps from the shells and spread green lobster goo on crackers."

"Tomalley," says Anne. "It's the lobster's hepatopancreas; functions as both liver and pancreas. Considered a delicacy like caviar."

"Really?" I say. "But I never had delicacies like whole lobsters with claws and tails."

"We never had goodies like this either. Mom couldn't afford it; all she was ever trained to be was a nun."

"Right. Ellen a nun? What a joke. She prays to the devil when Jesus doesn't help her. Besides, she's not in a convent."

"She was," adds Ed, "until her mom passed away and her dad got too sick to care for himself. She got a leave of absence to help out. But then along came Alfonzo."

"And who was he, a priest?"

"Nope," says Anne, "a professional boxer from Nova Scotia. They met and got hitched. Mom insisted Dad quit the ring. He'd say he did but then he'd come home with his face all wicked, and stories about the car breaking down and the car jack falling. He loved his boxing. He kicked the bucket ten days before Eddie turned four. I was five. He had a brain tumor and didn't survive the surgery."

"I don't have many memories of my Dad," continues Ed. "But when I worked the Prudential tower in Boston, I met a guy who had known him. He gave me *Ring* magazines that had photos of dad in his prime. Kid Schofield, they called him. He said Alfonzo loved bananas and used to go to Haymarket Square and buy entire hanks. He would stuff his bureau drawers full of bananas. I've wondered whether Dad's banana craving indicated some kind of deficiency or whether his death was related to all the punches to his head."

"Mom went bananas," adds Anne, "after he died. Up shit creek: a single mom with us two rugrats. She had never balanced a checkbook. Or driven a car. Jeezum, she'd stuff us kids behind the back seat of the car and scream at us."

"Still remember every word too," says Ed. "'You damn kids. Stay put. If I'm gonna die, you're coming with me.' She'd mat that pedal and scare us shitless. She was a horrible driver. Still is."

"That's probably why, to this day," Anne tells me, "we Schofield kids get tense when someone else is at the wheel."

"Criminy, Anne. You solved the mystery. I've always wondered why Ed got unglued when anyone else drove. But go on, Anne; then what happened?"

"Mom tripped down a set of stairs. Broke her back. The quacks swore she'd never walk again. She got shipped to a special hospital until she could even sit in a wheelchair. We kids got farmed out."

"Farmed out, as in foster homes?"

"Working farms," says Anne. "The first place was in Massachusetts. Then we went offshore to a place called Bakers Island."

"It's in a group of islands off Salem, Massachusetts, called the Miseries, Jan; well-named too."

"All I remember is being stuck in this dank Quonset hut with other kids. And being in the fields ten hours a day, picking beans, tomatoes, and corn. Our only entertainment was an old crystal radio."

"But that's child labor," I protest.

"Child labor laws didn't exist, Janzie. And what Anne's saying is the God's honest truth. After Bakers Island we got shipped to a family, the Smalls. Got memories of them pigging out on Thanksgiving turkey and pumpkin pie. All we got was a lousy slice of baloney."

"Remember how they'd lock us in the dark attic, Ed?"

"I was so scared I couldn't stop crying. And when that witch grabbed the carving knife and whacked you, I thought she was murdering you."

"How did you cope?" I interrupt.

"Anne was my whole world, Jan. I think that's why even today we usually know what's happening to the other."

"And why you were able to sense where she lived," I add. "That was weird. But finish the story. Your mom walks now, and doesn't even limp."

"Mom's a mule; you can't tell her what to do. I think she walked to spite that doctor. Plus she wanted us kids back. She got out of that hospital, rented the place near the cemetery, and brought us home."

Pieces of the Schofield past are now starting to fit. "Tell me, how come given your upbringing, you both ended up so sane? Folks with half the trauma are in therapy their whole lives. Or they end up mad at the world, or criminals."

"You let it break you, Jan," Ed says, "or you listen to Shakespeare: 'Let me embrace thee, sour adversity, for wise men say it is the wisest course.'"

"I'd say you both chose well."

After Anne's, we stop over with my sister Doris in Jackman, Maine, whose hardness toward Ed had melted after she met him. My parents and other southern New Hampshire siblings also approve my match. But next is Ed's mom, Ellen, at her Belmont, Massachusetts, apartment.

Ellen digs in stuffed cupboards for Blue Willow cups to serve us tea. Canned goods and toilet paper stack to the ceiling in the spare room. Drawers cram with clothes from Christmases past, labels still attached. Ellen wears a sweater missing buttons; she has safety-pinned it closed. A tall grandfather clock ticks time. Country house antiques dominate the space, mixing with fifties furniture.

"Take your poor mom to Florida, Eddie," Ellen wheedles. "Get your poor mother a house in Florida." She tugs her sweater tighter. "Damn it to hell, I'm cold as a pig on ice."

"Why don't you turn up the heat? It's worse than the Yukon in winter."

"That heater costs money."

"Let me get you that new sweater I bought you."

She shakes her head stubbornly. "Saving it." She takes another breath. "Florida."

"But you've got friends here, Mom. Your buddy next door."

"Witch."

"I thought she was your best friend."

"I caught her looking in my window."

"She was checking on you, Mom."

"I hate her. I want to go to Florida. Build me a house in Florida."

"I'll look for a house for you, Mom, okay? I'd be happy to fix one up for you."

For the first time, Ellen breaks a smile. She hugs Ed and glares at me. We depart, and run the gauntlet to the Blue Ridge Parkway. We camp on the summits, stretch our legs on the trails, rest, and rejuvenate.

"Ready for Florida?" Ed asks.

"Ready as I'll ever be."

By the South Atlantic ~

"Where might Ellen like to live?" I ask Ed.

"Don't know that she knows. Let's find someplace where we don't mind visiting her periodically." We boogie along Eastern shores; Jacksonville's too frantic, St. Augustine too pricey, Daytona? Like Kachemak Bay, Daytona's beach doubles as highway. But instead of Old Believers driving past Swift Creek to reach their village, the Florida beach sports Southerners on school break cruising for joy. We park by the sea, take a swim, and lie in the sun by the van.

Planes fly overhead towing advertising banners. Meanwhile, our small blue and gold Alaska license plates shout our presence. We attract more attention than the surfers, fishermen, and bikini-clad collegiates.

"How can you Alaskans stand that cold?" asks a tanned, middle-aged gent in swim trunks. "Ice and darkness all the time; and bears."

Floridians, we learn, can't stomach cold, detest darkness, and can't comprehend coexisting with bears black, brown, or polar. To them, we're Arctic counterparts of Tarzan and irresistible targets of talk.

We answer their questions but speak a foreign tongue. We try to translate bush, Lower 48, air taxi, mail shed, subsistence. "Alaska's not all ice," we say. "There are only five thousand glaciers. Bering and Malaspina glaciers are bigger than Delaware, but all in all, these rivers of ice blanket only 4 percent of Alaska's mass."

"Alaska does have summer," says Ed. "Farmers north of Anchorage grow cabbages that weigh almost as much as Jan."

"Yep," says the disbelieving Floridian, "and Santa Claus lives at the North Pole."

"Honest to God," I swear. "Matanuska Valley farmers win ribbons at the fair for eighty- to ninety-pound cabbages. It's the rich valley soil, and all that Alaskan daylight. Everything in Alaska is super-sized," I continue. "The state is five hundred times bigger than Rhode Island. Florida is about the size of Alaska's Southeast Panhandle."

"Is it true the state gives you money?"

"Yes. Alaska gets 85 percent of its revenues from oil. Governor Hammond created the Permanent Fund so that all Alaskans, present and future, continue to benefit from oil wealth. The fund's now one of the world's hundred largest investment funds. Each year every resident Alaskan man, woman, and child receives a check. Right now the annual check is one thousand dollars."

That tidbit is like a baited hook, along with the fact that Alaskan wages are double to triple Florida paychecks. But lest we start a northern exodus, we balance the picture, and tell our listeners, "The twenty-five-cents-per-pound Florida bananas are one dollar per pound in Seldovia. The large Floridian everything-on-it seven-buck pizza would cost an extra fifteen dollars or more. The forty-thousand-dollar beachside Florida home would be another hundred thou or more."

We tell a college girl the truth. Alaska does have more men than women. But we warn her of the local saying, "The odds are good, but the goods are odd."

We remind our keen questioners that weather can be fickle. Hiking to Rocky River, we have skied through snow in the pass as late as June, and as early as August. We tell them of the great flood, the month of rain, winter darkness. We see expressions change. Floridians like their shorts and citrus, their screened porch and suntan. But we tell them to take a visit.

Ed quotes the National Geographic Society president, the same words shared in the late 1800s to those wanting to go north:

If you are old, go by all means.
But if you are young, wait.
The scenery of Alaska is much grander than anything else of the kind
in the world and it is not well to dull one's capacity for enjoyment
by seeing the finest first.

By the time our audience leaves, so does the sun. Ominous gray clouds roll in. We snuggle onto our bed and listen to dancing raindrops. The rhythm transitions from waltz to mambo. The van quivers in gale gusts. I roll over and groan. The windows are dripping rain onto our down bed.

Camellia Drive ⟿

By morning, our mattress is as soggy as a baby's bum. We flee to Ormond-by-the-Sea Laundromat; while feather down dries, we treat ourselves to breakfast burritos. Next door is a realty office. We meet realtor Theresa and describe Ellen's needs: a place convenient to shops and good neighbors, with easy access to the beach, and under fifty thou.

"Camellia Drive," says Theresa. "The seller, Ted, retired, but then his wife's cancer forced him back to work. It's now the worst house in a great neighborhood, but all it needs is cosmetic stuff. He didn't have time for maintenance."

The home sits on a skinny peninsula between the Halifax River and the Atlantic Ocean, doors away from beaches. The house is a typical retiree structure: a hurricane-resistant, concrete-block home with a sunny Florida room.

"Ted's wife passed on a year ago," continues Theresa. "He's now remarrying a widow with a lovely house, and he's in a hurry to move. He's a motivated seller."

Ed calls Mom with the good news.

"I want you to build me a house, Eddie."

"No way, Mom. But this place needs work. I'll tidy it, paint it up for you, get you settled. You'll be able to sell it for heaps more if you decide you don't like it. You can't lose."

"How much do you need?"

"I'll tell you tomorrow, Mom. Won't be much, the asking price is forty-eight."

"I'm a poor woman."

"Mom, you've enough. Julia . . ."

"Don't you mention her."

"Your sister's dead, Mom."

"Got what she deserved."

Sisters ~

"Mom's sister was a judge," Ed tells me. "She had heaps of stocks in oil companies, utilities, railroads, all that Monopoly board stuff, but tight as the bark of a tree. When I was a kid I'd shovel her quarter-mile driveway, and she'd give me two cents. Mom stopped by to visit Julia once, right when Julia was sitting down to tea and lemon meringue pie. Julia knew it was Mom's favorite. Julia poured hot water on her used bag for Mom, and sat there shoveling pie down her gullet. Didn't give Mom even a sliver. Mom steamed like a kettle, and never went off the boil. She wouldn't say a word to Julia after that. She kept ranting how she hoped Julia would slip on one of her damn Turkish rugs and break her neck."

"That's terrible."

"Yeah, and believe it or not that's how Julia croaked. The maid buffed the floor and the rug slid and Julia broke her neck. You would think that with Julia being a judge that all her affairs would be in order. In her will, she had chunks of cash earmarked for Perkins School for the Blind, the Humane Society, orphanages, and a pittance for Mom. It was spelled out in detail. But she died before she signed it."

"Didn't her intention carry through?"

"Nope. The law took over. The million-dollar estate was set to be split between mom and her brother. Then some Canadians came out of the woodwork. They had proof they were relatives. Mom wigged out and hired a lawyer to fight it. And then the Canadians got lawyers. And then the IRS entered the picture. By the time things ended, the estate was in smithereens and Mom was a nervous wreck. She ended up with two hundred grand but still thinks she is as poor as a church mouse. But she has got more than enough to get herself a home in Florida."

Ed offers thirty-eight thousand, with no builder's report required, no restrictive clauses, and cash on the table. Ted can leave anything behind he doesn't want. The seller accepts. The papers transfer. We walk into the house, stunned. An easy chair sits in the living room, next to lamps and a television. The bedroom has a bed. The kitchen cupboards have pots, pans, silverware, and even the kitchen trash.

We scrape cockroach droppings off walls and paint each room. Ed builds a screen porch, repairs leaking taps, and makes the place pristine. I enroll in botany and journalism classes at the Daytona Community College. Each morning, I hop the bus for the fifteen-mile jaunt to school. I wear shorts, reveling in the balmy fifty-degree winter temps. Elders shiver in scarves and winter coats.

We celebrate Ellen's first Christmas in her new home. We join hordes buying trees. "What a funny way to live, Ed," I say. "Buying a tree. And wearing shorts and sandals for Christmas. The holidays are not the same without snow."

"I miss Rocky River too, Jan. I'll be glad when we're on our way again."

As Ellen settles, we grow more concerned. Back in Belmont, in the apartment she'd occupied for a dozen years, her mental abilities appeared intact. In Florida she's less adept. The buttons on the electric stove confuse her. The stove is left on. Food burns in the pans. Ellen is oblivious to the smoke. She is lost in the streets. She marches across the bustling beachfront highway, Route A1A, hand up in a stop gesture. Wheels screech.

"You can't do that, Mom. Kids race their rods here all the time," Ed tells her.

"They'll stop when I damn well want them to stop," she insists.

And she tells Ed, over and over, "Jan's not good enough for you, Eddie."

"Don't take it personally, Jan," he consoles me. "It's her broken record. I should be taking care of my poor mother." On some days, the barbs penetrate. Ed hears the door slam. I pedal off on the bicycle I bought at the flea market. It's getting a lot of use.

Ed's escape is the roof. He lies on the tiles, equipped with a Sony Walkman and hammer.

"Eddie? Eddie?" Ellen screeches.

"On the roof, Mom," Ed hollers. He taps with the hammer. "Working."

Our other escape is the ocean. We rise at five, walk to the empty beach with Max, and jog, chat, and savor pink skies and solitude.

At nightfall, Ellen glues herself to the television. We soon are bored of quiz shows and sitcoms, and head back to the empty beach. When we arrive home, Ellen is on the phone. We hear her through the open window. "Sharks got him. My son has been attacked by sharks. You have to save him."

"Mom."

"Oh thank Jesus, you're home. . . ."

"Mom, what were you doing?"

"Talking with police, Eddie. I was sure Jan got you killed. It's all her fault you're out so late."

"Max's fault this time," I counter. "He found some juicy perfume to roll in. I've got to bathe him." I sit Max in the shower and lather him with shampoo. His ears lie flat to his head in abject misery until the bath is over. I towel him dry, and release. He races in circles of joy, and dashes from the bath to the screen porch.

Crash. Ellen has closed the sliders to keep out the evening chill. Red rivers pulsate with each beat of Max's heart. Ed grabs a dish cloth, wraps it around Max's leg, and applies pressure. I grab the phone book and flip to the Vs. My heart hammers madly; finally, a vet with an after-hours number. I alert him we're coming, and get directions. Ed drives; I hold pressure, trying to halt the arterial flow. Max is rushed into surgery. Three hours later we're back, Max stitched and bandaged. Ellen has filed another missing person report.

I'm eager to leave Florida. To escape Ellen's barbs, I'm always on my bike, and now weigh a record low 103. "Can't eat more, Ed. Your mom's harping makes me sick to my stomach."

"Don't take it personally."

"How can I not?"

During the evening meal, Ellen lays another insult. I burst into tears, and dash out the door. When I return, the atmosphere is different. Ellen apologizes.

"I read her the riot act, Jan. Told Mom you're the only reason she has a house here. And that if she's not nicer to you, I'll cut her off the way Anne did."

Things improve, but still I fret. Light is growing, Alaska's calling. Ed worries how Mom will cope solo. Unbeknownst to her, he hires Marilyn next door to check daily, and assist Ellen with various tasks. Then we say good-byes and drive west.

Rosemary ～

Daytona's botany course whets my appetite for more schooling; we detour home via California for a weeklong herbal intensive. We traipse verdant meadows and forests, smelling, tasting, and identifying plants. A sea of names swims in our minds: mallow, manzanita, cattail. We heap our baskets with herbs and meander to the kitchen.

Rosemary Gladstar, founder of the California School of Herbal Studies, assures us that wild food cooking is like any kind of cooking. There are a few basic rules; the rest is creativity. Her rules:

Enjoy and have fun.

Use only quality, fresh wild plants. Use the same judgment as if in a supermarket shopping. Avoid the dry brown leaves, and plants that look past their "use by" date.

Be a good earth steward. Use only plants that grow in abundance. Don't over-harvest. Proper harvesting can help the plant community to thrive.

Don't poison yourself while picking or get shot while doing it. Stay away from busy roads, sprayed areas, and "No trespassing" signs. Get permission before harvesting on private land. And most important, know what you are picking.

Wild plants with mild flavors, teaches Rosemary, are useful for most any dishes. Sours add zest to dips and salads. Hot spicy flavors jazz up recipes. Bitters stimulate digestion and enhance a meal.

We gently rinse the plants, then cut and chop. Weeds become wonders: marinated Greek salad, wild herb pesto, and Rosemary's special spanakopita:

Rosemary Gladstar's Wild Herb Spanakopita

a. Cook 1 cup brown rice.

b. While rice is cooking, prepare your wild greens. You will need at least 3–4 quarts of them as they cook down considerably. (My favorite greens for this dish include nettles and lamb's-quarter but other abundant wild or garden greens can be included.). Wash, chop, and steam lightly. Drain well by placing the herbs in a colander.

c. Sauté onions and garlic in olive oil. Add Italian seasonings such as basil, oregano, marjoram, and thyme.

d. In a large bowl, mix all of the above ingredients together. Add 1 cup ricotta cheese, 1/2 cup grated provolone, and 2 eggs to the mix and stir well. This is your filling. You can adjust the flavors; leave out the rice; leave out the eggs; leave out everything but the herbs for that matter, but this is the filling I love the best.

Preparing the filo:
1. Melt 1/4 cup butter in a small sauce pan.
2. Place filo dough under a towel to prevent it from drying out.
3. Butter the bottom and sides of a 9x13 inch baking dish. Place a layer of filo on the bottom of the pan and brush lightly with butter using a pastry brush. Place another layer and butter lightly. Repeat this process until you have used half the package of filo.
4. Pour your filling over the filo and sprinkle the crumbled feta liberally on top.
5. Now back to the filo. Place a layer over the filling; butter lightly. Repeat until you have used all the filo or until you get tired of layering and buttering.
6. Cut in diagonals before baking.
7. Bake in a preheated 350 oven for about an hour. Serve with a fresh wild herb salad or Greek nettle marinade, French bread, and hearty red wine.

We satiate ourselves with herbal delights. Then, in Herbal First Aid, Jane Bothwell guides us in the herbal arts. We mash poultices for bee stings, and craft salves for soothing cuts and scrapes. We brew tinctures for colds, for insomnia, and for cramps. There are herbs for every ailment imaginable.

A field trip deepens our connections with coastal plants. Jesse Long-acre extracts shimmering strands from tide pools. "It's not sea*weed*," he tells us. "It's sea *vegetables*." He details their names, nutrients, and cooking tips. "Kombu's like a soup bone, great for making stocks." We retreat again to the kitchen and eat our creations.

The week fast-forwards; we form a closing circle and sing a tune by ceremonial songwriter Lisa Thiel:

The spirit of the plants, she comes to me,
In the form of a beautiful, dancing green woman.
Her heart fills me with peace,
Her dance fills me with joy.

We thank our raft of teachers. A week of eating wild weeds has forever changed us. As we close, a Cessna lands in the meadow. Rosemary boards, waves, and flies toward the setting sun. My heart leaps at the image. "That's what I want to do, Ed." I whisper. "Teach like Rosemary, share plant knowledge with folks, and fly off in a small plane."

"Well Janzie. Then we'd best get going. You've heaps to do on the book."

Home Sweet Home ⌒

Days pass in a blur of roads and campgrounds. We rise with the robins, and tank up on food and gas. Latitude changes pump our adrenalin. We escalate to ten-hour drives, then twelve; we race northward, tugged by the place where land ends and sea begins. On Homer Spit at last, we halt and queue for the ferry. The *Tusty's* late again.

"We've time to kill; let's get a few more groceries." Ed stops en route to the store at an all-terrain shop. He pauses by a shiny, red, three-wheeled Honda ATV, chats with the salesman, and shakes hands.

"Big Red is ours, Jan, along with a trailer for towing our stuff."

"We won't need to cart everything on our backs?"

"Nope. As long as the switchback is passable, we've got wheels."

We queue in line again, this time with Greenie, Big Red, and Red's trailer. Aboard the ferry, we pace the decks restlessly. "Can't wait to see Rocky River, Jan. And be back to peace and quiet at last. What a zoo out there."

"It'll be fun to check the guest book. Wonder if we've had any winter visitors."

"Probably a couple of stragglers, and Marsha usually takes a winter ski in the valley."

In Seldovia, May mountains wear winter coats; town roads are bare. I drive Greenie and Ed hops aboard Big Red. At the mill, we load packs, down bedding, and the ice chest into the trailer. The three-wheeler fires into action. We roar to the switchback and claw up the white slope. Snow deepens but the three-wheeler chugs onward. I lean into Ed's back, hug his waist, and smile at our newfound ease. Max dashes ahead and circles back like a border collie to herd us home.

The cabin looks well. I open the guest book: "Thank you for the shelter when we needed it most. We walked to Picnic Harbor and came out in the rain. All of us had sore, tired feet." A Soldotna resident adds: "Thank you again . . . The man who built this home undoubtedly has happy, contented hands and a warm heart . . . and the woman who lives and works here is in love with this cabin and this country . . . Thanks."

Ed opens cabinets. "Look. A heap of candles. New packet of coffee. Bags of pasta. Full wood box. Looks like housecleaners were here too."

"I'm glad we left the cabin open, Ed. We're richer than ever."

"Yeah, inside the cupboards. Our wallet is road-killed."

"And we've still so much to do on the place."

"Like insulating under the floor; the boards opened up over winter. Wind must have howled through like a banshee."

"And windows," I add, standing by the Visqueen-covered holes. "It would be so nice to see clearly. But at least we have light."

A loud "Halloooo . . ." interrupts. Ed opens to a duo with waist-length hair. He waves the men inside.

"I'm Steve Shultz," says the first, "better known as Shultzie."

"Willie Condon; call me Chile Willie, as in Chile, the country I'm from. Shultzie and I live out East Road, where we have a portable sawmill."

Willie pats the cabin walls affectionately. "Great logwork."

"Still plenty to do," Ed replies, plucking a piece of dry grass from the floor crack. "Needs insulation and windows, but they need . . ." and Ed rubs his fingers together, indicating money.

"Nah, you don't need it," starts Shultzie.

I launch into a spiel about Gulf winds and long valley winters. Shultzie laughs. "I meant you don't need money to get insulated. If you're hard up, you'll qualify."

"Qualify for what?"

"The state's new energy conservation program. Helps low-income people insulate their homes and save on heating."

The visitors leave us with contacts for the program. As they depart, I plunk down at the Royal, slide a clean white sheet between the rollers, swipe the lever to advance, and type:

To whom it may concern.

Income details: "Hmm, that's easy, two thousand in Permanent Fund checks. The few freelance checks. *The Alaska Story* proceeds. Sourdough sales. The dock job." I total the columns. The amount of our income is well within the program's parameters.

"Ed. Can you help, please? Bring a seat." Ed sets on the alder-spruce stool and rattles off the window sizes for downstairs wall openings and the number of items we need: bales of Fiberglass batts for sealing under the floor and sheets of four-inch-thick Styrofoam.

"What's that for?"

"A sandwich roof, Jan. The Styrofoam will go above the rolled roofing and be topped by plywood and roof shingles; it'll keep our wood ceiling and log rafters visible."

"Feels like a fantasy list. This is what we get for being broke?"

A fortnight later, we get a bush line. Our order is in.

"Feels like hitting the lottery." We drive Big Red and its trailer to the mill, trade it for the van, drive to Seldovia, ferry to Homer, load the supplies, catch the next ferry, and drive back to the mill. We transfer goods from van to trailer, taking special care to cushion the windows. Ed kneels on Big Red's seat as he balances the three-wheeler across washouts and through creeks. We exhale as we reach the cabin. We mindfully unload the windows and lean them securely against the cabin wall. We turn our backs, and grab batts of Fiberglass. Meanwhile, the winds laugh, catch a window edge, and slam it. We pick glass shards from the grass, then brew ourselves a comforting tea.

Afterward, Ed crawls on his belly under the cabin and lays the itchy pink batts between the floor joists. I follow behind, unrolling clear plastic sheeting; Ed drops back, staple gun in hand. I lie like an upended turtle, flat on my back, legs extended and anchor plastic in place while Ed staples. "The Visqueen," he explains, "will keep the batts dry, and keep out rodents." Two crawling hours later, I call a break. I brew hot water; Ed heads to the corner couch and lights his pipe.

I read the signs. "What are you thinking about now?"

Bush Essentials 〜

"Visqueen," replies Ed.

"What about it?"

"Do you realize how essential plastic is? I've no clue how pioneers survived without it. It keeps our firewood dry, makes windows, and pack covers. Even made Randy and Mike their winter hut. And then there's this bush necessity," continues Ed, as he holds a gray roll.

"Duct tape," I laugh. "Never even heard of it until Alaska. Its importance hit home for me on that commuter flight on Alaska Aeronautical. The woman next to me was wringing her hands, her forehead so ridged with worry lines it looked like corduroy. I asked her if she had aviophobia. Shook her head no, and pointed to the gray plastered on all the seams. Said she only gets nervous flying when planes are held together with duct tape."

"Probably why locals called that airline Alaska Scare-onautical. But back to duct tape, I heard on KBBI about a guy who went into the emergency room with his wound stitched with duct tape."

"And remember that car we saw on Jakolof Bay Road, Ed, its bumper duct-taped on? And the shirts we've seen in town, with duct-tape patches on the tears?"

"And the graffiti we saw: 'I was here,' written in duct tape?"

"And the model at Wearable Arts in the duct-tape dress? And the duct-tape wallets for sale on the Homer Spit?"

"What about duct tape and warts, Jan? Some medical journal says it's more effective than freezing them."

"I guess our uses are pretty mundane. But here's a challenge: if Visqueen is the first bush essential, and duct tape is second, what's the third?"

"Easy. Five-gallon buckets."

"Spot on, Ed, we use them daily to haul water and rodent-proof our food. Good old plastic. Awful environmental curse sometimes, but what would we do without plastic? Now there's one other essential we've been living without all this time."

"What?"

"A full-length mirror. We live in the bush, but we don't have to look like we crawled out from under a rotted log. Don't we still have one in the van on the closet door? How about bringing it in for me? Would you mind taking the three-wheeler out to get it? I'd like to stay here and do more edits."

"Sure Janzie, could do with some air."

Ed returns hours later with the mirror. "I've got smile cramps, Jan."

"You must have looked silly carting a mirror into the bush."

"No kidding. Met a hiker en route. He asked me about the mirror. I told him it was bear protection."

"Bear protection?"

"Exactly what he asked. I told him that if a bear charges you, all you have to do is flash the mirror. He'll see this big charging bear and it'll make him turn tail."

"He didn't believe you, did he?"

"He wasn't certain at first. But I was so convincing he showed me the hand mirror he had in his first aid kit, for flashing signals to airplanes in emergencies. 'Gawd, no,' I warned him, 'don't flash that at a bear.'"

"Why not? It's a mirror."

"With that tiny thing, the bear will see a spring cub. If it's a boar, it'll kill you quicker than you can say jack shit."

"He didn't buy it, did he?"

"Yep. Hook, line, and sinker. I drove off into the bush with my full-length mirror and he was still standing there dumb as a skunk."

Solstice ⟞

Summer's longest day and biggest party, the solstice, lures us to Homer. We arrive on the *Tusty,* shell-shocked by Homer hustle. We treat ourselves to pizza and beer, scramble for groceries, and hit the hardware shop. As Ed buys basics, I pace the aisles. I gleefully note the not-neededs: no plumbing, no wires, no appliances, no electric anything for Rocky River. "We'd flunk Consumerism 101," I tell Ed. "Our purchases are all so nuts-and-bolts."

We visit Mossy for a beach ride, then head to Wilderness Lane to see the Minnesota boys. Mike lazes in his hammock between spruce trees. He sees us and smiles and waves us in for tea. We admire his newly completed wood frame cabin, then tour Randy's log home. Evening brings gaggles of Homerites to the solstice gala at the local bar. Mike and Randy are there too, celebrating. "To our homes," we say, clinking glasses.

"And my new fishing job," adds Mike.

"To great catches, great life," we toast again.

Mike braves the stage and sings his localized version of Dana Lyons's folk song, "June is a coming.'"

> . . . *But sometime in May* there's a magical day*
> *When the perfume of Springtime appears,*
> *And the flowers and trees of Homer* all bloom in the rain,*
> *It's the time of the year that the money runs short*
> *And the smell of the sea is so strong,*
> *When the boats are all painted, the fishermen soon will be gone.*

The crowd joins in the chorus; so many identify strongly with the situation:

> *June is a coming, the salmon are running*
> *And I've got to be on my way,*
> *I don't want to leave you my darling*
> *But there's so many more debts to pay,*
> *They say that the catch will be bigger this year*

And we'll all come home rich in the end,
I don't want to leave you my darling,
But the nets will be loaded by dawn,
June is a coming and I must be rolling along.

* Dana's tune has *March* and *Seattle* in the lyrics instead of *May* and *Homer*.
Visit www. danalyons.com to hear the original.

The room erupts in a frenzy of clapping. Mike returns to his seat, beaming. We head off at midnight, the party still well underway, and drive to the Spit to camp. We snuggle on the bed, chatting. "Mike was amazing tonight, Ed, having the guts to get up before the crowd and sing."

"Yeah, Jan. He has come so far since living in the hut at Mossy's and the winter in the plastic palace. He has his very own cabin now, and a fine job."

In the morning we hear the news: after the party, Mike ended his life with his gun. We head to Wilderness Lane in a sea of tears. Randy melts in our hug. He has already scrubbed the cabin of blood, but the memories are harder to erase.

"I don't understand, Randy. Mike was doing so good. Why now?"

"I found this journal, Jan. Take it home to read."

I am riveted to the pages. Mike details Vietnam buddies dying in his arms, and the unfairness of it all: one moment sharing meals in the mess, the next dealing with limbs blown off, or bodies stiff and lifeless.

I expected Mike's despair to be deepest in darkness. But it is summer's shining light that deepens his angst. His most piercing pain is success, the having it all: home, job, money. And friends not even having life.

I expect the familiar reaction to death: crushing loss, shock, grief like a rogue wave. Instead, I'm a hissy wasp. I hike to the ocean and scream, "You bloody quitter, Mike. Coward. Ass-wipe! Why didn't you warn us? You sang to us like it was any old day. It was a fricking farewell serenade."

June is a coming and I must be rolling along.

I yell till I'm hoarse, then beat myself up. "I should have known. Maybe I could have said something, done something. Why couldn't I see what was happening? All that bravado, simply a veneer? I miss you. You asshole, Mike. I miss you."

First Fish ⌇

We head across the bay to lick our wounds. I want to be alone. We retreat to the cabin, and return to routines. A knock interrupts. I open the door and slam it. "You get it Ed. A damn salesman."

"Don't be ridiculous, Jan."

"It's a salesman!"

Ed opens the door to: "Dan Dee Dan, the Carpet Man, Chimney Sweep, all around Kreep. Here to get your chimney sparkling. You betcha." The banter thaws Ed. He sweeps Dan inside. Dan hauls pickled fish from his pack. "Easy to make, you betcha. Take one large Dolly or a silly salmon. Six pounds of vinegar. Throw in salt and sugar, pickling spices and turmeric. You betcha, she's good."

Ed bites and raves. My stomach growls. I take a nibble, then another.

Dan pulls items from his pack like a magician. "Korbel Brandy. You'll need this by the time you get done with me." He spots the guitar. "Got the perfect thing for you Jan. You can wear this when you sing the Windy River hop. You've got to supply the words and melody, you betcha."

Dan hands me a ridiculous mock tuxedo t-shirt. I crack a grin. We insist Dan stay overnight and share more of his wacky tales. Morning brings yet more from his pack. "This deer hide is from Afognack Island; a good rug for your floor. And this stainless steel coffee pot is a must for the cabin. And this Honda thermos wants to live here, too."

We try to refuse but Dan is insistent. "I'll be back, you betcha."

Our mood lifted, we hit Seldovia. First fish are running at Outside Beach. We join the line-up, cast and catch, and head home for salmon barbecue, and more pickling. Ed skins fillets, rinses them in the river, and cuts them into bite-size chunks. I layer fish and herbs in boiled canning jars, then top with the cooled vinegar solution. "Now I need the refrigerator to chill these for a few days."

Ed returns with five-gallon plastic buckets with lids. I stack the jars, Ed carries them across the meadow to the river and sets them in a pool. He weighs the tops of the buckets with large rocks. "In a few days, we can bring them in, store them in the cupboard, and have pickled fish all winter long."

"Can't wait; Dan's was so yummy."

In the middle of the night, we stir slightly. There's a pleasant thrumming on the roof. It's so lovely to hear while snug in a dry, downy bed. The rain drums on, and we sleep deeply. In the morning, it's raining big pelting drops. I pull on my raincoat and brown rubber boots and head to the river for morning water-hauling duties. The river has risen dramatically in the night. Our buckets are gone.

I tell Ed the bad news. "Our salmon took a swim," I pout. He pours me a cuppa as consolation. "You put so much work into it, Jan; what a shame."

"I'll go take a look, Ed. Maybe I can find some of the jars."

"Nah," he insists, "They'll all be washed out to the Gulf or smashed in the rocks."

"I'll take a look anyways," I persist. I chow down the hot oatmeal, throw on an extra sweater under my coat, and strike off into the torrent with Max. I wade into the river, peering to and fro. I glimpse a shimmer. Can it be? I peer closer. "Glass." The jar is intact, wedged between rocks. I keep looking. One more treasure. Ah, and now, a plastic bucket trapped in the branches of a fallen cottonwood.

I keep searching, finding yet more strays tucked hither and yon. I reload the bucket with the twice-caught fish and strut back to Ed. "Look," I say proudly, "the fish that didn't get away."

Doldrums ⁓

Summer routines become robotic: daily water, daily meals. Ed details the cabin, trading the chain saw for handsaws, hand drills, hand planes, and chisels. Window trim and corner cabinets progress like an inchworm.

Making haste slowly rules my days too. Writing shifts to rewriting. The typewriter is stern as a Puritan; one blot equals punishment. My purgatory is endless retyping.

Our solitude is a two-edged sword: unlimited time to write, too little inflow of ideas. "I need connection with other plant users," I complain to Ed. "I need to learn how everyday Alaskans use these plants. What happens in the bush villages? Are plants a lost art or do Eskimos and other Natives still use them?"

"You'd have to travel around, Jan. But we don't have the budget to do it. One flight to one village would set us back $500. And you'd need to go to a lot more than one."

Our mail sack brings a lucky dip; our solo-on-the-Yukon friend Helen details her summer plans to canoe the second half of the Yukon River starting from the Interior Haul Road. Then Helen is off on a bush village tour. "I've found an unbelievable fare deal with Wien Airlines," she writes, "a book of air tickets good for twenty-nine days of unlimited flights to all fourteen villages and cities where Wien has regular service. I can fly above the Arctic to Barrow, and Kotzebue, and as far south as Kodiak Island, and even Seattle. The grand total for the flying safari is only $500."

I'm gobsmacked. My brain spins with possibilities. If Helen wanted a companion, and if she and I camped, I could interview folks statewide about their uses of plants. I run my fantasy to Ed. "Go for it Janzie," he tells me. "Write Helen."

Helen is keen. I book with Wien, and make plans to rendezvous at St. Mary's where Helen will haul out her canoe in conclusion of her 1,300-mile Yukon River epic.

Ed too gets news of travel, a trip to Icy Bay in Southeast Alaska, adjacent to the Wrangell–Saint Elias Wilderness to work the log ships. Marsha Million's neighbors from Little Tutka Bay lure Ed with promises: three thousand dollars in three days. Quick bucks, plus all you can eat, and the food is on par with a deluxe hotel. Whisper your desires and the chefs prepare it: prime rib, steak, chicken, salmon, king crab. And pie, all the pie you can eat.

"A guy on the crew broke his back," Ed says, "and they need a replacement." Instead of warning bells, Ed hears food gongs. Pie. The log ship needs another hand. Pie. Ed volunteers.

The Call of the Job ⬳

Ed flies five hundred miles east to Yakutat in the Gulf of Alaska; Yakutat is Tlingit Indian for "a place where the canoes rest" but Ed's here not to rest (or recreate near this "surf capital of Alaska") but to work the Icy Bay log ship. Meanwhile I fly about six hundred miles northwest to the Yukon River delta, equipped with a tent, backpack, Nikon, and names of village contacts for potential herbal interviews. Helen meets me at the Wien terminal in St. Mary's, upriver from the mighty Yukon on Andreafski River; she takes me on tour.

"Only $450 folks," Helen tells me. "The village is approximately

95 percent Yup'ik. There's the Catholic Mission school and the fish-freezing plant over there." We head over to the combination grocery and department store and stroll the aisle. I stare at the freezer case. "It can't be."

"What, Jan?"

"Häagen Dazs ice cream, my absolute favorite. You can't even find it in trendy Homer, yet here it is nine hundred miles off Alaska's road system. The bush is more civilized than I'd expected."

"You've seen nothing yet. Wait until I show you where we're roughing it tonight." Helen strolls to the door of a modern home and walks in. "Jan, meet the Bradys; they've invited us to stay here with them."

The Bradys welcome us like long-lost relatives and indulge us with warm beds, running water (that we don't have to run for), hot showers, and a washing machine. Dinner is fresh-caught silver salmon, dessert is fresh-from-the-tundra blueberry pie topped with homemade ice cream. "Even better than Häagen Dazs," I murmur.

During dinner, Helen regales us with her personalized "Murphy's Laws" for paddling the Yukon River:

1. *No matter in which direction the wind is blowing, it's always against the bow.*
2. *Whatever I need is always at the bottom of the pack.*
3. *The best campsites are always found early in the day when you don't need them.*
4. *A short cut on the river channels is always longer.*
5. *Just about when I say "enough" (rain, bugs, whatever) it always changes for the better.*

In the morning, I'm introduced to a Yup'ik elder, willing to share her personal plant lore. I show herbal samples from the tundra and her daughter translates. Her eyes brighten as she spots wormwood *(Artemisia tilesii)*. The elder utters syllables deep in her throat: strong KKKKKs, gutteral GGGGGs, streams of words. Her daughter translates succinctly: "Stinkweed."

I sniff the herb; definitely aromatic, but not offensive. "What do you use it for?" I ask. The elder points to her stomach and grimaces. "Ah, stomach pains." She rubs her hands together as though crushing the herb and holds it to her shoulder. "Ah, poultice for sore muscles." She waves in the air and pinches herself. "Ah, for biting insects." Words fly in Yup'ik, are translated, and are confirmed by the sign language.

Afterward, I bubble with excitement, assured that this trip will be well worthwhile. From St. Mary's we must fly about 450 miles east to Anchorage, Alaska's hub, for connector flights to villages. Fairbanks, in the heart of the Alaskan Interior, is next; Helen needs to pick up her large backpack, left behind with friends due to size constraints in her canoe. Her pals Celia Hunter and Ginny Woods are readying for a raft trip but squeeze in time for a farewell dinner. Eleven friends surround the table. We dive into a delectable feast of moose meat, garden vegetables, and twice-baked potatoes.

Celia and Ginny hand Helen a card, and say, "When you're in Barrow, please give this to our friend Charlotte Rogers. She's a nurse and she lives at the hospital apartment complex."

The next day we are scheduled to fly 766 miles north to Barrow on the Arctic Ocean, the northernmost settlement on the North American mainland. Barrow is fogged in; we wait three days for clear skies. Meanwhile, we fiddle in Fairbanks, visit the University of Alaska museum and explore the Arboretum. Fairbanks is in the midst of an August heat wave; temps top ninety.

We finally get a flight and arrive in Barrow midmorning. We step down the open ramp and shiver. Barrow's temps hover at freezing. As soon as our bags unload, we dig frantically for overcoats.

"City buses," I exclaim to Helen, pointing. "Here we are, 340 miles north of the Arctic Circle and there's public transportation. Homer doesn't have anything more sophisticated than a taxi." We scramble onto the bus, laden with packs, drop coins in the meter, and ride to and fro, observing. Barrow is a creative anachronism. Sealskins stretch on plywood in back yards. Huskies on short chains sit next to snow-machines; an Iñupiat man builds a dog sled. An Eskimo woman in colorful Native dress walks the street carrying a plastic bag of groceries. A satellite dish perches on the roof of a plywood home next to stacks of caribou antlers.

Charlotte Rogers works nights; we drop by mid-afternoon to drop the note from her Fairbanks buddies. She welcomes us inside and plies us with hot tea and snacks. While we chat, my eyes study shelves laden with ivory and bone carvings and baleen baskets. "Gifts from my patients," says Charlotte. On the windowsill, tomatoes cascade like red waterfalls. Next to them corn grows.

"I love corn," Charlotte says. "I get only a few ears from the plants but they're delicious, and they remind me of home in West Virginia."

"Can you recommend a good Barrow campsite?" asks Helen.

"Right there," insists Charlotte. "My couch." Charlotte won't take no for an answer.

We abandon our packs and embark on area explorations. We visit an archaeological dig where a centuries-old frozen family was excavated from a collapsed sod home. While Charlotte works nights, we attempt to sleep on her fold-out couch. Since May 11, Barrow's sun has been stuck on endless day. The sun undulates slightly in the evening, but fails to kiss the horizon. Our eyes droop but our brains buzz.

During the days, we wander and wonder in the tundra's Lilliputian world. I kneel down and touch a leaf. I feel its undersides and peer at its margins.

"What are you checking, Jan?"

"This leaf has the shape of coltsfoot *(Petasites frigidus)* and the felty back. I'm sure it's coltsfoot, Helen, but it's no bigger than my thumbnail. Remember the coltsfoot in the boreal forest in Fairbanks, with leaves as big as dinner plates?" Plants peek from the tundra, heads low in Arctic wind; they adapt strangely, wisely to their harsh environment. Spring lousewort *(Pedicularis kanei)* clads itself in a woolly overcoat as it emerges from permafrost, then erupts into mad pinks. Its flowers attract hungry bees, as well as Iñupiat kids who are fond of sucking sweet nectar from its flowers. Sunny bouquets of yellow poppies *(Papaver macounii)* blaze, tucked snugly in sheltered gullies.

Our morning yields answers as to why Eskimo language has twenty-two words for snow and twenty-six words for ice. Though high summer, the sky spits flakes. Offshore are icebergs, the remains of last winter's ice-pack. I struggle to imagine life in Barrow. How does one cope in a Jekyll and Hyde world of endless day giving way to endless night, with the sun buried below the horizon from November 18 until January 24? With winter wind-chill factors equivalent to one hundred below zero?

Southern-born Charlotte tells us she has weathered fifteen years in Barrow and plans to retire to Homer. "I've got a plot of land by East Road. I'm going to build a log home. Do you know any builders, Jan?" I tell Charlotte about Ed; we exchange contact details.

Kotzebue, on Alaska's western coast, is the next stop on our itinerary. Helen tells me it was called Kikiktagruk (Iñupiaq for "almost an island"), and was renamed after the 1816 explorer Captain Otto von Kotzebue. Like Barrow, it lies above the Arctic Circle, but air connections require we first fly south to Anchorage.

Connections complete, we descend to undulating tundra, punctuated by clusters of dwellings. Helen reads her travel literature: "There are three thousand inhabitants, Jan, over 80 percent Iñupiat. Kotzebue is also center for NANA (the Native corporation) and headquarters for the eleven-million-acre Western Arctic National Parklands."

We set camp in a drizzle and struggle as winds play kite with our tent. At the park headquarters I chat with a young ranger about my plant project; we mount a four-wheeler, and scoot to the tundra to scout plants.

After lunch, I tentatively knock on the door of an Eskimo elder, Mamie, a friend of a friend of a friend. Mamie flings the door open and welcomes me like a sister. I show her my bouquet of tundra wildflowers. "Stinkweed," she exclaims, as she extracts an herb from my bundle. Mamie tells me she drinks stinkweed tea for flu, mashes the leaves and sticks it on sores, and whips bodies with it in the *banya* (sauna) to stimulate circulation.

From Kotzebue, Helen and I fly across the Seward Peninsula to Nome. We read that Nome is "Alaska's oldest continuous first-class city" and was, during the turn-of-the-century gold rush, Alaska's most populous city. Its naming came from a manuscript map where "Name?" was penciled next to a prominent point; during transcription the lettering was misinterpreted and "Nome" came into being.

We're counting on our home in Nome to be its youth hostel's five-dollar beds. Unfortunately, the hostel is locked with an "out of business" sign on the door.

"Shall we camp on a Bering Sea beach?" I ask.

Helen frowns. "It's pouring cats and caribou."

We march to the reception desk of the nearest hotel; its cheapest room is 120 bucks. We march out. On the curb are two backpackers, folks we had seen on the flight. "Where are you staying?" we ask.

"We were going to the hostel."

"Us too. What if we all chip in for a room? There's one more hotel we can check."

Hotel two has a bargain hundred-dollar room with one double bed. We sign the register, while the other couple stands outside. We get the key and tell them to meet us at room twelve.

We toss a coin to see who gets the bed. Helen and I lose. We sweep the floor of dust bunnies, then unfurl our sleeping pads. "Well, this beats that," says Helen, pointing to the rain pelting the window. "At least we're dry."

Evening brings in-house entertainment. Doors slam. Radios blare. Sounds of "Oooooh, yes yes yes!" percolate the skin-thin walls. "Like my college dorm," comments roommate Sarah. Sounds of the familiar lull her to sleep. I toss and turn on my thin foam pad and sleep in fits and starts.

The sounds of breaking glass waken us all. We hear screams, scuffles, banging, cussing.

Soon there is running in the hall. "Police!" There are sounds of a door pushed in and a person dragged from the room.

Morning shows baggy-eyed faces. "A hot shower will perk me up," says roomie John. He heads down the hall to the bath, with towel, toiletries, and his battery radio. He sets his treasured music on the shower ledge; it slips between shower and wall. It sits there still. But for ten hours in August, Nome's hotel added a star to its rating, offering the only singing showers in the city.

Our second day in Nome has us facing the dilemma again. "Tenting would be quiet. We have warm bags," I say.

"It's still pouring, Jan. Let's suit up and check out town. Maybe the weather will clear later." Nome windows display ivory carvings, a polar-bear-hide coat bearing a $10,000 price tag, and Iditarod race posters. We pop into a gift shop and chat with its owner, Mary, who quizzes us about our travels. We mention Barrow. Mary mentions Charlotte Rogers. "We slept on her couch," we say. "You'll have to do the same on mine," says Mary. She leads us upstairs. We sit and sip hot tea and watch the roaring rain in snug comfort.

I interview Eskimo Grace Johnson, who generously shares her plant knowledge. Dock *(Rumex arcticus),* a member of the buckwheat family, was traditionally stored by northern Natives in sealskin pokes in earthen caches. "Do you use dock?" I ask Grace. She opens her freezer and extracts a vacuum sealed package of blanched dock leaves. She uses dock as a boiled green, and in stir-fries and soups.

I hold up a sprig of *Ledum palustre,* an aromatic tundra plant commonly called Labrador or Hudson Bay Tea. Labrador Tea, I've learned, is "stinkweed's partner" and used for stomach troubles, chest ailments, and flus. "Yes, I use that all the time," Grace tells me. I lean forward expectantly, pen poised to record her traditional local use. "I use it to flavor my Lipton Tea."

And Grace too uses stinkweed. "It's good for anything that ails you."

Dillingham, in the Bristol Bay region on the southwest Alaskan coast, is next on our itinerary. It too requires a circuitous rerouting via Anchorage. In Dillingham, Helen and I set up camp in the grassy riverside park adjacent to the harbor.

"No noisy Nome hotel tonight," I say, "only the sweet sounds of the lapping river." We're deep asleep when nature's soundtrack alters. Motors hum, metal clangs rudely. "It's 2 A.M. What the heck is this?" Over breakfast we learn that the Army Corps of Engineers dredges the harbor each and every low tide, no matter the time. The tide rules.

Botanical Boggle ~

Each day's a living mystery, sorting out botanical clues. I peer at flower clusters, and stare at stalks radiating like an umbrella, with each ray sprouting a second umbrella. Double umbels characterize *Umbelliferae,* the parsley family, but have I found the family's Jekyll or its Hyde? The family is diverse, encompassing humble parsley and carrots as well as the most nefarious plants in the northern hemisphere. Even blindfolded, I'd know cow parsnip *(Heracleum lanatum)*, its platter-sized leaves and Herculean proportions a clear giveaway. I take care not to break stalks as furanocoumarin in its sap can trigger blisters similar to third-degree burns. Obvious too, but requiring more detailed observation is the smaller parsley, called beach lovage or *petrushki,* whose stem splits in three; each stalk bearing three leaves. I crush and sniff: its unique scent tells me it's definitely lovage *(Ligusticum scoticum)*. I selectively harvest leaves for today's sandwiches.

On another plant, herbal stalks taller than lovage but smaller than cow parsnip bend abruptly. The bent knee reminds me of genuflecting when entering Church. "Ah, bent-leaf angelica *(Angelica genuflexa),*" I tell Helen; "its roots were roasted by Siberian Eskimos and inhaled to relieve seasickness."

But now I'm confused by yet more double umbels, with varying leaf shapes and fragrance. I go on red alert. There is no casual tasting to aid identity with this family of plants. This family kills the careless. I've read of campers who have mistaken poison water hemlock *(Cicuta mackenzieana)* for marijuana; instead of a high they get spasmodic convulsions and death. *Cicuta* is rated the most toxic plant in North America. Thousand-pound animals eating one of its walnut-sized roots have died within fifteen minutes; a pea-sized taste fells a human. I check the leaf margins. Veins end in the bottom of the V between leaf margins, and I remember a rhyme: "veins to the cut, pain in the gut." This appears to be the deadly hemlock.

Yet another species bears a slightly broader leaf, with veins to the tip. Beach angelica? I head to the library to study Hulten's *Flora of Alaska and Neighboring Territories,* and confirm identities.

We leave Dillingham and hop an air taxi for a fifteen minute flight to Helen's friends in Manokotak; we skim low over rolling tundra to the dot of a village. Our host Marilyn Crace is a teacher and her husband Tim a pilot, playwright, carpenter, journalist, and skin sewer. Their kids introduce me to my first video game. We supper on moose, breakfast on caribou sausage, head outdoors to study neighborhood plants, and observe the community.

At 8 A.M., the air fills with the sounds of woodpeckers. "Hammers," Helen exclaims. "This is the first bush village I've ever seen that gets to work so early, and so diligently."

The Craces confirm that Manokotak is supremely independent and community-focused; its raft of community improvements, including housing and telecommunication networks, is completely village funded. "Unlike most villages, they say no to government. Don't want to be beholden."

From Manokotak we return to Dillingham, then back to Anchorage for commuter connections to the Kuskokwim River in southwest Alaska. "This district," reads Helen, "contains ten thousand square miles, with only one thousand inhabitants." Six hundred of those are in McGrath, a former Athabascan village and trade center for area villages. McGrath is also home to yet more friends of Helen's, our hosts Gordon Castanza and Beverly Cornet. Gordon and Beverly pick us up at the airport and welcome us to their log home. Gordon is in training for the Iditarod, the famous 1,049-mile sled-dog race from Anchorage to Nome. With summer in full hilt, Gordon harnesses lead dogs to his belt, and the trio run McGrath roads. "As soon as snow comes," Gordon tells us, "I'll get the whole team training with the sled. Meanwhile this helps get me and the leaders fit."

While Gordon trains, we make ourselves useful. Our standard repayment to hosts is helping with dishes and housecleaning. But Bev directs us outdoors. "Gordon needs help with that skiff," she points. "It needs to be scraped so he can do a repaint." We dress in men's overalls, strap on goggles and dust masks, and lie on our backs beneath the propped up skiff. Hours later, sweat pouring, we've barely begun.

Back from his run, Gordon heads to the bathroom. "Septic system has taken a crap," he tells us. "You'll have to use the outhouse round back."

Before I can poke Helen, she glibly volunteers our help.

Gordon hires a pump and a portable tank, but things go awry. Shit happens while we hold the hose. The stench is overpowering. Everything reeks, including our clothes. "Our next stop," Helen assures me, "will be even more memorable."

Close Encounters of the Furry Kind ⌒

Planes return us to Anchorage, and shoot us to King Salmon on the Alaska Peninsula. Helen insists we book a connector flight to Katmai National Park. "Free camping, and the rangers can help you, Jan, with botany."

Barren tundra gives way to lakes, forests, and hills. The plane flies low; our noses press the windows, our eyes captivated by herds of caribou and lone brown bears. The plane skims onto Naknek Lake, and speeds toward the trees. "Oh godfather, we're going to crash." My heart pounds; my head slams to my knees, I prepare for impact.

The engine revs. The plane lurches forward, spins and stops. I hesitantly raise my head. Our plane is now sitting on the beach, on wheels. The pilot laughs at my naïveté as he explains that our aircraft is a flying boat, a Grumman Widgeon with a boat hull for water landing and wheels for beach and bush strips. Our landing, he says, "has been perfectly routine."

"Katmai's weird," I tell Helen. "Boats fly. And look, floating in the lake: aren't those rocks?"

We scoop up featherlight, porous rocks. "They remind me of those pumice scrubbers for the bath, Jan."

"Lava," says the ranger, dressed in a green suit and tan Mountie hat. "Pumice is that light-colored one," he points, "made of dacite or rhyolite.

Pumice forms as gas expands in erupting lava. Katmai is home to the largest volcanic eruption in North American history. I'll tell you more about that in my evening talk. Right now everyone has to hear the bear rap."

"Be bear aware," continues the ranger. "There are approximately two thousand brown bears in Katmai National Park. Browns are normally solitary, but during peak salmon run they gang up to gorge on salmon. There can be forty to sixty near the falls."

Like a preacher, he hammers home the commandments:

Give way to bears.
Make noise. Sing, talk, or wear bear bells.
Walk in groups, not singly.
Never walk closer to bears for photos.
Don't store anything remotely edible in your tent, not even toothpaste or
shampoo; place your goods in the cache, on stilts near the campground.
Never set down a backpack when hiking.
If a bear approaches when you've caught a fish, cut the line immediately;
don't train bears to associate humans with dinner.
If a bear approaches you, talk loudly, lift your arms, look big; back away
slowly. If you run, the bear will think you're prey.

My ears rivet to the ranger's words. I recall the crabby charging blackie in the Yukon. Blacks look like cuddly kiddie toys compared to the Katmai browns. When standing they can reach nine feet high.

Helen and I depart for a hike, chatting loudly. We hike along the Mount Dumpling track and weave through a maze of head-high devil's club. I dodge their thorns, reach beyond for a soft twisted stem, and emerge with a handful of wine-red berries. "Taste these, Helen."

"Watermelon."

"Yes, and in spring the shoots are like fresh cucumber. So it's often called wild cucumber, or watermelon berry. See how the leaves wrap around the stalk, and the fruits hang like rubies. Look at the underside, that stalk is kinked too. So another common name is twisted stalk. In fact, the botanical name, *Streptopus amplexifolius,* means exactly that, the clasping leaf with the twisted stalk."

Helen shows me a fungus growing on a fallen balsam poplar. It looks like a frozen waterfall. "You can't mistake this for anything else," says Helen. This is precisely the type of edible mushroom I want to add to the book, the foolproof fungi. Helen says this is bear's head, a *Hericium* species. She collects the fungi, soaks it in water to encourage resident insects to evacuate, then sautés it in oil with chopped carrot. In another pot, I boil water and cook ramen. We combine efforts and jazz all with grated parmesan and chili pepper flakes.

In the evening we hike to the floating bridge across the Brooks River. A hiker, a hundred yards ahead of us, spots a grizzly. He drops his daypack, grabs his camera, and strides toward the bear. We backpedal to a discreet distance; with my longest telephoto I start to shoot. The brown halts, hackles vertical, and waves his massive head to and fro in a definitive no. Then it sounds off, a cross between a throaty growl and a woof.

We retreat further. "We'd best get a ranger."

The roar startles the photographer from his stupor. He backs up, stoops, and retrieves his pack. The bear hesitates and swings his body in indecision. The man retreats to the lodge, the bear to the river, and we to our tent.

Morning sends me to the lakeside water spigot to fill the kettle for coffee. I emerge from the forest, yawning and rubbing sleep from my eyes. The dawn dance of light on the lake hypnotizes me. I stare at the glassy lake mirror, glance down the beach to the right, turn to the left, and drop the kettle. A super-sized shrub is moving: it's a huge brown sow.

What do I do? Make noise? "This land is your land," I sing at the top of my lungs. "I'm leaving your land. You can have the lake shore. I'm here no more." The wall of bear halts six feet from me, shakes its monstrous head, and strolls on.

I refill my pot, spilling water with my shaking hands. Katmai is crazy. All these humans in the midst of a bear highway. Thank God for the tolerance of the bears that we've met and their gentle grace in face of human stupidity, mine included.

Our post-breakfast agenda is a jaunt to the infamous Valley of Ten Thousand Smokes. "It's the valley of ten thousand colors," insists Helen. The valley floor is a pastel painting, a forty-square-mile bowl of pinkish ash, one hundred to seven hundred feet deep. Rivers carve Grand Canyons through the ash, which was deposited by Novarupta Volcano in 1912.

Evening draws us to the platform established at the falls for bear viewing and photography. A bear stands on a rock, his neck stretched forward; he flicks his jaw and catches a silver salmon in its mid-air flight. Another bear, dubbed Diver by the rangers, plunges his head in a pool and snorkels for salmon.

"What a wilderness paradise, Helen. I'll have to bring Ed here some-day to see these brown bears. I so hate to have this trip end. It has been quite a month."

"We're not done yet, Jan, there is still one more adventure. Tomorrow, the Emerald Isle."

Pony Trails and Break-ins ⌒

The Emerald Isle, Kodiak Island, lies some 250 air miles southwest of Anchorage. "Kodiak," Helen informs me, "is home to the world's big-gest brown bears."

"Bigger than Katmai's monsters?"

"Yes, sized more like polar bears. A large boar, standing upright, can be thirteen feet tall."

"That's not a bear, Helen, that's King Kong. And I suppose there's one on every street corner?"

"Nearly one per square mile in the Kodiak archipelago. And Kodiak is huge, second only to the Big Island of Hawaii. That makes for around three thousand brown bears."

"And you expect me to sleep on this trip?"

"No problem, Jan; we're not camping. I've got . . ."

" . . . a friend. Why am I not surprised? You've got more friends than a wagging Labrador retriever."

We hop a taxi to the home of Bob Brodie, whom Helen had struck up a friendship with in the Nome airport terminal during our travels. "You must visit," he had insisted when we parted. "My door is always open. Drop by when in Kodiak and make yourself at home. Camp on my floor as long as you wish."

The three-story building matches Bob's map. "No answer," says Helen. "He must be at work." As promised, the door is open. We drop our packs discreetly in the corner with a note, and tour the City of Kodiak. What we discover is a town of six thousand folks, and a city of thousands of boats ranging from small pleasure craft to fishing vessels 150 feet long. Crab and salmon fisheries form the economic base for Kodiak, and its harbor houses one of North America's largest fishing fleets.

Stomach growls lure us home in late afternoon laden with groceries for a thank-you meal. Bob is still not home. The door is locked. Unable to cook, we dally over supper at the harbor café, and check back afterward to greet our host. There is still no one home, and no open door. We walk again, and return yawning. It's still locked.

We hear voices in the downstairs apartment; the residents there assure us Bob does indeed live upstairs. Beate, who lives downstairs, leads us to the deck. She stands on Helen's shoulders and pulls herself onto Bob's balcony. She slides open the glass door, enters, and unlocks the normal entrance.

"What do we do now, Helen?"

"We can sleep upstairs or go tent with the bears."

"Bob said we could stay. Let's sleep, and move on in the morning."

We unroll our camp mats and slide into our bags. Hours later, we startle awake. A strange man looms above us.

"Who are you?"

"Who are you?" counters Helen. "You're not Bob."

"I'm Bob's roommate; Bob won't be back 'til tomorrow."

"Bob said to stay here," I squeak.

"He's always picking up strays. Yeah, yeah, fine. Get some sleep."

The next afternoon, Bob is back, laughing over our tale of breaking and entering. He treats his intruders to a king crab and halibut banquet. We heap bowls with salad and pour wine.

After breakfast the next day, a miniature ferry transports us to a two-mile spruce isle, where a bridge link is under construction. Near Island is inhabited solely by a herd of semi-wild ponies. We hike the tracks, and duck through Shetland-high holes in the elder groves. I stop to shoot herbs and pick samples. Helen harvests salmonberries for tonight's farewell cobbler. We scour the tide line, study kelps, and taste-test beach greens, oyster leaf, and lovage while waiting for the ferry to transport us home to Homer.

For once, the *Tustemena* is on time. The Gulf of Alaska crossing is, praise God, uneventful; no Dramamine is needed on the Dramamine Express. We camp on the above-deck solarium, snug in our sleeping bags. My brain's a blur; I can't wait to see Ed.

Icy Bay ⁓·

Ed meets us on the Homer Spit, welcoming us with warm hugs; we drive to the Homestead Restaurant for cuppas and catch-up.

"How was Icy Bay?" I ask him.

Ed rolls his eyes. "You know, Janzie, how I told you about my old days working the Boston high-rises?"

"How could I forget—you standing on those freight planks, riding up fifty floors without a harness? And the time your buddy went to dump concrete and it stuck in the wheelbarrow and pitched him to his death. And when you got knocked from the twelfth floor and were plummeting to your death until you smacked into that rail that stove in your ribs but saved your life. What's that got to do with Icy Bay?"

"High-rise work was kid's play, Jan. Should have paid more attention to why I got the job: the fact that the last guy broke his back. Sure wasn't a garden party. Lots more to Icy Bay than pie. You should have seen Dave Seaman," Ed tells me, referring to our Tutka neighbor. "He'd leap from the log ship onto wet logs that bounced like bucking broncs. Rodeo riders who fall kiss dust. Log riders who fall get squashed like toads on the road. Only here they are squashed between logs and the ship. The new man on the job, namely me," continues Ed, "gets the hold deep in the ship's belly. He has to stand on spruce that's slippery as duck squirt."

Ed continues. "The trees don't stack like bricks on a pallet. They hang up and leave gaps to fall into, death traps. My job was to reach up, unhook the chokers, and leap out of the way. The hardware on the end of the cables would grab the logs, making them roll and shift. And the cables would stretch and spring out like rubber bands. That guy before me broke his back when a choker bounced and smacked him. I felt like a rat in a barrel getting blasted with buckshot. Most dangerous stuff I've ever done."

In three days, Ed frees the cables on 2.7 million board feet of timber. He works twelve-hour days and collapses into his bunk nightly with flashbacks of Boston in his head. "Easy money isn't easy, Jan. And I've already done my time in danger. But Icy Bay itself was amazing. You'll have to see it someday. It's like Glacier Bay minus the cruise ships, with eighteen-thousand-foot Mount St. Elias on the horizon, and icebergs everywhere. Up to 3,500 harbor seals in the bay. And the nightly entertainment, you wouldn't believe it, Jan."

"Entertainment? At the logging camp?"

"Yeah; after supper, we'd pile into a van and head to the dump for the show."

"What?"

"Each night the boss's kids loaded all the meal scraps onto a pickup and drove them to the dump. Four brownies would roar in snarling and fighting to be first onto the truck bed. The boys would jump out with a two-by-four and smack the bears on the nose to get them to drop back so they could empty the truck. Then the kids would jump into the center of the food heap as it was being ripped apart by bears. They'd pour fuel on the scraps, then leap back and toss in a match. The bears would back off 'til the inferno subsided, then paw through the barbecue."

"Mornings," continued Ed, "would begin at 4 A.M. While breakfast was cooking, we'd head over to the lunch bar and brownbag sandwiches and fruit and pie. Then we'd pick up scrambled eggs and stacks of hotcakes and bacon."

"You must have been stuffed like a tick all day."

"Nah, I couldn't get enough. By 5 A.M. we'd be on a bus out to the bay. We'd pick our way down a jetty of massive rocks and leap from them into an open skiff bouncing in six foot swells. We'd dodge ice floes, then clamber up rope ladders onto the ship. Then we'd bronc logs, dodge chains, be on red alert every single second. Work and stress ate up every calorie. By nightfall we'd be so exhausted we could hardly crawl to bed. It was great money, three thou in three days. But I'll never do it again, Jan. It's not worth the risk."

"Glad you're home safe, honey."

"And how'd your trip go, Jan? You and Helen look all smiles."

Return to the River ⌒

We fill Ed's ears with our adventures and comic mishaps. "Katmai's a must-see," I tell him, "some day. Right now all I'm hungry to see is home."

Helen and her pal Ed Berg, a geologist and botanist, join us when we return home. At Rocky River, we waken to Tarzan cries as Ed Berg braves an early bath in the ice-water river. Berg is keen for a trek to Red Mountain. We splash warm water on our faces, belly up to breakfast, load packs with lunch, then trek to its rusty red chromite peaks. Berg stops often to chip rocks and scribble notes. At nightfall he writes in the guestbook: "The geology of the land here is of especial interest to me—the chromite of Red Mountain, the slates and graywacke of the McHugh Formation of Rocky River, the elusive fault of Rocky Bay. This area is a sort of fossil subduction zone, where the Pacific Plate plunged under the North American Plate some 150–190 million years ago and piled up the rocks that were later uplifted to form our Kenai Mountains."

Berg's botanical eye brings new plants to my attention: Thrift *(Armeria maritima)*, a dainty beauty common on Arctic shores and strangely out of place inland; more evidence, Berg tells me, of Red Mountain being a geological upthrust. Maidenhair fern *(Adiantum pedatum)* is yet another area oddity with its delicate foliage, common in temperate southeast Alaska.

Yet, here it is before us, thriving in harsh Red Mountain conditions.

As Helen and Ed leave, more visitors arrive, luring us to holiday in our vast backyard. I'm keen to share my Red Mountain shortcut. "It's not far," I tell my fresh-from-the-city guests, "only about a mile and a half. It's about eight if we take the road." They opt for short. "Memorable," guarantees Ed. "Jan's Pass is memorable. But I'll stay here, and have supper ready for your return."

At Wolverine Creek, we enter old growth spruce, weave between devil's club, and scramble ever upward. We snake through tangles of alders, thankful for handholds on the steep slopes. We pause and pant in grassy openings and gaze beyond the hills behind the cabin into the vastness of Kachemak Bay State Wilderness Park. Still we climb and then meet a wall of rock. We skirt the edges, wading our way to an alpine meadow that stairsteps upward. We peel off shoes and socks and stroll barefoot in the thickly piled carpet of heathers. Rested, we shoe up, and crest a Rocky River summit. Below us lie emerald meadows lined by Windy River and shadowed by the pyramid of Red Mountain.

My guests opt for the long, road way home. Eight miles later, we collapse on the couch. Ed hands us wine. "A toast," says one of our visitors, "to Jan's Pass. I've been on adventures around the globe but never anything as magical as this. What's it like to live in heaven?"

Neighbors ⌒

Summer's stream of visitors reduces to a cold-season trickle. We ferry to Homer for bulk food and arrive back at Rocky River. Halloween has left new treats in our journal. Tasmanian Kent sets the record as our furthest visitor, but it's his companion's entry that most intrigues us:

Ours were the only human tracks in the freshly fallen snow, although
there were many critter tracks as my friend and I walked along today.
The sun shone off icicle waterfalls. Like a trimmed toenail the moon
hung for a time above the snowy peaks. What a great life! I am just
beginning to build my house on the lake. I hope you'll come by someday.
  Steve Hughes

"The lake," says Ed. "I wonder which lake Steve's referring to?"

"He seems to imply it's local."

A fortnight later, we strap on our packs, wax skis, and head to
Kasitna Bay for mail. Below the switchback, we freeze. Smoke. We stare
at the cottonwoods and the glimmer of orange below. We weave through
tangles of alders toward the smoky plume. A man in a woolen sweater
with a kingfisher design sits on a stump by a campfire, next to a pumpkin-
colored pop-top Volkswagen camper. He pumps our hand enthusiastically. "Hi, I'm Steve. Grab a stump, have a cuppa."

Steve is rapt to learn that we are the Rocky River residents. He is the
mysterious journal scribe and now our closest neighbor. "I'm settling
down," he tells us. "I'm building a home back there," he points, "on Kingfisher Lake. It's Seldovia Native lease land. Living here with Nellie while
I get started."

"Your girlfriend? Where is she?"

Steve reaches out, pats his Volkswagen affectionately. "Nellie," he says.
We laugh.

"Bought Nellie in Germany five years ago," he continues. "We've been
round the world together."

"Where will you winter?" we ask.

"On my land at the lake. I'm setting up a wall tent with a woodstove
while I build."

While we sip tea, Steve spins yarns, describing his work doing mineral exploration on Admiralty Island in Southeast Alaska, work that ended with a helicopter crash. "I'm lucky to be alive. When I finally recovered, I decided it was time to see the world. The settlement money got me Nellie and five years of adventures. But now we're parked. We've hit paradise."

"Can't wait to see the lake," we tell Steve. "But right now we've got to boogie or we'll miss the tide and the mail. We'll come see you next trip out."

"If Nellie's here and I'm not, you'll know I'm at the lake. There's a stack of rough-cut piled at the trailhead. If you don't mind, grab a couple boards on the way in."

"Easy; we're great pack mules."

"Seems like a real down-to-earth guy," says Ed afterward. "Have a feeling we'll see lots more of him."

"That crash he had was quite a wake-up call. What a life he's had since."

"Staring death in the eyeball tends to do that, lets you know what's important." Ed pauses, looks around at the Jakolof Bay views; he reaches across the seat and takes my hand. "This is important, Jan, you and me, living this, together."

My eyes mist. "I'm so glad I'm with you, Ed. I had no clue life could be this alive, this free, this rich."

"Rich? On eight thousand dollars a year?"

"Yeah. It's nothing to do with the money honey."

Ed squeezes my hand.

Changing Season ⌁

The season of white brings solitude. "You create your own reality," Ed reads aloud from *Seth Speaks* by Jane Roberts. "Exactly what I've been telling you, Jan."

The reality we've created is a world of wood fires and simple chores.

Daily I research, write, and rewrite. Each interlibrary loan shipment brings new data, new manuscript changes, new fire starter. I delete with scissors, tape the new, redo, and do again. I glue my butt to the spruce stool and bang on the keys of the ancient Royal.

"This typewriter is as portable as a boat anchor," I complain. "And I so wish there was some way to change words without retyping."

"You'll have fingers of steel by the end of winter, Jan."

"I only hope I don't have buns of Jell-O."

Max interrupts, whining and heading for the door.

"Come on, Jan," Ed coaxes. "Can't let you lose that sweet ass."

We step off the porch onto our skis, and set off on the valley's endless miles of trails. "Our very own wilderness playground," says Ed. He points out tracks: wolverine, lynx, coyote.

We return revived, put soup on the boil, and play the latest cribbage challenge. Days ditto. While I write, Ed builds. His latest project is a chess table, a spruce slab with alder legs and a wood-burned pattern.

Out at Kingfisher, Steve Hughes is now encamped in canvas tucked under a wooden roof. A slab boardwalk leads to his paradise.

"So glad we're past that stage," I tell Ed when we arrive back after a visit. "Rocky River's getting downright civilized, except . . ." I say, squeezing my legs together.

"Yeah, yeah, the out. But we need to haul in more rough-cut from the mill to build a real outhouse. And we can't get supplies in until we can use the three-wheeler and trailer again."

"Yeah, yeah," I say, grabbing the broom to brush the seat of the new snow. "No big deal."

A fortnight later we waken abruptly. We dash to the river. Ice sheets shatter and crash. Ed hugs me. "Spring, Janzie. It's on the way."

"I sure wish we had a lottery like the one in the Interior on the Tanana River: Guess the minute of break-up and win $100,000. But merely witnessing this spectacle is wealth enough."

"This is what living now is all about, isn't it?" Ed grins.

As the light gains strength, my fingers fly on the keys. "Need to get this draft done before field tests and photos start."

"Think you'll be done this season, Jan?" Ed asks.

"No clue, Ed. It's not the six-month project I had imagined. I wonder if we'll ever recoup what we're putting into this. But I can't stop now. Besides, we need this book in our life; I only hope other folks need it too."

Yo-yos ~~

"I've got a problem, Ed. How do I show differences between species of plants?"

"Aren't you doing that with your photos?"

"Yes and no; in some cases the differences are too subtle to show. Or too wordy to describe. If you use botanical terms, only botanists understand them. But it takes a sea of words to get the ideas across otherwise."

"A picture's supposed to be worth a thousand words."

"Perhaps a drawing is that talkative. But I don't draw well enough."

"Doesn't that Pioneer Avenue art studio sell botanical art?"

"Great idea. Which means . . ."

"I'll ready for the ferry."

In Homer we wade through Toby Tyler's studio on Pioneer Avenue. Inside are plants painted on driftwood, plant prints in frames, fireweed portraits, regional flora posters. I tell Toby my illustration needs. "I can't pay cash," I warn. "But I can give you a percent of royalties. You'll get a check every time I do."

Toby is amenable; we write up a contract. Ed and I yo-yo across the bay. We steal time at Rocky River. I race with the camera to click first specimens. I mail slide film to Kodak and await results. I gather greens for recipe tests and head to the kitchen.

In Homer again, we gather first illustrations from Toby, who is living in his basement apartment by East Road. One glass-lined wall is a virtual botanical garden.

"Try this," says Toby, handing us wedges of pie.

Ed's face lights up. "My favorite, pumpkin."

"Rosehip," beams Toby.

"Scrumptious; this recipe is a must."

"Use a standard pumpkin pie recipe, Jan, but substitute rose hip puree for the pumpkin."

I scissor the rose chapter, add Toby's tips, tape pages together, and retype the chapter.

While in Homer to sort out book details, our home is Greenie. With the mattress and stove at Rocky River, we now sleep on camp pads atop the plywood frame, and cook outdoors on a Coleman stove.

"Primitive again, Ed."

"But look, Janzie. Grewingk Glacier's right there, and the beach below. And those courting sandhill cranes give me ideas."

"I need that Laundromat first; time for another shower."

Ed wraps me in his arms. "Ah, my grubby wee bear. Feeling cranky?"

"Missing home."

As the Tide Turns ～

Morning brings a bush line from Marsha on Little Jakolof Bay. "Come play plants." Girl time with Marsha has become an annual event. With each meeting, the stage changes. Instead of a rickety plywood shack, her home is now a two-story marvel. Banks of floor-to-ceiling windows overlook Little Jakolof Bay. Her new copper-tone ceiling bounces light and warms the scene. "The ceiling is made from antique printer's plates, Jan. I ordered them from a heritage home catalogue."

Redwood tongue-and-groove boards line her bathroom wall; black and white checkerboard squares tile the floor. A flush toilet and bath/shower await hook-up. In the kitchen, water gravity-feeds to the kitchen sink. "Tomorrow we'll take a walk to the lake," Marsha says. "I want to double-check all the water lines."

An ice chest parks on the porch, shaded by spruce canopy, and cooled by bay winds. "I had to bang pots and chase a blackie out of it last week," Marsha says. We explore the network of tracks and then load into her skiff for kelp gathering. We challenge each other with wild foods. Who can make the most exotic dish? The competition is keen and friendly. Marsha's still the only full-time resident of Little Jakolof Bay, but in green season the cove's cottages bustle with doctors, dentists, and guests. Summer weekends are a whirl of parties, barbecues, and potlucks. My visit coincides with Marsha's turn to host, providing the perfect opportunity to test our newest wild recipes.

"Wait 'til you taste this one," I say as I grind up flesh from a conical shaped shell.

"Aren't those Chinaman hats, Jan?"

"Yep. Limpets. I watched a Native woman in Seldovia eat them straight from the rocks." I sauté and season limpet paste, add fresh chopped beach lovage, and smear it on crackers. Marsha munches, and smiles with approval.

The table piles with platters: Jakolof Bay oysters Rockefeller, Kachemak coho with hedgehogs, fresh goosetongue greens, yarrow-spiced mussels, kelp chutney, and bottles of blueberry cordial and lingonberry liqueur.

I offer some German guests crackers with beach pâté. *"Nein, danke,"* they say as they reply. Marsha offers oysters. *"Nein, danke."* They move along the table, plates still empty. They stop at the end, and peer into the slow cooker; the contents look and smell like canned chicken noodle soup.

I dash to the end, and hold the ladle. *"Ja, bitte,"* they say, pushing bowls forward. I give them a smidgeon. *"Ja,"* they repeat, nodding, holding their bowls for more. I fill their bowls to the brim. They hoe in. I lack the language skills and the heart to warn them their soup swells with seaweed and gumboot chitons, which are mollusks even more primitive than the limpets they bypassed.

The next night, Marsha hauls me to a potluck at the Seamans. I carry food; Marsha bears towels. Perhaps she's loaning them to the neighbors. We head into the moss-draped forest, traipse across a bog, and emerge finally at Dunning's Lagoon. A two-story houseboat sits on the shore; my attention rivets on a small wood hut. Smoke pours from its chimney and naked bodies swarm on the deck.

"We'll take a sauna before we dine." Marsha steps on the deck and strips.

Be naked with strangers? But what's that saying, "When in Rome . . .?"

I turn my back, remove my clothes, fold my arms across my chest, slide inside, and head to the empty corner. There are bodies everywhere, all sexes, all ages, even a very pregnant woman. Everyone's starkers.

The stove blasts like a steel furnace. I erupt into sweat, uncertain whether it's from roasting temperatures or nerves. People pile on benches and chat as casually as folks at a dinner table. Marsha does intros and I'm swamped by names. Dave. Dick. Billy. Barb. Mary. Paulie. Handshakes of welcome force me to shift my arms. I don't know if I like this sauna business.

Folks laugh, heat tins of water on the stove, sweat, dash outdoors for a high tide plunge, reheat, lather up, and rinse clean. They chat and chortle.

No one stares at my boobs or at me. No one seems to notice my embarrassment. No one notices fat, thin, sag, or firm. No one seems to see bodies. Chats are congenial, laden with laughter. Is talk more real when clothes are abandoned? Nothing to hide? Maybe this sauna business isn't so bad after all.

Port Dick ～·

Plants race from flower to fruit. Salmon swell the river. "We need to hit Port Dick soon, Jan, to fill the larder."

"Why hike all the way there? The Rocky's outside."

"Time for our annual pilgrimage." A pilgrimage is a "journey to a sacred place," alternatively defined as a "tedious, wearisome time." Port Dick is both. Access requires crossing a wasteland of clear-cut spruce, clogged with deadfall tangled like pickup sticks: branches, whole trees, and logs infected with red heart fungus left to rot by loggers.

After a run into town, our Port Dick expedition grows. Ed meets Tom Walker buying tickets to Anan in Southeast to photograph black bears for his new book, *Alaskan Wildlife.* "Save your money, Tom. Join us at Port Dick. Sure, it's okay to bring your daughter Mary Anne."

I see buddy Norma Dudiak who wants bear photos for her Ptarmigan Arts gallery exhibition in Homer. "Come along," I encourage.

We lead our crew past Rocky River and head southward. We pull up onto three-foot-wide horizontal spruce and plummet into brush. Max tangles with limbs. We cuss at the mess. Finally, we step through a fairy tale portal onto moss carpet beneath towering moss-draped limbs. A musty perfume hits our noses. "Smells like . . . bear."

"There," points Ed. A cub sits above us on a limb.

"Watch for Momma," warns Tom.

"Hey bear," Ed bellows. "Passing through, bear."

"Home, home on the bay, where the moose and the black bears play," I sing.

We creep forward loudly, eyes darting like fireflies.

"Bear," says Norma. We yield and shift to the creek's gravel bar.

"Bear," says Tom.

We're wedged between two bears. Tom's blackie crouches on a rotted log, its head dropped behind a twig.

"He looks petrified. Bet he has never seen humans before."

"With big backpacks."

"And dog. Let's stop scaring the poor thing."

We walk into the wind, Tom in the lead. A large sow emerges and strides toward us, nose in the air, sniffing. We call loudly, lift our arms and wave like flags. The bear walks closer. And closer still. Tom cocks his gun. The bear stops; the stink of humans bangs her nose and she spins to the forest.

The Port Dick cabin is open, as always. It was originally built by Alaska Fish and Game for salmon studies and now available for public shelter. Rough bunks fill the corner; a simple table sets by a picture window, next to a woodstove and propane cooktop. We step outside to explore. We pass the roofed outhouse and follow a whispery track behind the cabin. An elfin log hut tucks into the greenery. Foot-deep moss blankets the roof. A corn broom sets on the deck by a wooden bucket and firewood rounds. Inside, a fifty-five-gallon drum sits horizontal, attached to a stovepipe. Twin benches line the wall of the sauna.

The Gulf rain begins to twang and do drum rolls on the roof. We retreat to the main cabin, fire up the stove, and put soup on the boil. The next day is a downpour. We sauna, sweat, wash, chat, and rainwater rinse. We eat, play cards, and eat again. The following day is a rerun. We chow food for sustenance, food for comfort, food to shake off boredom. "If only this rain would ease," says Tom.

"Forecasted to improve," says Ed, "but we're running out of food."

"Let's forage," I say. We pile on raingear and head out. The late August greens are limp and berries have been stripped by bears. In the forest, though, I spot dinner. "Chicken!"

"Spruce hen? Where?" Tom raises his gun.

"No, 'chicken of the woods.'" I lead everyone to a Sitka spruce covered in layers of orange. With pocket knife, I demonstrate. "Feel how the edges are soft and carve like butter. Move a bit further in and the texture hardens and gets less digestible." In the hut, I coat the tender mushroom morsels in flour from the cabin canister and add seasonings. I squirt dredges of oil in the skillet, and sizzle the 'shrooms to golden-brown.

Ed enters with brown ribbon kelp. We plunge it into boiling water; the blades change like an iguana to kelly green. We chop blanched algae, and sauté it in leftover oil with a stray carrot. We've now fresh salad. Dessert's a packaged cheesecake salvaged from the bottom of my pack, topped with wild blueberries found by Norma.

The next day clears. Tom races out for the magic dawn light. He dens behind a log, armed with a long telephoto. He clicks bears, bears grazing beach greens, bears catching salmon. Meanwhile, we women forage on the beach. I wink to Norma. "Let's make rock soup," I tell Mary Anne. "Find a rock covered with seaweed. Norma, you get mussels. I'll pick oyster leaf, and now more chicken of the woods." Back at the cabin, we fill the kettle with everything including the rock.

The ladies head back out to scour hillsides for hidden berries. Meanwhile I tend soup, discard the rock, and set the table. "Look, Mary Anne," I say as I serve the hungry crew, "mussels are open, and the rock is dissolved."

Evening meal is mushroom-stuffed salmon, spiced with lovage, along with hot kelp salad and blueberry cobbler. While all bakes, Tom returns to his vantage point for evening light. He returns, thumbs up. We feast in celebration, and depart in the morning to Rocky River's sweet comforts and a final night with guests.

The wheel of the season spins onward. Nights bring stars. First snows fall. Ed's chain saw is cranky. He is cranky. I'm sad. Already we're sleeping longer, getting less accomplished. My writing well is as dry as an old shoe.

"Go to New Zealand," advises friend Kenton.

"If only we could."

"Your Permanent Fund checks will get you there."

"We can't live on air."

"The whole country is a half-price sale. One U.S. dollar buys you two kiwi ones. Campgrounds are everywhere, plus you can free camp along any waterway."

"Still gotta eat."

"Gotta eat anywhere, and food there is heaps cheaper than Alaska. There are roadside fruit and veg stands with honesty boxes. And all the kiwi pie shops."

"Pies?" says Ed.

"Meat pies. Good though."

"Maxwell . . . what do we do with him?"

"We could ask Marina Schaum and the Caldwell brothers to dog-sit," suggests Ed. They are our new friends who live at McNeil Canyon east of Homer.

We do, they agree. We call the travel agent, book tickets, drop off Max, and migrate like shearwaters: Homer to Anchorage, Anchorage to Honolulu and on to our next stop—clean green New Zealand.

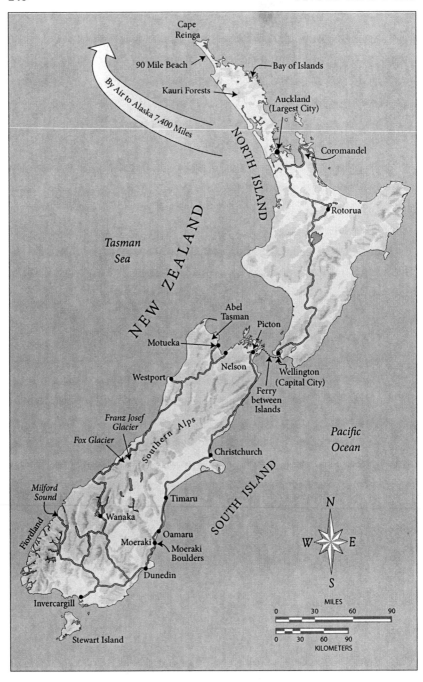

Cape
Reinga

90 Mile Beach

Bay of Islands

Kauri Forests

Auckland
(Largest City)

By Air to Alaska 7,400 Miles

NORTH ISLAND

Coromandel

Rotorua

Tasman
Sea

NEW ZEALAND

Abel
Tasman

Picton

Motueka

Nelson

Westport

Wellington
(Capital City)

Ferry
between
Islands

Franz Josef
Glacier

Southern Alps

Pacific
Ocean

Fox Glacier

Christchurch

Milford
Sound

SOUTH ISLAND

Timaru

Fiordland

Wanaka

N

Oamaru

Moeraki

Moeraki
Boulders

W   E

Dunedin

S

Invercargill

MILES

0   30   60   90

Stewart Island

0   30   60   90

KILOMETERS

Summer Down Under ⌇

Kiwi air hostesses parade the aisles with free fizzy drinks, fresh-perked coffee, and complimentary goblets of Marlborough Sounds Riesling and Nelson pinot gris. We devour real meals: rosemary-crusted lamb, roasted pumpkin and potatoes, and crisp salads followed by spongy pudding. Stewards hand us headphones for free movies. Half a day later, steaming hot towels freshen our faces, then the jet powers down and wheels to the Auckland gateway.

Our noses press to the windows. "Here comes the welcoming committee," Ed says, as uniformed attendants board the cabin.

"What's that they're holding?" I ask. "Looks like cans."

"Don't know Jan. Air freshener?"

The loudspeaker blats. "Welcome to New Zealand. Our country is highly susceptible to pests. Please keep your seat belts fastened while we take precautions to keep New Zealand clean and green."

The cans fire. We duck noxious spray, slam noses to knees, and struggle to not breathe. We finally escape into the gauntlet of customs.

"Do you have camping gear?"

"Yes."

"Hiking boots?"

"Yes."

"Have you been in forests?"

"We live in forests."

The officers confiscate our backpacks, and haul them to an inspection and fumigation room. While we wait, Ed scans a newspaper and points to the upper right-hand corner. "'Fine.' The weather is 'fine.' What sort of stupid forecast is that?" he complains.

"As dumb as American weathermen with 'partly sunny,' or 'partly cloudy.' Ever figure out the difference?"

"Forecasters everywhere must like to cover their bases."

The agricultural inspectors return our equipment; we stride to the exit. Airport doors slide open. Stale air breaks to floral perfumes and scents of new-mown grass. The sun's warmth coaxes us to strip layers. "Great temps," says Ed. "Not too hot, not too cold."

"Fine, Ed. It's a fine day."

We board the northbound coach. "Never knew there were so many shades of green."

"Or so many sheep in the world. The guidebook says there are four million people here and over twenty million woollies."

"Check out that sign, Jan."

"Kindly refrain from smoking on this bus."

"Quaint way of saying 'no smoking.'"

Road markers flash by. "Such funny place names, Whangaparaoa. Orewa. Waiwera."

The driver's microphone interrupts. "Waiwera is Maori for hot water; Natives often called it 'te rata,' meaning 'the doctor.' Battle-wounded warriors were taken here for healing at beachside hot pools. In 1875 a European style resort was built, and travelers came far and wide, many testifying to miraculous healing of asthma, typhoid fever, and rheumatic conditions. We'll be stopping briefly for exiting passengers."

"Let's get off, Janzie," beams Ed. "A hot soak would be great."

"It should cure our jet lag, anyway."

We hike to the campground, pay our fee, and pick up the map. "Tent sites are here," points the owner. "Kitchen, showers, hot pools here." The kitchen is fully equipped with dishes and rows of stoves, plus a strange Zip water heater. We watch as a fellow camper tugs its chain and triggers instant boiling water.

We spend hours soaking in the sulfurous bluff-edge pools, basking in steamy comfort with surf stereo. We peer at stars and struggle to decipher our first Southern Cross.

At breakfast, I walk to the counter to make toast. "What is this? How do you operate this thing?"

Ed laughs. "It's like the one I had as a kid."

"You're a decade older than me, Eddie."

"It's easy, Jan." He flops down the side doors, slides in the bread, lifts them back up. He scratches his head. "Nothing's happening."

A fellow camper walks up. "You've got to flick the wall switch. Power's on two-forty. All the outlets have safety switches."

The toaster clicks on. Ed waits and watches. "Then you've got to turn the bread over, Jan, and do the other side."

"What a blast from the past."

We hike by day, soak by night, eat hot mutton pies, and sizzle lamb chops and fresh corn on the barbie. Ed discovers ice cream New Zealand style: a dollar buys a double scoop; his favorite is the classic kiwi hokey pokey, vanilla with toffee chunks. Two days later, our waterlogged skin is like a prune. We stand by the roadside and thumb north.

A car pulls over, bound for Waipoua Forest, home to the largest remaining tract of ancient kauri trees in New Zealand. "Kauris," the driver tells us, "are the dinosaurs of the forests; they once covered four million acres of New Zealand. Then Cook came and blathered about the finest timber on earth; now there are only about eighteen thousand acres left."

We hike the track to Tane Mahuta; kauri lord of the forest. According to Maori lore, Tane created everything that dwells within: forests, birds, humans. "It's like being in a cathedral," I whisper.

"This tree was a seedling when Jesus was born," Ed reads.

"And it's more than sixteen stories high," I add. "Makes me feel as small as an ant."

We wander and wonder, imagining pre-European times and a plethora of flightless birds and deafening birdsong. "Immigrants brought so many problems with their stupid stoats, possums, deer, gorse, and saws."

The next ride leads toward Dargaville, to another kauri reserve; we pitch our teacup of a tent and wander the tracks. Ed leads me roadside to a farmer's driveway. "Sign says 'wood turner.' Let's check it out."

Tony the turner shows us his workshop, demos his lathe, and takes us on a farm tour. Kauri stumps line the field edges. "The last owners tried to burn them," he says, "but fire preserved the kauri. It's my gold mine for my wood-turning."

Tony's real work is raising sheep and sheepdogs. "Times are bad," he says. "You've got to hang a five dollar bill on every lamb that goes to market; Kaye and I are selling off the sheep, and switching to dairying."

We retreat to camp to prepare our evening meal when Tony shows up. He chortles at our tiny tent. "Good thing you're as small as hobbits; Kaye said to invite you to evening tea."

We expect a bag in hot water and slam into another language gap. The table is set: a rack of lamb, roast spuds, salad, Swiss chard (which our hosts call 'silverbeet'), and bread and butter. Then, hot apple pie. Ed grins as wide as a barn door. I let out my belt another notch. Tony gives Kaye a hilarious description of our tent. She drags us to the guest room and won't take no for an answer. "Have a night of luxury," she insists. We love their wholesome happy clan, Tony and Kaye, their two boys, and Tony's mom, who lives with them. We promise to stay in touch.

The bus takes us to Northland, to where land ends and seas collide at the tip of Cape Reinga. A lighthouse perches on the rocky promontory, towering over the meeting place of the Tasman Sea and the Pacific Ocean. "Next is Ninety Mile Beach," says the driver. "But it's really ninety kilometers, only sixty miles in length. It's a natural theme park built by nature, the only beach in New Zealand deemed open road." We motor along the beach, with nothing in sight except towering dunes, surf, and sand. Ed leans over and chats with the bus driver. "Grab your bag, Janzie, we're getting off."

"But there's nothing here."

"Precisely. Let's camp. Tomorrow, we'll catch the next bus by."

We tent in the dunes and splash ocean water on our faces. We stand at the tide line barefoot and casually wiggle our feet. The wave washes away the loosened sand.

"Look, Ed. Clams."

"Tuatua," he says. "I read in the guidebook that they're a delicacy." We steam them in our camp pot in ocean water, and drizzle the clams with melted butter. We stare at our campfire and listen to a surf serenade. There's no one in sight; we have our own beach paradise.

Noon brings traffic and stray cars, followed by our bus. We flash our ticket to the driver, board, and journey south to Ahipara, a small community popular as a start, or endpoint, for Ninety Mile Beach adventures. We hike to the local campground and socialize in the kitchen. Pia from St. Gallen, Switzerland, tells us she is biking New Zealand solo. She is keen to do a horse trek. Ed is reluctant.

"But you used to ride at Swift Creek, Ed."

"Necessity, Jan. This isn't."

We sweet-talk him along. Ed's appaloosa sticks in low gear and lags behind our willing mares. The guide hands Ed a stick. "Whack him; tell him who's boss." Ed taps. No response. Taps harder. The horse knows. We meander through the brush, and upward.

"Kauri gum fields," the guide tells me and Pia. "In the late 1800s, amber-colored kauri gum was dug from this swampland by immigrant Croatians and Dalmatians, and sold for the manufacture of varnish." Ed is too far behind to hear.

We ascend to the dune plateau, the horses struggling in the knee-deep sand. We dismount at the summit and photograph the vistas, while resting the mares. As we remount to head back, Ed arrives. Homeward bound, Ed's horse shifts to overdrive. "Haul on the reins," yells the guide. "Tell him who's boss."

Ed and his appaloosa crash through brush and hit the beach in full gallop. The footing is as firm as a Kentucky Derby racetrack. Around us is a carnival of activities: wind surfers, land kites, hang gliders, motorized dune buggies, body boarders, sunbathers, hikers, and surfcasters. The frenzy spurs Ed's galloper onward. Watchers cheer.

"Home sweet home sweet home," the horse races. Back at the stables, Ed dismounts, gingerly cradling his crotch. "You must be a sadist," he tells the guide, "making me pay for such torture." The guide belly laughs as he empties Ed's wallet. Pia and I pet our lovely horses, and feed them the carrot treat we've saved.

Ed is sore in all places. He studies the guidebook and stabs at the map: "Hot Water Beach." We bus to the east coast of Coromandel Peninsula, and arrive at low tide. We mimic the locals digging bathtubs in the sand. Hot water seeps in from underground volcanic reservoirs filling our trough.

"There are hot pools at Rotorua too," I tell Ed. "It's south of here in the Bay of Plenty region."

"Great; that's plenty of reason to go there. That'll be next. I don't think there's an inch of me that doesn't ache."

We smell Rotorua well before we arrive. "Like rotten eggs," I complain.

"Sulfur pools, famous for their therapeutic benefits," Ed reads from the guidebook. The pools set Ed right; by afternoon he is keen for a hike to Hell's Gate. Water burps from gray mud holes bearing names like Sodom and Gomorrah, and Devil's Cauldron. "It's a perfect location for shooting an Armageddon film," Ed notes.

"Check that out," I point. A vile bubbling inferno bears a sign: "Please do not drop anything into this pool. You will be kindly asked to retrieve it."

"Leave it to the kiwis. Americans would say 'No littering.'"

We return to the resort for an evening soak. We simultaneously start to speak. "You first," I say.

"Jan, I know we've only begun to see the North Island . . ."

"Yeah," I jump in, unable to restrain myself, "it's time to head south isn't it?"

Ed nods. We share the same strange impulse; the South Island calls our name.

The Other Isle ～

Wellington is the world's southernmost capital, dubbed the Windy City due to its placement in the Roaring Forties latitudes. We blow to the beehive dome Parliament building for snapshots, shelter in the Botanic Gardens, then queue for the nineteen-kilometer (twelve-mile) Cook Strait crossing, headed for the northeast corner of the scenic South Island. "Just like home, Ed. Waiting for the ferry again."

The boarding call sounds. Ed checks his watch. "Not like home, Jan; this ferry's on time."

We stand at the rails during the three-hour crossing, and click images of green islands, azure seas, sunny skies. Once across the strait, we set camp in picturesque Picton, home to the ferry terminal, walking tracks, and ecotours. The morning mail boat takes us on a tour of Marlborough Sounds. Residents emerge from coastal cottages and collect mail, newspapers, and crates of milk in glass bottles. I elbow Ed. "Red Mountain mail, kiwi style."

Days swell with fine weather. We tour where our thumb takes us. At Lake Wanaka, we stop for snacks at the natural food café. It is closed. A middle-aged couple weeding shrubs in front tell us, "It'll be open for evening tea."

Ed's stomach rumbles in protest.

"Where are you from?" they ask. "Alaska" opens the door. Bev and Brian wave us inside, pour cuppas, and slice pie.

"This is our son Mark's café; we're on holiday and helping out. Mark is mad about Alaska." We answer their questions, they answer our kiwi ones. "You must visit us in Timaru when you pass through," they insist. Brian grabs a map and Bev scribbles contact details.

We continue south, hotfoot through adrenalin-pumped Queenstown, then leisurely wander in Fiordland, New Zealand's largest national park. We flightsee the Southern Alps, then mosey east to Pacific shores. We hit Timaru, a port city set on rolling hills created from ancient lava flows from Mount Horrible. Today's weather is horrible too, with pelting rains and cold winds. "Should we say hello to Bev and Brian?" Ed asks.

"We'll ring first, and make certain this is a good time." Brian insists we drop by. The map leads to an imposing brick home. "This could be on the cover of *Home and Garden* magazine, Ed."

"We're rather grubby and wet as muskrats. Let's make this quick."

Bev and Brian ply us with tea and biscuits. The aroma of roasting lamb fills the kitchen. "You're staying for evening tea," says Brian. "We won't take no for an answer." Platters heap with food; wine flows. Afterward, Bev pulls me aside and leads me to a bodacious bedroom. "The bed is already hot," she says, pointing to electric liners under the bed sheets. "This is where you and Ed will sleep."

"We weren't planning to stay over."

"Please do," she says. "Tomorrow we'll show you more of our beautiful country."

After breakfast, Bev makes sandwiches. Ed offers to help. "You can put the chilly bin in the boot," she says.

"What?"

"Ice chest in the trunk," I translate.

We visit turquoise-blue Lake Tekapo, a highland lake surrounded by golden tussock grass. The nearby Church of the Good Shepherd honors the glory of God. At lake's edge a statue honors New Zealand sheep dogs "without the help of which the grazing of this mountainous country would be impossible." Our hosts then take us to little Lake Alexandrina. "Filled with trout," says Brian. "And only rowboats allowed."

That night as we snuggle, we dream aloud. "Wouldn't it be nice, Ed ... "

"To have a summer cottage in New Zealand," he finishes. "Alaska's awesome, but winters are endless. Wonder if it'd be possible?"

"We could build a teeny tiny cabin; what do kiwis call it, a crib?"

We spin ideas with Bev and Brian. "What do you imagine?" they ask.

"A place by the sea, some quiet spot."

Brian gives Bev a knowing look. "More ack he," he says.

"More what?"

He grabs the map and points to Moeraki. "On a wee peninsula south of here. Check it out tomorrow," Brian says. "You'll like it. You can take our car."

"No way," says Ed, refusing Brian's keys. "You kiwis drive the wrong side of the road."

"Then we'll take you ourselves. We could use a holiday." Brian calls the bicycle factory he owns in Pleasant Point and tells the office his plans. An hour later, we cross candy cane–striped railroad poles into a dreamy world. At Moeraki, rainbow-colored fishing boats dot the harbor. Kiwi cribs line secret coves. A lighthouse beacon marks the point.

"Moeraki is Maori for Sky of Dreams," explains Brian. We stroll the beach to Moeraki's keynote attraction, six-foot boulders shaped like bowling balls. We wander roads and turn about on a dead-end above the campground. I spy a faded sign covered in vine: "For Sale by Owner."

"Don't waste your time, Jan," Ed says. "Must be long gone. Besides, look at that sea view; must be worth a bomb."

"It won't hurt to check."

I exit the pay phone. "It's still available, Ed. The owners got it as a wedding present decades ago. They're too busy to do anything with it. It's a kiwi quarter acre, and ours for eight grand."

"Forty-five hundred U.S. dollars," Ed calculates.

"We do have my book advance; that would help cover it."

"We'll camp on the land," we tell Bev and Brian, "and check out the neighborhood before we commit." We tent under the apple tree on the property. At nightfall, as we slip inside our bags, Ed erupts in a spastic fit. His hands flail wildly.

"What's the . . . ?"

"Flashlight," Ed stammers. "Grab the flashlight."

Ed peers into his bag, pinches forefinger to thumb, and pulls out a mangled cricket.

"Thought it was a spider."

"You live with bears and freak over a bug?" I ask.

"Shh." We listen. Raindrops patter, then change tempo to a drumroll.

"Nice to sleep by; at least this new tent stays dry."

Morning brings more tempests. We huddle in the tent, cramped and cranky. "The campground has tiny cabins for rent, cheap," I say. "We'd be more comfy and we could use the kitchen for meals, plus take hot showers."

"Great idea, Janzie. Let's do it." We drop the wet tent and start walking.

"Helloooo," a raincoat-clad body calls. "I'm Alex from next door. Come have a hot tea, mates." Alex and Hazel Joll set us down with cuppas, cakes, and questions. "Looking at buying the lot next door," Ed says. Alex pulls Ed and me aside and leads us around the house to a nail tucked behind a board. "This is where I hide the key."

What an odd duck, showing us his hidey hole. In the kitchen, Alex leads us to the refrigerator. "This is where I keep the beer."

"Okay," we say.

"We're driving home to Mosgiel." says Alex. "You folks can stay here as long as you want."

We protest. The Jolls insist. "Our door is open in Alaska," I nudge Ed. "Maybe karma is paying us back."

We settle into the three-bedroom holiday home. Next-door neighbors Bob and Pauline invite us for morning pikelets, tiny pancakes topped with jam and cream. Bob shows us his art studio and his gallery of landscapes. "I've always wanted to try oil painting," I natter. "Someday."

Bob hands me a brush and grabs a blank canvas. "Give it a go. I'll coach."

Later, Ed and I talk. "Great neighborhood."

"A dream place; let's do it Jan." We call, confirm the purchase, and go to the solicitors to sign documents.

"Time for one last adventure, Jan. What would you most like to see?"

"We've still that contact in central Otago," I say. "We've not been there yet. I read that central is like Alaska's Interior: big open spaces, record-setting summer and winter temps."

"A dose of heat would be great after this soggy patch," Ed agrees.

We call and get directions to Bob de Berry's farm back of beyond. A milk truck delivers us to the general area, then we wait roadside. Hours tick by; a pickup truck finally passes, cab crammed. "You can hop in back with the goat, if you want." We want. We exit at the sign: Cambrian. Population five.

Bob's home is mud brick, made distinct by a flame-red dragon. Bob looks as though he stepped from Tolkien's *The Hobbit,* with a flowing beard, long hair, a gentle spirit, and a ready wit. His farm is a fairy tale of braying donkey, laughing pig, gardens, and beehives.

"My life mission," Bob says, "is to plant trees. Not for commercial purposes, mind you; only for beauty and diversity." We step into his grove of towering oaks and maples. Homesickness stabs us; memories of New England life.

Bob grimly shows us his sleep-out, a cabin for visitors; the roof is crushed. "Tree limb stove it in that storm."

"Let's fix it," Ed says. We hop into Bob's truck, and drive to neighbors to borrow a winch. While the men work, I volunteer to make supper. I wander round the kitchen looking for a stove. Dominating one end of the kitchen is an antique wood-fired cookstove. It's hot as Hades out, but I split kindling and bank the stove. The men return, Bob bearing a bottle with dragon label: "Bob de Berry's El-deBerry Wine."

We toast to new roofs, new friends, new ideas. I'm keen about Bob's pastoral life and his creative winemaking with elders; he is intrigued by my plant project.

"Here, this might help you, Jan," Bob says as he hands me a book.

I read the title: *Simply Living: A Gatherer's Guide to New Zealand Fields, Forests and Shores,* then glance excitedly through the pages. "Wow, it even covers how to prepare lichen species that occur also in Alaska. This would be a fantastic reference; where can I buy a copy?"

"Read the frontispiece."

"To Jan and Ed. From one mighty grateful kiwi. Travel in peace."

Days later, we travel onward, emotions on boil. "I'm sad we're leaving, Ed, but relieved we'll come to New Zealand again. And Rocky River, it'll be so good to see the cabin again. Wonder how it has fared in our absence?"

Open Doors ⌒

We time-warp to yesterday; summer below becomes winter above. We grab overcoats, hitch a lift from Homer Airport to McNeil Canyon to pick up Max, who has stayed with our friends Marina Schaum and Glenn and Doug Caldwell. Max leaps to greet us, tail waving like a windshield wiper on high.

"What's New Zealand like?" asks Marina.

"America thirty years ago. We never saw a single shopping mall; only tidy towns with mom-and-pop shops: butcher, baker, fruit and veg shops."

"And pie shops, Jan; don't forget them. Mince pies, steak pies, potato top, and mutton. And so many sheep. Twenty million. At the butcher, fifteen kiwi dollars buys you half a lamb."

Ed and Glenn chat construction while I help Marina in the kitchen. Her welcome-home meal is a feast of local delicacies: smoked salmon dip, marinated moose, and Kachemak stir-fry. "You're such a whiz in the kitchen, Marina; I wish you could help test recipes for the book."

"Why not, Jan? That'd be a buzz."

The next day, the *Tusty* is late as usual and the trek to the mail shed takes longer than expected. The pass sits deep in snow. By the time we reach Rocky River, we're exhausted, and overwhelmed by what greets us.

A week later I sit at the typewriter by candlelight, and hammer on the keys.

To: *Anchorage Daily News,* "Letters from the Bush."

WELCOME HOME

For the past four years, the door to our bush home has been open to passers-by who need shelter from storms. During that time, we've had nothing but kindness. We've been left candles and champagne, art supplies and inner tubes, cabin slippers and rain pants, caribou steaks and fruit leather, and warming thank you notes in our guest book. And then this!

We'd heard a vague rumor regarding a surprise waiting for us. As it turned out, there were three. The first was left by nature: a fall flood had gobbled another culvert and bridge, reducing our three-wheeler trail to a footpath.

Surprise two was more inspiring: a welcome plaque left by an anonymous visitor in thanks for our open-door policy. As we probed through cabinets, getting reacquainted with home, we found the usual diminishment of coffee, cocoa, and tea, and a substantial upgrade of food stocks from packs lightened before leaving. Examining our guest book, we discovered we'd had a few visitors, all who obviously subscribed to the leave-it-better-than-you-found-it philosophy. All looked well indeed, as though a crew of maids had been diligently scrubbing, sweeping, and polishing throughout our absence. One entry was a wee bit peculiar, signed by fourteen strangers, and one signature read "Homer Glass." Odd.

After scanning how well all inside had wintered, we began checking the cabin exterior. A bit of roofing paper from the dormer had been blown away by the infamous valley winds. The logs were weathered and dry, thirsty for a fresh coat of oil. All else looked okay. But no! Wait! The plastic covering the gable openings was gone! My heart sank to my socks as I imagined the damage upstairs from a winter of weather. The books and bed must be soaked! All my family photos must be ruined! I plunged into depression, while glancing casually at Ed to see how he was handling the crisis. He was acting strangely, standing with gaping jaw, quietly muttering, "There's glass up there. There's glass up there." Glass?

We scrambled up the steep stair-ladder to the loft, gawking in disbelief at the Thermopane glass filling the Visqueen void. Our dream of loft windows, which had been postponed year after year, first because of finances and later due to the unreasonable logistics of physically transporting such awkward, oversized, fragile creations, was now a reality. But how?

By asking about, we've finally begun to piece together the details of the window party. A stranger who'd previously discovered our cabin during a blizzard, and used it with his son during the storm, spearheaded the surprise. He and a friend, both glass shop employees, custom-cut the windows, and then each backpacked the eighty-pound, eighty-eight-inch triangular glass the eight rough miles from sea to cabin. Then, standing precariously on railings and cans and stumps, they hoisted the delicate

cargo into its lofty perch. Finally, so we hear, they popped corks and
toasted the success of the challenging mission with their friends. As we
lie in bed, gawking at the gift, we reflect on the kindnesses returned to
us by the window party and others.

Had our door been locked to the wet and weary, had we not taken the
chance to trust and share, our lives would be minus all the joys that have
brightened them so dramatically. Our cupboards bulge with gift goods.
And we no longer strain for a glimpse outside through cloudy plastic. We
can see clearly now, and what we clearly see is love. We are very thankful.

Two weeks later, we pick up a copy of the Sunday *Anchorage Daily News*. Today's "Letters from the Bush" column features a rebuttal to our "Welcome Home" window story, written by Achim Jahnke, perpetrator of the deed. Achim insists that challenge, not kindness, provided the motive. He writes:

Far away from the little cabin in the woods with the new windows,
I read the article "Open-Door Policy Sometimes Opens Hearts" and
lo and behold found out for the first time that our surprise to the
Schofields really did work.

What Janice didn't stress enough is that none of us had ever met
them and, due to circumstances at the time of this writing, we still
haven't had the pleasure. So, for clarification, I feel compelled to explain
the motive of the whole expedition a bit more. It was hardly caused
solely from the goodness of our hearts.

Two years ago my son and I barely escaped harm in an early spring
blizzard because someone had built a cozy cabin and decided to take
the chance to leave it open for everyone. We simply fell in love with it.

This winter I found myself again in a similar predicament, in
terrible weather, with a cabin again close by.

That night in the loft, trying to watch the storm through two triangle openings of some barely clear plastic, I had this little conversation with myself. How could one ever get glass the right size to fit into these windows? I got myself all worked up—the challenge was on.

Measuring the rough openings with a three-foot piece of rusted tape measure was only the beginning. Deciphering the all but washed-out results on the back of my map half a year later was another.

But all my friends were gung-ho enough to make it happen. Since two of us work at the local glass shop and our boss has a warm heart, that end was covered also.

The other end was not so simple. Transporting two odd-shaped windows like these is not unlike carrying two raw eggs in your pocket while running the Boston Marathon. Also, they each weighed about eighty pounds and were eighty-eight inches across on one side.

We trucked them to the harbor, carried them down the ramp onto a sailboat and tied them up. They survived that.

They also survived a twenty mile trip in rough waters with a boatload of people, including kids and two dogs (and I'll tell you: the tail of a black Lab can break any window).

They lived through being lowered onto the pack-boards of two of us, standing deep in mud on the beach. And then it was eight miles of rocks, mud, snow, places to duck under, trees to climb over, steep grades to climb, creeks to cross and wind to lean into. And where did you put your fragile load when your back was starting to turn into mush? And then that little voice that kept saying louder and louder: "What if you didn't measure right? What if they won't fit?"

It was a moment we will never forget when the corks were flying and we were toasting the installed windows and the sauna was hot.

We have to thank you for that, Jan and Ed. All that's missing now is to know you.

Now that we know the true culprit of our experience, we pen a thank you. The next mail returns a note with pressed flowers and handwritten invitation from Renee, Achim's wife, to visit when next in Homer.

"Gotta meet these folks, Jan. Don't quite believe all Achim's ranting of it only being a challenge."

"Yes," I agree. "I bet he's a bit like that Far Side cartoon, where the polar bears are crunching an igloo."

"What do you mean?"

"The cartoon with the caption about being crunchy on the outside, soft and gooey in the middle. I bet it's like Achim, you know, typical German reserve, crunchy outside. But heart soft as butter."

"We'll have to see for ourselves. Next time in Homer we'll look them up."

Coming Attractions ⁓

Our next Homer jaunt brings us out East Hill to a dead-end road, and onward to a narrow walkway suspended above a gulley. "The Jahnkes must be as crazy as us, Ed, living out here like this."

A storybook log cabin, similarly sized to Rocky, nests beyond the bridge. The open plan boasts a kitchen with running water piped from a spring, a sitting area with glacier view, a center wood-fired stove, and a corner double bed lined by bookshelves and CDs. An upstairs loft sleeps their children Nina and Uwe. Sounds of Enya set the mood.

Renee is Alaskan born; Achim is from Germany. The couple, we learn, lived in California for a time and then headed to the high seas on their trimaran that they built themselves.

Achim details the window story. "After the glass was cut, we had to figure how to transport the glass triangles over challenging terrain. My buddy Gary and I puzzled over that in my shop, armed with hammers, saws, scrap timber, and wine. With pack frames ready, all we needed now was support crew."

Neighbor Johanna precooked beans to reduce cooking time at the cabin; her generous handfuls of dry legumes swelled to forty pounds of bulk. Talk of the foray attracted more helpers, more food, more drink. Adults, kids, dogs, packs, and sleeping bags piled onto the Jahnkes' catamaran and departed Homer harbor.

The evening ends with the Jahnkes' promise to visit us at Rocky River. For now, it's time again to catch the *Tusty* and return to our home with the clear view.

In the cabin, I clank again on the typewriter, typing and retyping the ever-expanding manuscript. Each fortnight we trek to the mail shed and collect the latest interlibrary loans. Ed's dip in the mailbag scores news: "Steve Unsworth is coming to visit, Jan. Steve was my childhood pal. Steve's mad about fishing and hunting, can't wait to see Alaska. He's a bit younger than me," adds Ed. "As kids, whatever I said was the way to go. There were three of us that hung together, me, Steve, and Gary G. Funny how we all turned out. Steve became a top cop. Gary G. went to jail."

"And you're dancing between the worlds," I retort. I'm edgy. Ed's less-lucky dip in the mailbag was a letter from the Internal Revenue Service. He tossed it unopened into the fire.

"It's what you have to do, Jan. You can't recognize the IRS. Treat it like it doesn't exist."

"It doesn't exist for me," I counter, "but only because my earnings are poverty level. I don't make enough to have to file. You monkeyed up the works when you filed as tax-exempt on the Homer Spit job."

"The job was only going to be a week, Jan. Not enough to owe tax."

"But you ended up working longer, Ed. And from what I've read, filing tax-exempt is like waving a red flag at a bull. You could have opened the letter to see what's up. Maybe you owe tax."

Ed shakes his head and heads out the door.

"Where are you going?"

"To get my chain saw; build an outhouse."

"I'm getting rather used to our box over the hole."

"Steve is bringing his wife Sandy; she's great, but a real city slicker. It'll be quite a jolt for Sandy to use even a 'propa' outhouse."

That's how Ed says *proper,* the soft, slurry Boston way. The letter *r* evaporates like steam: "Pahk the cah in the yahd; Bah Hahbah." I love his lingo, the sweet purr of his voice.

The coming visit spurs yet more construction. Until now bathing has been primitive, the round tub set by the barrel stove. Ed wedges in it so tightly I do his soaping and shampooing. "Sandy will freak, Jan. It's time to upgrade our lives. Let's build a propa bathhouse."

We grab paper and scratch a design: a four- by eight-foot sauna with attached guest room. I'm assigned the mole role, digging four-foot-deep holes on the river knoll to hold foundation posts. We ride the three-wheeler to the old sawmill and scavenge abandoned two-by-fours. While Ed frames walls, I head to Homer for supplies. I board the *Tusty* as a foot passenger, taxi to Spenard Builders, stuff insulation into Ed's pack, and strap on a second bale. Pockets fill with nails, screws, and glues. The next day, Ed meets me at the ferry terminal. I'm impossible to miss, a moving mountain of pink batts.

"Take your load, hon?"

"Nah, Ed. I've adjusted all the straps for negotiating the ferry stairs. The van's not far."

A local stares at Ed, trailed by a towering backpack with legs. "Nice looking pack mule you've got there," he drawls.

Back at Rocky River, it's mule time again. Ed needs rocks for the sauna hearth. "Piece of cake," I smile. "The river's right by the sauna door;

not like Blueberry Hill where I had to walk three miles of stone walls."

"Can't use river rocks, Jan; they'll explode from the heat."

"But there are no rocks in the meadow."

"There are twenty miles of Rocky River Road. Pick flat rocks for the hearth, with a flat front edge; and large corner rocks."

"With two flat edges?"

"Exactly. Enough rocks for two waist-high walls. And don't forget flat rocks for the top shelf . . . covered with Fred and Alice."

Max accompanies me on the great rock hunt; he races joyously while I find and fetch. Ed stays home to frame window openings. Ed mentions our project to Herb, the Red Mountain welder who tells him, "Kids have been smashing windows in the old mine sheds; you folks should salvage some for your sauna before they're all destroyed."

We drive the three-wheeler and trailer through the washouts and over the Windy River log stringers. We take a left at the wild chive meadow and continue onward past Herb's place. The road narrows and dead-ends before the final alpine ascent where the track still lies deep in snow. Ed sinks to his knees with each step. I trudge behind and step in his footprints.

As the track switchbacks and gains altitude, the snow crust hardens. Relief turns to terror as all becomes ice that slopes precipitously forty-five degrees toward the valley floor. Ed scuffs his heels and digs for footholds.

At the summit, fist-thick chain encircles the mine shed roof, anchoring the building to the mountain. "Winds must be wild up here," I say. "Looks like kids have been wild too, Jan. Only a couple windows left intact." Ed crowbars the precious glass from the building. We clasp the fragile cargo to our chest and begin our descent.

The ledge is as slippery as cow pies. Wind batters our windows with kitelike thrusts. We struggle to keep from tobogganing with the glass. Relief floods when we finally reach soft snow.

On the flats, we wind through the cottonwood lane and stop at Herb's trailer to show our prizes. "Would you folks like some fresh milk?" he asks.

"Oh yes, please; all we ever drink at the cabin is that awful powdered stuff. I've never had milk straight from a cow."

"No problem," he says. Herb heads to his shed and emerges with a plastic bottle and a rope. "I'll pinch some off that cow." He circles the rope like a western cowboy as he advances on a beefalo in the unfenced field. The cow dodges. Herb's rope snags on the alders. He untangles it, throws again, misses, tosses again, and scores. The cow struggles as Herb tethers her to a spruce. He tugs on her teats. She kicks. He dodges and tugs. "Ah, dry as an old bean. Calf must have pinched it."

"No problem, Herb," Ed tells him. "We've got plenty of powdered at home."

"You wait, I'll get some." The next cow tows Herb like a water skier. She darts around a spruce; Herb dodges the tree, throws his body sideways, and wraps the rope. As he tugs, she kicks at his crotch. He dodges, dives in, and tugs. Squirt. Tug. Kick. Squirt. Dribble.

"That's plenty, Herb. We don't drink much milk." Ed's stomach is growling. It's still a long way to the cabin.

Herb snags a third beast, gets more squirts. He beams as he hands us the bottle bearing tablespoons of milk. We thank him profusely. "You'll have to stop by for a cuppa and a meal," says Ed.

We drive to the cabin slowly with the fragile load. We unload at the washouts, reload on the other side. Finally, we reach Rocky, with materials safe and stock-piled. During the next month, construction flows. Ed installs the salvaged windows, then scrambles onto the roof and starts laying rolled roofing.

I hang quilted curtains on cord lines, oil the plywood bench top, and set shampoo and soap on the wooden spool table, next to a ceramic wash basin. Foam pads stack on the plywood bed, with fresh bedding, books for bedside reading, and candles.

"Looks homey, honey," says Ed. "Like a honeymoon suite."

"Perhaps we should christen it, Ed. Let's give Steve and Sandy the main cabin when they come, and test this ourselves."

"Can't wait for them to arrive."

The *Water Rat* ~

"You know, Ed . . . ," I say, as I lift my morning coffee.

Ed shudders; such sentences foretell a wild hare of an idea.

"We spend half our life waiting for the ferry. If we had our own boat, we could come and go at will across the bay."

"Boats are holes in the water you sink money into, Jan. They're always blowing motors."

"Randy has the *Water Rat* for sale. With sails, you don't have to sweat the motor. The wind's free."

"Don't know a thing about sailing."

"Randy invited us to go sailing this weekend; we could have fun and learn and check it out. Besides, we've got the time; we don't have to pick up the Unsworths until Tuesday. We could go fishing."

"Suppose; could do with a mess of halibut."

We drive to Seldovia, bush line Randy, and buy beer and snacks for the sea-camping adventure. Randy picks us up at Jakolof Bay and gives Ed lessons on lines and rigging; I relax on the sun-splashed deck. The only sounds are wind-flapping sails and seabird squawks. "What a life," I think.

We cruise to Tutka Bay, toss anchor, and catch halibut. We sauté the fillets with beach lovage and wild chives. At low tide, we hop in the inflatable, row to shore, and dig clams. We cruise to new grounds, and anchor for yet more fishing. Randy drops to the galley to brew coffee. "A boat is really a necessity for us, Ed. Look at all the seafood we can harvest, the money and time we'd save on ferries. We could dock the *Rat* for free at Jakolof Bay, and do more of our major shopping in Homer. And do more sea camping like this."

"A boat isn't all fun," Ed protests.

I'm about to pitch harder when I look at Ed; his mouth is open like he's catching flies.

I follow his gaze. "Yowser. Look at that wave."

"Randy, check this out."

"Nah, busy." We hear clanking in the galley. "What is it?"

"Looks like a green wave. It's way bigger than any of the others."

"Nah, must be a boat wake."

"Randy," I add. "You've got to see it, it's a monster."

"Nah, nothing to worry about."

"Randy," Ed insists. "It's about to . . ."

The wave whams the sloop. Galley pots crash, mugs smash; Randy hits the deck. The boat rights itself; Randy emerges from the cockpit, dazed. "What the hell was that?"

"A rogue wave."

Randy returns to the galley and refills the coffeepot; we help pick up the mess. Fortified with coffee, we talk turkey, negotiate the purchase, and make plans. Randy will return to Homer, and dock the *Water Rat* in the harbor. We'll ferry with Greenie to pick up the Unsworths. We'll store the van in long-term parking on the Spit, then head home by boat with our guests.

"See Ed. No more waiting for the ferry. Easy as pie."

Crossing the Bay ⁓

We meet the Unsworths for breakfast, then head to their hotel room to pick up their gear. "I thought I told you to travel light," says Ed.

"We did. We've only got a backpack and duffel bag."

"Each. That makes four bags."

"So?"

"Oh, we'll sort it out; we've got gear too; we might have to make two trips with the three-wheeler."

"I'll go return the room key," says Sandy.

"Before you do, would it be okay if we use the shower?"

"The shower?"

"It'll save stopping at the Laundromat."

"You're going to wash your clothes in the shower?"

"No, we're going to bathe ourselves, of course."

Sandy is puzzled, and anxious for what lies ahead.

We hop aboard the Rat, exit the no-wake zone and hit chop, typical end-of-spit conditions. Waves worsen as we head toward Yukon Island. There's now a marathon of monsters. Bottomed in the trough, we can't see land, only walls of water.

"These are worse than that green wave that broadsided us, Ed." Ed keeps the bow pointed directly into them. The rat climbs radically and pitches over the crests. The engine roars as the prop bites air. I gasp.

"Let's go back."

"Can't turnabout," Ed whispers. "We'll breach."

"Should be better in Eldridge Passage; hope we can reach there okay."

Ed glances at our guests. Sandy has a death grip on Steve's wrist. Ed turns to them and smiles broadly. "See, Sandy," says Steve, "Look how happy Ed is. This must be normal conditions."

The seas calm behind the islands. We calm when we disembark in Jakolof Bay. We carry gear to the three-wheeler. Ed stares at the mound of packs. "I'll load," I offer. I stack packs, wedge food into crevices, and finally lift the last box. Ed secures the mountain with ropes. "Jan has to come with me to help carry the load across the washouts. You'll have to walk," he tells our guests. "Cabin's that way. Watch for black bears."

Sandy pokes Steve. "Ed's kidding, isn't he?"

"Make noise," Ed continues. "Blacks will scram. I'll be back for you as soon as Jan and I unload."

"Great, you can pick up our remains," says Sandy.

"Oh, don't worry, Sandy. We'll make noise."

Screams of "Nanu Nanu" reverberate behind as we drive off.

The drive to the cabin is as slow as snails. The load is unbalanced. At Windy River, we unpack the trailer. Ed drives the bike and trailer across the stringers. Then we cart gear, reload, rerope, drive to the next washout, and repeat the dance.

At the cabin at last, we carry supplies inside. Ed hits the radio button and pauses to listen. "Typhoon Holly is battering Japan; four boats were lost near Homer. The marine advisory is for sixteen-foot seas."

"Better not tell Sandy. We're lucky we made it."

I remain at Rocky River to start supper while Ed drives back to find Steve and Sandy. Sandy straddles the bike and wraps her arms around Steve as the bike bounces through the first washout.

"Okay, hon?"

Sandy beams. "Better than any ride at Disneyland."

They drive into the meadow filled with fluorescent fireweed. The cabin gleams in evening sun. Smoke drifts to the peaks. The smell of baking halibut fills the cabin. We gather round the table with goblets of wine. "Welcome to Alaska."

"Can't wait to wet a line," says Steve.

"Can't wait to hit the bed," says Sandy. "Long journey." After supper, Sandy nudges Steve. "I've got to use the facilities." Steve talks on. Sandy nudges him again. "Bear's out there," she whispers. "Take me." They walk out, calls of "Nanu Nanu" filling the air.

After morning porridge, we pack lunches. Then I mount the three-wheeler behind Ed; Steve and Sandy ride in the trailer. "Okay?" asks Ed.

"Feel like a tennis shoe bouncing in a dryer," says Steve.

"Delicious," adds Sandy. "We're riding."

At Fish Hole, I forage spring beauty and fireweed blossoms for salad. The others perch on the rocks with rods and catch Dolly Varden. Even Sandy catches a fish. Ed is changing lures as a scream erupts. "Fish on!" Steve's rod bends like an *n*; a flash explodes from the river and cartwheels like an Olympic gymnast.

"A silver, Steve."

"Feel like I should get the gold for this one."

Steve lands his silver salmon, strokes it reverently, and releases it.

"You let it go before I even got a picture."

"No need, Jan. I'll never ever forget this fish."

Back at camp, we feast on herb-baked fish and wild salad. All rave over the apple cobbler. "Had to use them up," I say. "Voles had them all half-eaten."

"Those voles must have a death wish," says Steve.

"They're hungry." I tell him. "Everything's got to eat."

Morning brings a trek to Red Mountain and to the saddle overlooking the Gulf of Alaska's fiords and virgin rain forest. "All that land. No one lives there?" says Steve.

"Not a single mall?" adds Sandy.

"Nada; not in Boston anymore, guys."

We hike up the abandoned mine road that's now devoid of snow. "My hands are freezing," says Sandy. Steve hands her extra socks from his pack.

"My feet are okay," she insists.

"Wear them like mittens, Sandy."

They stare at the barren summit. "This is like a red rock planet."

"Chromite, Sandy," says Ed. "It's what makes this mountain so red. Tons of ore were extracted from here until 1957. That shed with the chains is one of the last historical remnants.

"What trucks carted out the ore?" asks Steve.

"None. Ore traveled from mountain to sea on a poop-a-lina."

"Poop-a-what?"

"A cart on tracks driven by compressed air. The escaping air created a pooping sound. Later, after World War II, Jakolof Road got built so that ten-wheel trucks could cart out ore."

"People really lived up here?"

"Yes, over fifty, but in green season only. According to Herb, the mail shack at Kasitna Bay was established to service the miners; that's why the address is Red Mountain. Sunday was the only day off. There was an airstrip down by Herb's; sometimes the miners would fly home to visit family."

Back at the cabin, Sandy dozes in the hammock chair; she startles to a rap on the door. "Oh hello," I say. "No thanks, we don't need our honey bucket cleaned." I stand back laughing, and introduce Gordon Castanza from McGrath. "Remember, Ed? Helen and I cleaned his septic tank."

Sandy is shocked to see company arrive with no advance notice. "This is Alaska," I explain. "Folks drop in."

"And stay," she whispers.

I set another plate and make room for Gordon's bedroll on the couch.

"Gordon's a computer programmer," I say.

"Office geek, eh?" jokes Steve.

"And an Iditarod musher," I add. "The sled-dog race from Anchorage to Nome."

Their questions prod Gordon. "One thousand forty-nine miles," he says.

"Dogs need three thousand miles of training before the race; sixty-eight teams began the last race, each with a minimum of eighteen dogs; you need five dogs remaining to finish; dogs can only be dropped at checkpoints."

"Expensive?" asks Sandy.

"The entry fee is twelve hundred dollars; it costs fifteen thousand to prepare, another two grand afterward, mostly in travel expenses. Most have sponsors who help cover expenses."

"Temperatures this past year," continues Gordon, "ran from unusually warm (fifty degrees) to twenty below. Despite the trail-making team's best efforts, rain and snow messed up the trail. If you ran off, you hit hip-deep slush. A plane dropped my supplies on a frozen lake but the lake was uncrossable, so I never got them. Another time I had to lead my dogs across a lake covered with two feet of water. I slipped and fell on my lead dog; he bit my hand. It swelled to double its size, so at the next checkpoint the vet treated me. Later a female dog decided to mate, which raised havoc with the other males. Next came a snowstorm. I couldn't see through the whiteout, so I camped on the sea ice but it kept rising and falling like a monster breathing, and breaking up the ice. Then two hundred miles from Nome, my sled wrecked; I had to wait for a charter plane to fly out another. I tried to catch a nap on the sled, but the Northern Lights were so bright I couldn't sleep. Best sound in the world is the air raid siren; it screams every time a musher hits Nome. Folks go wild welcoming mushers home."

"Prizes must be awesome to go through all that," says Sandy.

"Only the top twenty get cash, but all finishers receive a patch and an official belt buckle."

"You do all that for a patch and buckle?"

Gordon shrugs his shoulders.

"I didn't get it either, Sandy," I said, "until I was in Nome watching a video of last year's race. I bawled when the dogs hit that finish line. Those dogs are bred to run, they live to run. And it's an ultimate high for mushers. It's not the money; it's love."

"Well said, Jan," says Gordon. "Well said."

With so many mouths, our cupboards grow barren. Town meat is long gone. "No worry," we tell the Unsworths. "There are fish in the river, rice in the cupboard, and heaps of oatmeal."

"No coffee," says Sandy.

"There's plenty of spruce tip tea."

Sandy sighs, but smiles.

In the morning, I set the table with tea, hot oatmeal, and the last carton of boxed soymilk that's been stored in the vented cupboard under the propane-powered stove. We pour milk on our cereal and start eating. Sandy is last to the table. She pours but nothing happens. "Doesn't feel empty," she says. She gives it a shake. A drowned vole falls into her bowl.

We roar with laughter, then stare despondently at our cereal. "How about some breakfast in town?" I suggest. "With coffee."

Two hours later, we reach Seldovia. First stop is the flush toilet at the harbor for Sandy, then bacon and eggs at the café. Steve points to the customer wearing a beanie hat with a plastic propeller. "Bet he's the local pilot."

"How'd you know?"

"You're joking, right?"

"No. That's Snoopy. You'll be flying with him back to Homer."

"This place is chock-full of characters. Not to mention fish. My boy Dan would love this, Ed."

"Bring him sometime. When we were Dan's age, we would have given our eyeteeth to experience this."

"We'd be welcome back?"

"You're always welcome, bud."

Goat Mountain ~

"There are two seasons in Alaska," Ed says, "green and white." Though the August valley is still green, summits warn of impending change.

"What about meat this winter, Ed? It'd be a break from all the salmon."

"But there are so few moose in the valley and it would be far more meat than we need for ourselves. And we love seeing black bears. If only there was something like deer where we could utilize an entire animal."

"What about a mountain goat? They're about the same size as a white-tail. And there's supposed to be plenty at . . ."

"Goat Mountain; must be named that for a reason."

We pack tent, tarp, and gear and trek south, then scramble up the mountain. Ed halts at a flat grassy area nestled under a canopy of spruce. "Good site for base camp."

While he unloads, I scan the summit. "Aren't those snow patches moving?"

"Good eyes, Jan. Yes, eight goats. We'll set camp, then do an evening hunt."

I gather rocks for a fire ring while Ed steps aside for nature's call. He drops his drawers and is engaged when he feels a presence. He pivots and stares. Brown eyes set in a hairy white head stare back. Ed moves. The goat spins and bolts, and powers up the mountain.

"My gun, my gun!" screams Ed. He grabs his rifle; we tear up the slope after the goat. We stop and scan with binoculars. The goats are at the peak, peering down.

"Tomorrow," says Ed. "Let's go back and have supper. We'll hit the hay early and do a dawn hunt."

Back at camp, we start a canned salmon stir-fry. Our plumes of smoke lure visitors. Eight shaggy shapes peer from low rock ledges; they stride in our direction. Ed silently grabs his gun. He cocks the trigger. The click is like a cannon blasting; the goats race to the tops. I stare at the gallopers. "They're such beautiful animals, Eddie. Don't know that I want to eat one."

"Think how great it'd taste, Jan, later this winter, when it's salmon after salmon after salmon."

"Remember Deiv's goat?"

"That was old and not mountain goat. These are antelope cousins. Remember that steak those hunters left you? Scrumptious."

That night I dream of succulent roasts. I waken salivating. After breakfast, Ed solos to the peaks. I stay in camp with Max and watch through binoculars. Ed squats behind alders, crawls on hands and knees to the next cover, moves only as goats are busy browsing. He freezes when they glance up. He creeps within range, then lies flat on his belly behind a boulder. He slowly slides his rifle over its crest. He peers through the sighting scope. I wait breathlessly for the bang.

Nothing. Ed stays in position. He must be waiting to be positive of his target. The goats move even closer to the rock. I inhale. Ed rises. He begins descending the slope; goats trail after him. Ed arrives leading the goat parade.

"What happened Ed? Didn't the gun work?"

Ed hugs my shoulders and turns me to face the mountain. "Look at them, Janzie. Look at their eyes. One stared at me with total trust. How can you kill that? We've got the finest Alaskan salmon, all those Omega three oils. Who'd want to eat goat anyways?"

"Yes," I agree, relieved. "Alaskan salmon's the very best."

Snowed In ⌒

We winter in record comfort, snug as bunnies in a rabbit hole. Our new windows, insulation, and seasoned firewood warm us by day, our sauna by night.

I perch at my desk, scissor words, tape changes, retype yet again. The plant manuscript sprawls across the loft, one thousand double-spaced pages. "If only I could cut and paste automatically."

"Home computers, Jan; they're getting as common as telephones."

"Yeah, for those who have electricity. If only."

The sound of footsteps interrupts our chat; then a soft tap.

"Herb. Great to see you. Come in."

"No, no. I was trapping up the valley. Checking to see if you're alright."

"Doing fine. Come in. Have a tea," I insist. Herb shuffles inside.

I set our china teapot on the tablecloth and fill the teacups. Herb struggles to grasp the dainty handles with his banana-size fingers. His stomach rumbles. I grab bowls and ladle stew from the pot atop the barrel stove. Ed slices hot bread.

"Oh no," says Herb. "I didn't come to eat."

"We've been wanting to thank you properly for a long time: for the windows, the milk, and fixing the mill's bulldozer. The least we can do is give you a bowl of soup."

Herb's stomach growls again. He takes a bowl and inhales the contents. I refill his bowl. "Oh, I couldn't."

"I'll be offended if you don't."

Herb dives into the second bowl; we all take seconds of the bread.

"What are you doing now that the mill's gone?" asks Ed.

"Trapping, selling a beefalo now and then. Might go crabbing; saw a skiff I liked, called 'Oh My.'"

"Oh, my. Another cuppa?" I ask.

"Nah. Gotta get back to my critters." Herb bolts for the door. "Thank you ma'am," he tells me. "That was good."

"Typical Alaskan hermit, Jan; afraid to socialize."

"He looked petrified of the tablecloth and china."

"Wish he would have stayed longer. Haven't seen anyone else all winter, except the rare times we hit town."

"That's okay, Ed; you're all the company I need."

Blood Red ⁓

River ice crescendos spring's arrival. Fiddleheads peekaboo. Northbound flocks blacken the skies. Our mail-shed trek scores a parcel, the return of my plant transparencies from Alaska Northwest Books. They had requested slides for starting the color separation process. "Wow, that was quick, Ed. The company is so efficient. I didn't expect the slides back for ages."

At the cabin, I open the package and gape. My crisp caption sheets bleed red ink. "Look like the pages hemorrhaged."

"I don't understand, Jan. You put so much time into those pictures. You've sold photos time and again. What's the matter with the company?"

"It's me, Ed. I thought plants were easy because they don't run away like animals. But close-up photography has its own challenges. The editors keep complaining of poor depth of field."

"Depth of what?"

I hold my slide to the window. "See how the plant exists on multiple planes. It's tough to get the flower and leaves in focus simultaneously, especially for low-light forest plants. And see here," I point again, "this one was taken in noon sun, and shadows are too harsh. I have to shoot 80 percent of them all over again."

"Jan, I read in *Homer News* that Tom Walker is teaching a photography workshop this weekend. Want to go?"

My eyes light like flashbulbs. "Oh, yes."

We migrate across the bay. I emerge from the workshop and my personal consultation with Tom buzzing with knowledge and equipment needs. At the Salvation Army, we buy a white umbrella to smooth light for less contrasty images on bright sun days. "Tom says I also need a tripod, one that spreads its legs like a gymnast so I can get nose-to-nose with sundews and violets."

"No problem, Jan, what does that cost—fifty bucks?"

"Four hundred. Plus I need a 2.8 105 mm Nikon macro lens for crisp close-ups. That's another five hundred smackaroonies. Plus I need to travel again, redo my photos, and make certain I get plant portraits in each stage of growth: the big view of them in their habitat, close-ups of plants in flower and in seed, and spring shots of peak edibility."

"Crap. But you can't stop now, Jan. No clue how we'll fund it all though."

"Time for an angel?"

"Big time."

Bush Lines 〜

A bush line airs to Ed from Charlotte of Barrow. "Call me." We hit the harbor pay phone. "Find me some logs," says Charlotte. "Build me a home."

We ferry to Homer and stop at Fritz Creek printers for another print run of *The Alaska Story;* owner Jim is keen to have his spruce selectively harvested. We walk Jim's land, and mark cabin logs. Glenn Caldwell teams with Ed to fell, move, and stack logs; they need to season the trees before Charlotte's construction can commence. Meanwhile there are site details and foundation work.

Ed earns, I spend: new lenses, tripods, film, processing. I scout plants by day, shoot photos, and harvest; models become meals. I dry and grind seaweeds and wild herbs and blend as seasoning. I carefully record the measurements and dub it Land-and-Sea-soning:

½ cup dried sea lettuce
½ cup dried lovage
¼ cup dried bull kelp blades
¼ cup dried nettles
¼ cup dried dulse
¼ cup dried sorrel
¼ cup dried sweet gale leaves
¼ cup wild chives

I make repeated batches, and pack the surplus. "I'll take this seasoning and my massage oils and teas to the fairs this fall," I promise Ed, "I'll market everything as Rocky River Herbal Products and help recoup some of the book expenses."

I hand artist Toby the changes to the book's illustrations list. "Publication is another year away, Toby. I have to redo the photos."

"This will never be published, Janice."

"Of course, it will, Toby. Good things take time."

Each month, we retreat to Rocky River to rest and recharge. Steve Unsworth joins us with son Dan. The guys fish while I forage. They hit the Rocky River's pools and smoke the results. "I need new photos of buckbean, Ed. Best site I know is the Port Dick bog. Isn't it time for our annual . . ."

"Pilgrimage," Ed finishes up. "It's a great place, Steve. Lots of bears, Dan. We'll head out in the morning."

"Glad we did so much preparatory hiking around town with our packs," Steve says.

Ed lights his pipe and nods to me anxiously.

We walk south from the cabin and turn left into hell. We pant through tangles of felled trees; two hours later we reach the Port Dick bog. The men pause for tea while I belly down with my tripod. "Bear!" shouts Ed.

"But I'm all set for this buckbean," I insist.

"Jan, the bear's getting closer."

"One more shot; it's taken me ages to get this set up."

"Jan."

I stand and wave my arms and bellow. "Get lost, bear. Scram."

The bear bolts. I nose back to the buckbean.

"Wow, Ed," says Steve. "Hope I never get her pissed at me."

We mosey into the woods, the air thick with eau de bruin. We traipse single file on a narrow ledge and come head-on with a big black carrying a salmon.

"Nanu nanu!" Steve screams.

The salmon drops at his feet as the black spins and bolts.

"What a way to fish, Steve. Only next time choose a bear that likes something better than old spawned humpie."

We wind onward through devil's club, up slopes, and over ledges. "We're knackered," say the guests. "Almost there?"

"Not far," encourages Ed.

"Guess we should have practiced climbing more than sidewalk curbs."

Port Dick revives all with its cabin comforts and fishing excitement. The creek is choked with fish. "Looks like we could walk across on their backs," says Dan.

Max wades in, excited by the swirls. He dips his head underwater and emerges with a ten-pound salmon. "Great work, Maxie. Looks like you've caught supper."

"We'll cook tonight," says Steve. "Go play, Jan."

I sit under a spruce in the Gulf's evening light and dreamily relax, awaiting the call for supper. Wind whispers in the boughs. And then I hear a piercing scream.

Cry of the Forest ⌒

The scream resounds again. My head tilts, trying to get a bearing on where it's coming from. It sounds like someone or something desperately needs help. Didn't Ed say that a rabbit in distress sounds like a human scream? Could it be a rabbit?

An answer drifts into my consciousness, landing like a feather: "The forest; it's the cry of the forest."

"Nonsense," I argue with myself. "Has to be a rabbit."

"It's the forest," insists the voice. "It's crying for help."

"Shut up," I tell the voice. "Don't be stupid. There's no danger here."

I head back to the Port Dick cabin and tell Ed about the scream.

"Rabbit," he assures me.

"See," I tell the voice. "Only a bunny."

We return to Rocky River the next evening, sauna until our skin is as wrinkled as raisins, and retire to restful sleep. I waken at 4 A.M. parched with thirst. I step downstairs for a drink. The water jug's empty.

I head out in dusky light to the river, stand on a river rock, and squat to drink. The alder bush explodes. A bald eagle flies in my face. A white feather flutters to my hand. My heart hammers and my mind hushes. Eagle feathers are Alaska's version of lucky horseshoes; it's good fortune to find one. Is this connected to the forest cry? Is the eagle giving me courage?

"Must be another coincidence."

Vision Quest ⌒

The guys fish; I head to Wolverine Creek to forage. My skin prickles. The trees have eyes. Something has eyes. They're boring into me. My head swivels like a bobble dog on a car dashboard. I stare at the surroundings but see nothing. But the sensation remains. I'm being watched. I'm certain I'm being watched. I gaze again at the forest, looking for lynx, wolverine, bear.

Beady eyes stare back. A red-tailed hawk perches on a limb. I laugh in relief; only a bird. Cheery pink blooms beckon from the seep. I kneel to photograph spring beauty. I forget about my stalker until I move on. The hawk flies spruce to alder. He tails me. Where I go, he goes. This is too strange. Is he rabid? Do hawks get rabies? My feet spin me back to the cabin.

The men return with salmon for supper.

"You should have been here today, Steve. You could have busted my stalker." The hawk becomes a joke, but my gut still pinches. When our company departs, I tell Ed I want to spend a few days solo. "Spirit is trying to communicate something; I need to be alone to meditate. I'll take the tent and go camping, but I'm a tad nervous, Ed. I can get turned around in a closet."

"Oh Jan, back East our land was a maze, all stone walls and trees. But here, once you cross the river, you're hemmed in. There's the peak that looks like Max's ear. Use that as a landmark. You can't get lost." Ed gives me a hug. "You're a big girl. You'll be fine."

I load my pack with sleeping bag, tent, raingear, toothbrush, and bear bells.

"You forgot food, Jan."

"I'm going to fast. I'll do like the Natives and drink water only, chew on devil's club stem and root bark. It's supposed to help you see."

"See what?"

"Whatever the scream, the feather, and the hawk are trying to show me."

I ford the river and head up the slope toward the waterfall. I rub my pocket of devil's club. "Keep me safe," I whisper. "Help me see."

"Waterfall left," I remind myself. "Note the sun position. There's Maxwell's ear. Wish he was with me," I babble. "But he'd be a distraction. I must focus."

I pause by a cascade and rest. My nostrils fill with the earthy aromas of wild Alaskan ginseng. Thick tangles of the spiny shrub block my way. I hold arms aloft, and weave onward, smiling. "Teacher plant, teach me."

I crest the knoll. Below are emerald meadows ablaze with yellow arnica and purple irises. I choose a flat spot, dump my pack's contents, and assemble tent poles. Jeezum, the grass is flattened; the bed of a very big animal. I search a new spot, not too wet, not too rocky, flat, free of impressions. Tent erected, I gaze about. Alpine ridges rise to my right and ring my meadow; thousands of acres of wilderness park cradle me. My mind bounces like a tennis ball, batting from bears to moose to Ed to manuscript deadlines. "Breathe. Inhale like a wave." My mind flits again. I bring it back.

My skin prickles. I feel eyes; there in the spruce perches a red-tailed hawk. I stare at the hawk staring at me. I chew on the bark. I watch. I wait. "What's this all about? This hawk keeps appearing. Am I being followed? Summoned? What about the scream in the Port Dick forest?"

A varied thrush trills by my tent. "Won't someone please answer my queries?"

My stomach rumbles. I gnaw on the spicy bark and cool my palate with icy mountain water. "Am I being prepared for some coming event? How long do I need to sit here? This is boring; I miss Ed." I force my mind back to my breath. It ricochets. I spend the night in the alpine meadow then hike back to the cabin for breakfast, still wondering.

The next day, Ed and I hike to the head of Jakolof Bay. Since my fast on spicy devil's club, I'm hankering for greens, and most especially for goose-tongue, a coastal plantain "narrow as a goose's tongue" and chock-full of salty flavor, crunchy texture, and vitamins. Our favorite patch lies seven miles north on the coastal flats.

When we reach Jakolof Creek, I halt and point. "Jesus Christ."

"What's wrong, Jan?"

"That shrew's walking on water."

"Think you fasted too long, honey. Maybe I'd best take you out to the doc."

"Ed, I mean it. LOOK!"

Ed follows my finger. "Christ," he echoes. "It's walking on water like Christ."

When we return back from the coast, I steam goosetongue. Ed meanwhile studies the mammal book. "Look honey," he tells me. "This time there is an explanation. What we saw is a water shrew. Their hind feet have stiff hairs that trap air bubbles, giving them the ability to walk on water."

"Weird world we live in, Eddie. Shrews skating on water. I guess the real miracle is that we even saw it. And right after my vision quest. Can't help but wonder what's up next."

In the Sardine Can

We transfer back to Homer for construction of Charlotte's cabin. The book now requires phone access, too, for frequent exchanges with the publisher. "Where will we live, Ed? Greenie's fine for a few days, but she'd be a beast long term. Especially now that we've gutted her amenities for the Rocky River cabin."

"Don't want to spend all our profits on an apartment, Jan. What about that twelve-foot travel trailer we heard about, with bed and burners?"

In Homer, we check out the camper. "Judy's horses back in New Hampshire lived in spaces bigger than this," I tell Ed. "But it's quite the luxury after Greenie. We can stand up."

"And sit down," he adds, "and lie full length, and cook. And we only have to take a single step to do it all. All this for nine hundred."

We park the trailer on Charlotte's lot adjacent to her newly installed Homer Electric meter. On the job site, Ed time-warps to a modern world of power drills, power planes, and power saws.

Within the cramped kitchen, I set to work with herbal crafts. I whiz my newest creation: "nesto," a nettle pesto, in my blender purchased from the Salvation Army. And I plug in Marina's loaner, an electric typewriter she insists will be a godsend for finishing the manuscript. God's name comes up a lot as I use it. I'm accustomed to poising fingers over my Royal's keys and plonking like a sledgehammer. The electric frustrates me. The lightest touch, held a tad too long, and rrrrrrrrrrrrr rrrrrrrrrr. The keys repeatttttt themmmmselves. And I must still do the type, edit, cut with scissors, tape, retype, find new data, retype, make a minor change, and retype routine. At Rocky River I consoled myself I was generating BTUs for the fire. But here in the camper all I generate is trashhhhhhhh.

The temps in the caravan plummet as autumn advances. Condensation from cooking turns the tin can into an icehouse. "My bag's frozen to the wall," I wail. "This is ridiculous."

"Ah, she's not so bad, Jan." Ed stretches his arm and reaches from the warmth of his down sleeping bag to turn on the kettle for morning tea. "I'll brew you a cuppa, thaw you out."

I dance on the cold floor as I dress, swat myself for warmth, and tug on thermals. "I miss Rocky River."

"Best get used to it, Janzie; we'll be here all winter."

The next day Ed leaves me solo in the icebox. Mail brings a letter from Florida. Ed's mom is in crisis; he heads East to deal with it.

Crisis by the Sea 〜

I work on the book in Homer while Ed's away; I get a bush line on morning radio: "Call Sourdough ASAP."

I dial Ellen's house in Florida. "Mom's in a bad way," he tells me. "Her memory's so poor, Jan, that she forgets to turn off the stove and the neighbors have had the fire department out three times. And the other day Mom ran out because she heard the trash truck and she forgot to put on clothes. The doctor who checked her said she can't live on her own. She needs nursing care. In her lucid moments, all Mom talks about is 'good old New England.' She wants to go back North. So I'm making lots of calls to see about nursing options. And seeing the realtor about getting the house on the market."

"Crap. Sounds like you're not having much fun."

"No. But I do have some good news. Talked with your brother Jim. He wants to build himself a home. Wants to know if we'll sell him our two acres in New Hampshire."

"I suppose we could, Ed; I doubt we'll ever live back East. But you'll have to dig up the gold before he takes possession."

"Which is under four feet of frost."

"Do we ever do things the easy way?"

"How's the weather in Homer?"

"Still freezing to the walls; while you've been gone I've been thinking…"

"Yes?"

"What if we look for a bit of land in Homer and build ourselves a camp? Something insulated we could heat with a match? This tin can of a trailer is getting to me."

"Great idea, Jan. See what you can find."

Looking for Land ⁓

By the time the call ends, the priorities are clear. I'm to look for land with good access to town, as our intent is a simple cottage as work base. Rocky River will still be our main home. I'm keen for something with good gardening. And Ed insists on privacy. We both want to make certain Max can play without our worrying about traffic.

And our absolute price limit is under eight thousand per acre.

I tell realtor Roberta Highland our requirements. "You'll have to keep your head low," she warns. "Forget about the great Homer view."

"No problem. We live in the view at Rocky River; this is only a work base."

Roberta takes me atop the bluff where I strut the spruce, eye potential cabin logs, and inventory the flora. *Vaccinium* shrubs promise blueberry pies to come. *Viburnum edule* will yield highbush cranberry ketchup and crampbark teas. Cacophony erupts.

"*Ahooooooooooooooooooooooo. Ahhhhiiiiiiiiiiiiiiiiiiiiiiooooooo.*"

"Heck. Ed hates barking dogs."

"But sled dogs sound off mainly at feeding times," encourages Roberta.

"Yeah or when the moon is full. Or when they smell a moose. You know how often we see moose. Find something else."

I ride around daily with Roberta and her sidekick Diane. We walk piece after piece.

Too far.

Too dear.

Too wet.

Too bare.

Too dense.

Too many neighbors.

Too many barking dogs.

Next place to view is in Timberline Subdivision; the three-acre section is in Fritz Creek, seven miles east of downtown Homer. A creek trickles through the property. A view peekaboos Grewingk Glacier. The land is a medley of birch, spruce, and meadow.

"Neighbors?" I ask.

"Lots of moose. This section borders Fritz Creek moose-calving grounds. That track," she points, "leads to Stone Steps Lake."

Ed returns from Florida; we rendezvous and drive east. "You missed our turn," he says, puzzled, as I fly past the driveway that leads to the trailer.

"Nope," I say. "Wait 'til you see this. I've been busy."

We park in the cul-de-sac at Mile 7. I lead him through the meadow, down to the creek. Max splashes in the water; he freezes as a moose and calf stroll by.

We trek up the rise and eye Grewingk Glacier through the window between the spruce. "Imagine what we would have given for a view like that in New Hampshire, Eddie. It's not dramatic by Homer standards but certainly amazing in other places. And this fits all our criteria."

"You've done well, Janzie." He wraps me in a hug.

"Come on, there's more."

Hobbit Hole 〜·

We drive back toward town, turn right at Kachemak City community hall and down a side street filled with suburban-style homes. We sweep into a hidden drive into storyland.

A Hansel and Gretel cottage nests before us, walls covered with ginger-breadlike shingles. A round wall adds a Rapunzel-in-the-tower touch. The door opens to walls of pink cotton candy. I nod at the exposed batts of fiberglass insulation. "Look how warm we'll be, Ed."

"But whose is it?" he asks.

"Ours for three months. The owner's away; we're house-sitting."

In the loft is a futon on the floor. Downstairs is a wood stove, adjacent to plywood counters. "It will be great for finishing products for the Christmas fairs. There's even a kitchen table, Ed." The table is buried under my book manuscript and Marina's typewriter.

Outside, we tour the amenities. "Over there," I point, "behind the alders is an A-frame outhouse. Pretty flashy too; it even has a Visqueen roof."

Ed surveys our palace. "Good job, Janzie."

In town at the realtor's, we seal the land deal, then order rough-cut from Small Potatoes Lumber. During Ed's free hours from working on Charlotte's home, we dance construction and nail together our twelve-by-sixteen cabin frame. Ed drives the last nail and pauses. "Janzie, let's perambulate the bounds."

"Take a stroll," I translate mentally. Ed's favorite thing in New Hampshire was perambulating the bounds of our property, parading like a king overseeing his domain. While we walk, Ed puffs. He stops in the western corner. A grandmother birch sits kitty-corner to a massive Sitka spruce, with glacier view beyond.

"Nice spot," I say.

"Let's build the house here."

"Here? But the frame's out by the driveway, weighs hundreds of pounds."

"We could do it, Jan."

"It's not like shifting furniture."

"Nice spot," repeats Ed.

"It's so quiet here," I admit. "This is rather nice." We head to the driveway. The frame is rough-sawn and whale-wet.

"Lift, Janzie. You can do it," insists Ed. "Don't be such a wussy."

I bend my legs, and heave. Ed hefts the other end. We shift-drag-push-pull the frame across the icy meadow, then down the swamp, across the creek, and up the other side through the alders.

"Better?" says Ed.

I stand breathless and stare at the mountains across the bay; ancient trees stand sentinel. "Now we have to stack firewood," adds Ed, "and thaw the ground so you can dig postholes for the pilings."

"Me dig them?"

"You're great at it; I'll start framing another wall."

Payback comes with the cabin plans.

"What about adding a jog as an entryway?" I ask.

Ed agrees. Jogs breed like rabbits on Viagra. The plan grows a dining nook jog with skylight. "You know, Ed, upstairs, if you built a gable shed roof, you could add a jog for a built-in bed, with storage underneath. And if you surrounded the bed with windows, we could lie and watch the stars, and the squirrels in the treetops."

Even with modifications, the cabin stays teeny-tiny, five hundred feet of living space yet replete with built-ins like a yacht at sea. Dwindling light slows construction. Ed and Glenn chip ice from Charlotte's logs. At Gardensong, our name for our new property, Ed erects plastic tents to dry rough-cut beams in order to plane their edges.

Money is the only element in gallop mode. Products I make from wild plants sell well at fairs but inflow is a dribble compared to the outgoing tide. Everything costs. Every nail. Every ream of paper. Every call to the publisher. "Can't stop now," I tell Ed, as I retype the manuscript yet again.

"We'll get through this, Jan. Back to our sweet Rocky River life."

This is temporary, we remind ourselves, only temporary.

Hitching Up ～·

"You know, Jan," **begins Ed,** as he sets down his handsaw and lights his pipe.

I twitch, knowing that whatever's coming will cost money or time.

"Life would be easier if Gardensong had electric. There are utility posts in the cul-de-sac; we should be able to get Homer Electric Association to hitch us up for free. Might be worth a monthly utility cost for the convenience. Why don't you go sign papers so they can put us on the grid."

"We can connect you," the HEA secretary tells me. "No problem." She hands me a contract and asks for a check for eight thousand dollars.

"What?" I sputter. "There are utility boxes right there."

She rechecks her map. "Telephone only; electricity runs through Timberline Subdivision but not to your cul-de-sac."

"But we're in a bona fide subdivision. There's no electric to the lot?"

"No."

HEA is adamant. Pay or don't connect.

"They can stick it up their bum," retorts Ed. "Has to be another way."

"Like an angel?"

"Don't know that there are electricity angels, Jan."

"There are flood angels, why not power angels?"

Our angel is neighbor Shoshanna, who wants to sell her solar system. Ed positions the four panels, installs four fat batteries, and wires the inverter. We harness the sun to run electric lights, radio, and my latest loan from Marina, a 512k Macintosh computer.

"It's a bit of a beast, Janzie," she warns, "really slow." Marina coaches me as I type a sentence, point and hold the mouse as I drag across a word, and go to the edit menu to cut. I click. Words vanish and reappear magically with another click. Words drop in place where needed; letters reform to fill the gap. "Slow, Marina? This is warp speed."

Ed also time-warps forward with the addition of a Honda generator. "This will boot up the solar batteries during the dark times, and run the high-drain electric drills and chop saw."

With the help of the power monitor, we become conscious of every kilowatt of electricity we use. "How come, Eddie," I ask one morning, "the digital display's showing a discharge? I'm not running anything." We hunt like voles searching for crumbs. Lights are off. Stereo's off. Computer's off. Printer's off. "There nothing else, Ed. But we're still draining."

Ed ferrets out the answer. "When the radio's off, it's actually on. Has a warming element like in televisions, so that it powers on immediately when you hit the switch." Ed installs a cut-off directly in the line; off is now off.

One night, as we're working late, I gape at the power monitor. "Look Ed, we're charging."

"Like you, Janzie," says Ed. "Must be the full moon; it affects the panels as well as you."

"I had no idea that a full moon charged solar batteries."

"So much to learn."

"No kidding, about everything. With this book, I feel that I could go on forever and keep learning, but the publisher is pushing for me to complete it this season."

"You can always do updates in future editions."

"It would certainly be sweet to have a future edition. Right now I'll be relieved to complete this one."

Ed yawns. "I'm off to bed, Jan. Coming?"

"Still buzzing, Ed. Think I'll take advantage of the energy. Spring's coming soon; another four hundred pages yet to edit."

Last Chance ~·

Spring breaks. The cottages grow. The manuscript is refined, but plant portraits continue to thwart me. The eagle eye of the magnifier reveals flaws, scratches, blurs, and the damn depth of field. The marching buds force me to higher altitudes and more northern latitudes.

"Come across Cook Inlet with me," insists friend Norma Dudiak. "I'm heading over to shoot some wildlife photos for my exhibit. Plants are earlier there; you can reshoot what you've missed."

"This is my last chance," I tell Ed. "Have to do it."

A fisherman watches as we disembark from the floatplane with tents and packs. "Watch for bears," he warns. "The big browns are everywhere." He points to the beach sand, imprinted with clawed tracks the length of loaves of bread.

The Cook Inlet plants are prime. Waves of purple-flowering peas *(Lathyrus maritimus)* sweep the beaches. Oysterleaf *(Mertensia maritima)* displays a palette of pink buds and blue blooms. Norma scans for brownies as I belly low to the flowers. The gray light is like an umbrella in bright sun; harsh shadows dissolve. As the wind takes a breath, I gently squeeze the shutter; yes, the perfect picture.

The light changes and darkens. I glance up anxiously. A storm front is sweeping toward us. I race to a beach pea plant, splay the tripod legs, belly up to the ground, focus, change position, and shoot. Rain drops plink. I dart to a lovage flower. Norma spreads her raincoat to shelter my Nikon. The winds intensify. I manage one more shot and pray it's as crisp as my view-finder promises. Rain changes tempo to a fat pelting cascade.

"Let's get shelter, Jan." We dash past the fisherman clad in full rain-gear. "Where you gals going?"

"To set up our tent."

"The brownies will chomp it for breakfast. Stay in that hut," he points. The hut's a hovel; rain pours through gaps between the boards. Narrow plywood bunks, blanketed by mice droppings, line each side. We balloon Norma's tarp over the peak, and arm-wrestle with the wind. We heave and anchor the ropes. The indoor faucet turns off.

Norma finds a broken broom and sweeps. I inflate pads. A knock interrupts. "Here," says a raincoat-clad woman. She thrusts a plate covered with foil into our hands. "Thought you might want some hot razor clams. And if you want to bathe later, the sauna will be hot all night. You'll see the smoke down the beach."

Norma picks up a clam and inhales deeply. I bite into mine; juice squirts and flavors tango on the tongue. We scavenge every clam, lick crumbs, and sigh. "Ecstasy," says Norma.

"Ready for agony?"

We pile on raingear and throw open the door. Cold rain slashes. We duck our heads, tighten hoods, and fight the wind. We walk down the beach, searching. Norma points; another hovel, only hot inside. We hang wet gear on hooks, strip to our birthday suits. Our bodies thaw, our tongues relax. We swap yarns, and bake. Sweat breaks and runs rivers down my body. "I'm going for a shower," I tell Norma. I step out into the gale and dart back laughing. "Like being in a drive-through car wash." I reheat for round two.

Hours later, we face the music. We re-dress into still-damp gear, and with wind at our back, head to our sleep shed. "The rain is lightening. It'll be a nice lullaby." I drift deeply into dreamland. I waken refreshed. Norma's groggy. "Never got a wink," she complains. "Too much snuffling."

"Sorry my snoring kept you awake."

"Not you, Jan; something else."

Outside, Norma points. Tracks circle our hut.

"Coastal grizzlies. That fisherman wasn't joking."

We head off on our photo mission. Norma is on alert while I crawl and click. "Bear," she cries. I bolt upright; we arm ourselves with telephotos and shoot bears.

We exit on the afternoon plane, laden with tales for our husbands, and, I dearly hope, the perfect photos for the book. I deposit my films in mailer envelopes and post them to Kodak. Two weeks later, bulging envelopes return. I tear off the wrapping and stare dumbly at images: a cute toddler at her birthday party. I pen an angry letter back to Kodak and describe what I'm missing.

"Don't get your hopes up, Jan," says Norma. "I've lost slides before. Kodak never finds them."

The birthday folks are furious with their slides of stupid plants. Kodak rights its bloopers. We reconnect. The slide submission heads to Alaska Northwest Books. "Thumbs up," writes the editor. We dance a jig of celebration.

Fetish ⁓

Work progresses, but Ed pines, and points across the bay longingly. "Can't wait to go to Rocky River again, Jan. It's real Alaska over there."

Max hears "Rocky" and lets out a rare woof. "Motion made and seconded, Ed, let's go." As we depart Homer Spit, town concerns fade. I frolic along the Rocky River road. "Hi wormwood," I tell my favorite plant. "We're back again. You're looking well."

"Some people might think you're weird, Janzie, talking to the plants."

"Look who's talking, Eddie. If they only knew what you do." Ed, I've discovered, has a quirk. Some men do things in secret like wear women's clothes or play bondage games. Ed's compulsion is even stranger. Ever since returning from the East Coast with the gold bar, Ed digs holes in the yard, and buries and unburies his treasure. The meadow has as many holes as a cemetery.

"Where's the gold bar now?"

"On the river bank by the sauna."

"Do you think that's wise? Remember the great flood?"

"You're right, Janzie. I'd best move it."

Ed shifts the gold while I make supper. Then we relax with a nip of brandy. We're chatting gaily when Ed slumps.

"Ed! Oh help. A doctor! How do I get a doctor? We've no radio. Oh my God, how do I get help? What's happening? Is this a stroke?"

Ed revives, but is dazed. What questions am I supposed to ask at a time like this? What's that memory trick? STRoke. S stands for smile. "Ed, can you smile?" He smiles. I remember the R, for Reach. "Ed, can you lift your arms above your head?" He stretches. "Good," I tell him. T. What's T stand for? Oh yes, talk. Can Ed talk? "Ed, where's the gold bar now?"

By the next morning Ed's back in regular form. He takes me to the meadow and points out his newest gold cache. But I'm worried, wondering the cause of his mysterious malady. Is there something going on with his health that we don't know about?

We hike to Fish Hole and stare at shadowy bodies in the pools. "Dollies," Ed whispers. "Still too early for the salmon."

The sky screams. Two bald eagles meet mid-flight, lock talons, and freefall. "What a love dance, Jan." Before I can respond, a tail feather flutters, and falls at my feet. My skin prickles.

"What's the matter, Jan? You look pale."

"I'd forgotten, Ed, about the last time a feather fell like this. Back when the hawk was following me. And the forest screamed at Port Dick."

"Quirks of nature, Jan. You're making too much of it."

"You're probably right, Ed. But my gut aches like bad fish."

Hoodlums ~.

A mail run induces us to depart Rocky River; a surprise awaits at the van. "Some idiot broke the mirror Jan. And the door's all scratched. They dragged nails across the paint."

I giggle.

"Not funny, Jan. What 'til I catch that scumbag."

"Track him. There are his prints."

"Black bear." Ed opens the door. "Oh. Forgot about this." A half-eaten peanut butter sandwich sits on the dash. "Must be what the bear was after."

"Remember when there were chunks and scrapes in the cabin's kitchen wall? You were livid until you realized it was done by a bear."

"It's why we live here, Jan, because of the wildlife. We'll stop at the dump and see if we can find another mirror."

"And buy rubbing compound for the scratches; it's the price of living here."

The mail shed brings more fire starter from the IRS, and news from my dad, Jean, saying he's coming to visit.

"Your pestering worked. You've been nagging him to come for years."

"Yes, and he's always had an excuse. No money. No one to go with." I continue reading. "He's coming with Ray."

"Your cousin on crutches?"

"Yep."

"And they're planning to hike into Rocky River?"

"And beyond; I promised you'd take them to Fish Hole. Dad says he has been going dancing, getting fit for the trip."

"Dancing the switchback. Can see it now. Hope they're ready."

"And raring; Dad's as excited as a boy scout going to camp."

"Write back, Jan; warn him and Ray to travel light."

The Very Best ～

We drive to the Anchorage airport to meet the dancing duo. Ray is armed with crutches, Dad a walking cane. Beside them are four fat suitcases. "Oh Dad, I told you to travel light."

"Brought it."

"What?"

"Lite. Got four cases, Bud Lite. Got steaks too: a whole case of T-bones, double wrapped in newspaper; still frozen solid."

Ed rolls his eyes and shrugs. He hefts the gear into the van. I climb in beside the suitcases. Dad and Ray alternate in the front passenger seat, exclaiming at Turnagain Arm vistas. We stop for glacier close-ups, then scan mountain goats on the slopes above Cooper Landing. We pause at the Baycrest overlook of Kachemak Bay.

"We'll rest up in Homer. You can see Gardensong, the cottage we're building. You and Ray can have our bed tonight. We'll camp on the floor, along with Hilde and Guido. They're some Germans we adopted last week."

"Krauts? Alone in your house?"

"This is Alaska, Dad. Folks trust each other."

We arrive to a warm cabin and hot Bavarian meal. Then Hilde and I tidy dishes while the men chat.

"Outhouse?" asks Dad.

"Cross the creek and follow the path through the spruce. Can't miss it."

Dad returns. "Can't find it. There's no building out there."

"There isn't one. Only a box over a hole."

"What if it rains?"

"Wear your raincoat."

Morning brings showers. After breakfast, our guests vanish. I glance out the window toward the scrap pile. "They must be getting firewood, Ed."

The crew returns two hours later, empty-handed.

"Did it," says Dad excitedly. "We built you an outhouse."

"And we didn't have to cut a single board," adds Ray. "Everything was exactly the right length." Ed looks at me, worried.

"The outhouse even has a name, Jan. *Früchtekorb.* Guido named it after a peach basket. Come see."

The foursome point with pride. Wood scraps are latticed like a basket; Visqueen is tacked to the frame. "Thanks so much, guys," I say. I can't bear to dampen their enthusiasm. "And good timing. I'll give it a go." I sit and reflect on the strangeness of time: Dad in a world war with Germans and Japanese; today he's building outhouses with them.

I book tickets on the *Tustemena.* "You've got to experience the ferry and Seldovia." The visitors glue themselves to the rail and squeal as otters and pups play in the kelps. "Always good to have company, Jan," Ed tells me. "Makes us see this place with fresh eyes. Sometimes I forget how special this is."

After the *Tusty* docks, we tour town. Shutters click at the Russian Orthodox church on the hill and sea shanties by the old boardwalk. We drive to the mill and transfer beer, steaks, gear, food stocks, and backpacks into the trailer. Ed secures the mountain with ropes and drives off.

The three-wheeler strains heading up the switchback with the load. Dad and Ray strain as they walk behind, taking frequent stops for breath. We walkers pause halfway up the winding hill and rest on rocks at Thunder Creek. I point to the pinnacle rising from the falls. A gray bird, sized like a robin, alights. It bobs like it's rocking to a disco beat. Dad starts to murmur.

"Shh. Watch," I tell them. The bird plunges into the pool and forages underwater, turning over rocks. It emerges with a flapping larva. "It's feeding its young; it's a water ouzel, best known as a dipper for its bobbing behavior. It dips up to sixty times per minute. Sometimes it's called a water thrush, or *Turdus torquatus.* See where water's spraying off that rock pinnacle; that's where its nest is hidden. Some nests are in use for more than a century." The ouzel beelines behind the rocks, and emerges with empty beak. It wades back to the pool for more tidbits. "They have an oil gland by their tail that keeps feathers waterproof."

I remove the mug hanging on my pack, dip into the ouzel's pool, and hand it to Dad to drink. He hesitates. "It's pure," I assure him, "from mountain springs. We drink here all the time."

Ray takes a sip. "Best water I've ever had, the very best."

Ed vanishes over the crest. "We'd best keep going," I tell everyone. "We have to make it at least as far as Windy River. Ed will be able to pick up Dad and Ray there after he unloads." We stop frequently for rests and water. I check my watch, and try to hurry the men, but they're going as fast as possible. When we reach Windy, Ed is parked, waiting on the cabin side of the bridge. Bare logs span the rushing waters. Dad and Ray stare. "Can't Ed come get us and give us a ride across?"

"Too dangerous to cross with extras aboard. We have to cross on foot."

Guido steps first and takes Dad's hand; I follow behind holding the other. "Hi Ho, Hi Ho, across the bridge we go," I sing. We step over the expanse. Dad glances dizzily below. "Eyes up," I whisper. "Hi Ho, Hi Ho." We exhale a collective sigh as we exit onto terra firma. Ed returns for Ray; he and Hilde serve as crutches and confidence.

Safely across, the men chatter like songbirds, and excitedly mount the three-wheeler. Dad straddles behind Ed; Ray mounts behind Dad; they drive off. I walk with Hilde and Guido and Max.

At the cabin, Dad sheds worries like a dog sheds hair. The next day we all head out to fish. The three men pile on the three-wheeler, with Ray's crutches strapped on the front. I stride behind with Max and the Germans. At river crossings, the guys dismount. As Ray lifts his crutches in the current, they float, Ray wobbles. Ed grabs Ray's elbows to steady him. The men scream as Rocky River's ice water needles their flesh. The promise of salmon eggs them on. The fish hole becomes the elixir of youth. They stand on the ledge, staring into the pool. "Salmon," says Dad as he sees a shadow.

"Nah, only a Dolly Varden," counters Ed. "Now that shadow," he points, "is a salmon."

Dad's eyes stand on stalks. "Thought that was a boulder; it's huge."

Ed pulls pink pixie lures from his tackle box and sets the lines. The men cast; a salmon strikes. "Tip up," says Ed. "Keep it steady." Dad's eyes mist as he reels in his first Alaskan salmon. "The very best," Ray says again.

Back at the cabin, Guido hauls wood for the smoker while Ed guts salmon. Ray and Dad chip alder and cottonwood. Hilde and I marinate salmon steaks for supper.

Dad is excited I'm writing a book. "That's plantain by the door," I tell him.

"Plantain," repeats Dad with a French accent. "My mother used that when my brother got shot. We couldn't afford the doctor. She used that on the wound."

"Yarrow," I show Dad. "We use this to stop bleeding. It's *Achillea millefolium.*"

"*Mais oui, milfoil.* Thousand leaf. My mother used that too."

I'm flabbergasted. "But you and Mom never did anything herbal with us. I had no clue Grandmother Desclos was an herbalist."

"She died when I was still a boy; never did much with plants after that."

Ray, I notice, keeps rubbing his leg. "Problem?" I ask.

He lifts his pant leg. "Skeeters; must have scratched them."

His leg is red and swollen. "You need plantain." I soak *Plantago major* leaves in hot water to soften them, then mash them into a poultice and apply it to the wounds. I photograph the process for the book.

Dad picks goldenrod in the meadow for tonight's tea. I grab the Nikon again. By the river, Dad rests, and leans on grandfather spruce standing sentinel. I click again.

Ray and Dad joke constantly. Our faces have laugh cramps. By night, we play cards, sip Lite, and reminisce. "Remember Ray's bait business? Going to the country club after rainstorms to hunt night crawlers by flashlight?"

"And our fishing trips? Catching catfish by the full moon."

"Those horned pout were ugly as sin, but tastier than fried chicken."

"Nothing like Alaskan salmon, though." Ray dips again into the smoked salmon spread. "The very best."

We promise a final adventure before their departure, a trip to Marsha Million's. Marsha has agreed to transport us to Homer on *Harlequin,* her new water taxi, and to host us overnight beforehand.

"You built this house solo?" asks Ray incredulously. "Alaskan gals are awesome."

"Yes," Ed pipes in. "Alaska is where men are men, and women win the Iditarod."

"Marsha," I prod, "tell Dad and Ray some Toksook tales. And tell them about how you got your skiff."

We've laugh cramps, until departure. "Bad news," says Marsha. "Marine advisory. Can't cross the Bay. I'll drop you at Jakolof Bay dock. You'll have to get an air taxi in Seldovia." Even in Jakolof's protected waters, the boat leaps like a bronc, splattering icy spray. We're relieved to reach the dock; we cram into the Land Cruiser and drive. The Seldovia airport is closed; winds are too high to fly. We use the harbor pay phone, call airlines, change flights, and head to the local café for a consoling cuppa. "Now what?" Ed asks. "It's a long way back to Rocky River for a night's sleep."

"Hi Susan," I wave, as a friend enters.

"Dad, Ray, remember the Rowing Club Bed and Breakfast we saw along the old Seldovia boardwalk? That's Susan's. It was the first bed and breakfast in Southcentral Alaska."

During intros, Dad mentions our dilemma. "Stay at my place," she insists. "I've stayed at Rocky River before. What goes round comes round."

The men's eyes brighten as we step into her nautical Victorian world. "It's like a fairy tale," says Ray. "Featherbeds. Light-catchers. Vases of flowers. Susan's wonderful watercolors."

Their faces press to the window like kids at the zoo. "Otter," says Dad. "Soaring eagles," points Ray. Morning brings calm. Dad and Ray hug us, eyes soft. "I don't want to leave, Jan," Dad tells me.

"I know, Dad. You'll have to come back again."

"Once you've been to Alaska, Jean," adds Ed, "Alaska is always inside you. If you feel down, just remember: 'the very best.'"

Flashback ⟶

"Now I have to bring Mom to visit," I tell Ed, "and see what Alaska does for her."

"Tell me more about your Mom, Jan; you don't say much about her, or about your childhood."

"Where to start, Ed?"

"You said it was a piece of cake next to mine."

"Yes, but I didn't have yours to compare to at the time. The hardest part was around puberty."

"Usually is; all those raging hormones."

"But the hormones were Mom's. She was in perimenopause when she had her fifth and final baby, Jamie; he arrived November 15, my eleventh birthday. Everyone joked he was my present. I feel like my sisters and I nearly raised him."

"So Mom fell apart? Postpartum depression?"

"That's what the doctors thought at first, especially since her mom, my *mémère* Lagasse, had recently passed away. Docs told her to get plenty of rest and take some pills. Our home on Monroe Street became a cave. I'd get home from school to locked doors, drawn shades, and Mom scuffling around the house in the dark in a blue jumper. She wore that same blue jumper for over a month and never washed it or herself. She acted allergic to water. When we'd head off to school, she'd grab our arms and beg us not to go. We had to force food into her. We girls had to take care of the two babies and do all the cleaning and meals. Doris and Vivian, my older sisters, dropped Girl Scouts and all after-school activities. 'You kids have to help Mom through this,' insisted Dad.

"Then Mom turned into Cinderella and scrubbed the house top to tail. Windows gleamed. Floors glowed. Spices on the shelves stood at attention like little soldiers. She emptied closets, starched shirts, and tucked mothballs in nooks and corners."

"Good for you, Jan; that was a short crisis."

"If only; then Mom kept going. She started babbling about bones, stones, and ice cream cones; anything with rhythmic word associations. She got a job selling Amway and said she was going to be their top saleswoman and take us all to Europe. She started doing bizarre things, like taking clean clothes out of drawers and washing them; she would run the washer until three in the morning. She'd go on shopping sprees and come home with news. 'An in-ground pool is being installed next week; a new Studebaker is on order.' Then Dad would come home and pop the bubble. He took a week off, cancelled contracts, and regained control of bank accounts. But Mom had already flattened them in her mania.

"So Mom was shipped off to the state hospital in Concord. It was on Pleasant Street, but visiting her each Sunday was not a pleasant experience. We'd wade into a stark room and search for Mom. Everyone was in baggy dress, with glazed eyes like a landed trout. They wobbled like ducks, quacking gibberish, or they'd screech like banshees. It was a true-life cuckoo's nest."

Ed relights his pipe. "So what was the diagnosis?"

"Manic depression: alternating bouts of depression and euphoria. Docs said they'd set her right with electroconvulsive therapy. That's a fancy name for electroshock. They hitch electrodes to the temples and zap with 140 volts. ECT actually triggers grand mal brain seizures. Patients waken like Mom did, confused and with headaches, and missing chunks of memory. The most recent troublesome events go first, so patients often initially feel somewhat better, which Mom did for a while. She got discharged and came home."

"And then?"

"Began all over again, but worse; if Mom had a drink she'd fight like a tomcat. But when Dad refused her alcohol, she'd call the cops and tell them her husband was a rotten bastard who wouldn't give her a martini. The cops got so used to her calls they'd set down the phone while she ranted. Then one night we kids called. It took a while to convince them Mom was really hurling encyclopedias at Dad, and threatening to knife him. The cops escorted her to Concord. Docs did electroshock again."

"Barbaric," says Ed.

"With enough treatments, electroshock totally zaps memory. Events slowly return, but there are permanent gaps. And ability for new learning is permanently impaired. But Mom seemed to feel better again, and came back home."

"So life settled down?"

"For a bit. Then it was Bay of Fundy time again: hormones like Nova Scotia tides. Mom was shipped back to un-Pleasant Street, and to the newest miracle treatment: lithium. Mom felt so well she convinced herself she was better and stopped taking it. So back on the merryless-go-round for treatment. Docs restabilized her and shipped her back, with marching orders to stay on the meds. She was better, but flat, not the Mom we grew up with. She lived in la-la land, never quite herself, always thirsty, not hungry but gaining weight. Dad wigged out anytime she got a touch feisty, afraid it was happening again. They finally divorced. Mom is now living in state-subsidized housing. I wonder what a trip to Alaska would do for her?"

"One way to find out, Jan."

I hit the harbor pay phone and drop coins and call my sister Doris. "Mom go to Alaska?" Doris says. "There's no way she can travel on her own."

"I know Mom can't fly solo," I respond. "Let's think outside the box; how can we get her to Alaska? Can't someone travel with her?"

Ed finds the answer. I write my family excitedly. "Mom can come; she's going to be escorted by the police."

Mount Camille ⌒

The escort service is courtesy of Ed's friend Steve Unsworth who is keen for another Alaskan expedition. Steve delivers Mom to Homer, then heads off with Ed for halibut fishing; I head to Rocky River with Mom. She has been forewarned she'll have to walk, as I've never learned to balance the three-wheeler through the ravines.

Mom's gear is divided into my pack, and Max's. Mom carries only cigarettes and meds. We stroll along the flats past the mill, wind slower up the switchback, and rest at Thunder Creek. At Windy River crossing, Mom brakes like a mule, and balks at the log stringers.

"Hold my hand, Mom. We'll take it step by step."

"I can't."

"We have to, Mom."

"Can't."

"Can't stay here in the middle of nowhere."

Above us, dark clouds gather; a breeze stirs from the south. "Oh blast," I mutter. "Gulf squall en route."

"Come on," I plead with Mom. "Five steps, and you can have another ciggie."

Mom grabs my hand. We step one, step two. "See where the stringers come together like a platform? We'll stop there for your puff."

Mom lights up, drags deeply. I point at birds, distract her from the rapids below. "Okay? Five more steps. Eyes up," I remind her as we walk forward. Solid ground welcomes us. Mom celebrates with another smoko. We meander onward.

"Are we there yet?" asks Mom.

"Not far," I lie. We're barely halfway. Mom's steps slow like a kiddie crank-up toy that needs a wind. By the time we hit Wolverine Creek she's shaking like an aspen leaf. "Please God," I pray, "don't let her have a heart attack."

"Mom, how about a rest? Drink of water?" Mom lights up again. "Take my hand," I say. We balance on the single board spanning the creek and slowly cross. "The cabin is at the bottom of this slope."

Finally at the cabin, Mom collapses on our couch and lights another cigarette. I fling open the door to exit the smoke. Tomorrow I'll ask her to smoke outside. We sip tea and chat about childhood moments like the trips to Silver Lake to see our cousins.

"Mom, remember how I'd swim underwater and you'd scream."

"I was afraid you had drowned. I'm afraid of water over my head. *Mémère* was too."

Generational fear, I think. That's how it works, passing on like genes.

"Do you have any beans?" asks Mom. "I'll make you some tomorrow. And gorton too."

My mouth waters. I've not had gorton in years, a French-Canadian tradition in our family. "Remember the pork pies you'd make at Christmas? We kids couldn't say *tourtières* and called them *toot kays*. Can you make *toot kays* too?"

"We need pork butts for both."

"I doubt Seldovia will have any ground pork. But we could grind pork chops with the hand mincer."

I stroll with Mom along the river, picking wild salads and berries. Mom admires the mountain rising behind the cabin. "We'll call it Mount Camille," I tell her, "in your honor. Want to take a sauna?"

"Okay."

I stoke the stove and head to the riverside for wormwood. I fill the foot tub, for rinsing feet before entering the sauna, and set pans on the stovetop for hot water for bathing. An hour later, the sauna is hot. We strip in the dressing area and huddle on the benches. The heat frees memories; Mom chats about childhood in Nashua, New Hampshire, and about my *pépère*, Victor Lagasse, and his cigar-making and taxidermy hobbies.

"How did you meet Dad?"

"I was working in a bank; he was so handsome in his Air Force uniform. It was love at first sight," she sighs dreamily.

Sweat pours like a faucet. "Let's take a cold plunge in the river."

Mom balks.

"Okay," I tell her. "But you should close your pores. How about a cold splash?"

"Okay."

I grab the five gallon bucket of icy river water. Mom stands on the deck. I heave the bucket onto her. She screams.

"Want me to whip you with wormwood?"

"What?"

"Wormwood's a medicinal herb; whipping stimulates circulation and rewarms the body."

"Okay," she agrees, shivering.

I take the stalks of *Artemisia tilessi* and gently flog her back, arms and thighs. Then we dive back into the sauna for another round.

Pouring sweat again, we emerge. I do a quick dip, and return with another five gallons of water.

"Want me to splash you again?" I ask.

"Okay."

Mom hoots again. I flog her again with wormwood and step back into the hot box. Finally we're satiated, clean from inside out. We're ravenous for fresh salmon dinner and more of Mom's baked beans.

Ed and Steve are due to be picked up after their fishing trip. I ask, "Mom, do you want to walk with me or stay here?"

"Here." I leave Mom behind and walk to the mill for the van, then drive to Jakolof Bay to pick up Ed and Steve. The guys brim with fish tales; proof is in their packs. Before returning to Rocky, we run to Seldovia for pork and spices. Then Mom and I grind chops. I take notes as she prepares her family classic:

Mom's Gorton

Break 1 pound of ground pork into a saucepan. Add enough water to cover meat and simmer until cooked (about two hours), stirring occasionally. Add salt, pepper, and minced onion as it cooks. Season with cloves and cinnamon to taste. Skim fat. Remove from heat and let cool.

In the morning, we spread gorton on toast. Ed takes Mom for a three-wheeler ride to Fish Hole. She catches her first salmon. All week long she beams, inspired by the kudos, the cabin comforts, fresh air, and exercise. Like Dad before her, she's reluctant to leave Rocky. Steve dittos mom's sentiments. Steve pens in the guest book: "Thanks for another opportunity to share your special life. It is great fulfilling childhood dreams with my childhood friend and his very special lady."

Departure day brings us all to Seldovia airport. En route home we visit the Red Mountain postal shed. The mail brims with news. Brother Jim is coming to visit, along with three Yankee buds.

The Boys from Back East ⌒

"Book an air taxi in Homer," I write Jim. "Have it drop you at Kasitna Beach at low tide. Send a bush line with your estimated arrival time."

"Let's leave the three-wheeler and trailer home," suggests Ed. "Jim and his buds will be traveling light. And they're keen for adventure. Let's walk them into the valley."

"Great. They'll love stretching their legs after the long flights. It's awesome in the valley without motor noise."

We strike off from the cabin packless and gobble miles like peanuts. The track is dry, the skies clear, a fine valley day. As we near Kasitna Bay, a Cessna breaks the stillness. The commuter plane hurls toward the cliff, banks steeply, and swoops for touchdown. The guys exit white as chalk.

"Crazy," says Jim.

"Yeah, Crazy Larry's the pilot. Good though," says Ed.

"Thought we were hamburg when Larry went for the cliff."

"Standard landing approach, Jim; the pilots have to do a loop and scan the beach for flotsam and jetsam from each tide."

"My guts are looped too."

The gear parade begins. Jim and his friends Keith, Pete, and Gordon grab backpacks that soar like Mount McKinley. Attached with clips are barbecue grills, axes, bush knives, fishing poles, and machetes. "You're like Dad, Jim. You don't know what 'light' means. Hope you didn't bring a case of beer."

"Nah. That's silly. Only essentials."

"What do those packs weigh?" asks Ed.

"Eighty pounds or so; piece of cake." Jim reaches into the plane again.

"There's more?"

"Yep." Jim extracts a stack of flat white boxes.

"Look like pizza boxes."

"They are pizza boxes," says Jim.

"With pizzas?"

"Of course, and piping hot."

"We'll head to Steve Hughes for lunch. You have to meet our neighbor and check out the place he's building."

We hike the Jakolof Bay flats; the guys tug straps, adjust waist belts, and struggle to ease the strain of their load. We reach a clearing. "Drop the gear here; this way." We negotiate the log spanning the creek and melt into the forest jungle. The track is as skinny as a knife; stately shrubs lean inward for light. Jim swings at the plants.

"Damn thing bit me."

"Got more thorns than a cactus," adds Pete.

"Devil's club," I explain. "We'll give you a needle when we get to the cabin to extract the prickles. Otherwise they'll fester."

"I'm going back for the machete. Get rid of this shit."

"Steve will be pissed if you cut it; that plant is a kind of ginseng. It's great medicine. And it's not bothering anything. So long as you don't bump it."

"You're joshing us," says Gordon. "No one really lives back here. This is a big Alaskan joke."

"See that pile of rough-cut lumber?" says Ed. "Grab a few boards each; we'll cart them in to Steve; he is still under construction."

Jim holds up the pizza boxes and grins. "My hands are already full."

Our lineup of wood-bearing Sherpas emerges by the lake and dances across spruce slabs perched on pilings.

"Pizza," bellows Ed. "Pizza delivery."

Steve steps from the cabin and chortles as he spots the white boxes. "Stop, Jan," Steve yells. "Get the beer." I kneel on the board, reach into the net bag hanging in the feeder creek, and lift a six-pack of creek-chilled beer.

We pile on the deck, pile into pizza, and pile-drive the brews. The guys are awed at the hidden lake, hummingbirds darting at the feeder, the cabin Steve is constructing. We spin tales, feed bellies, then regroup with gear and grunt up the switchback.

"Don't step in the scat, Pete."

The guys poke at the pile of dung.

"Bears," recognizes Jim. "Oh shit."

"Yep, bear shit. Scat."

"I mean shit, no gun."

"We never carry one. Make noise." The dangling pack tools are like cymbals, enough ringing to drive every bear from the district. But the guys add catcalls and hooeys to the din. They power-walk noisily, determined to make it all look easy.

At the cabin, we settle in. With extra hands, chores are done swiftly: water hauled, wood-box filled. Tonight's meal is steak hauled from Homer. "From now on," I promise, "it's salmon."

"I drool like a baby thinking about it," Jim says.

"Rest well," we advise, as beds are assigned; two in the guest room, one on the couch, one on the floor. "Tomorrow we'll take you to Port Dick. But," Ed warns, "you'll want to lighten your packs."

"Nah; it's why we brought everything; we're ready for anything. Piece of cake."

Morning sends us gulfward. The guests are on foot, carrying clanging mountains; Ed bears his standard thirty-five-pound pack. I'm beaming, as I'm on my nifty new mountain bike, my gear strapped in its panniers. I reach Rocky River quickly and await helpers to ferry my bike across the rapids. Once across, my bike is out of sight before they've even reloaded.

It's easy cruising to the Port Dick pathway; I park in the alders, shift gear from panniers to backpack, and forage while I await rendezvous.

We all cross through clear-cut hell, collapse at the Port Dick cabin, fish 'til we drop, and sauna 'til we're raisins. The guys down sweets for treats; I secretly stockpile extras. Days later, they're chomping for a change of diet. Back through the bog and bears we hike, back through the cursed clear-cut to road's edge.

I've the sole grin; a ride home awaits on my sweet bike, with sweet treats. Every hundred yards, I brake and set leaves on rocks in the middle of the road. Atop the leafy platter I drop goodies: candies, chocolate, muesli bars, making a candyland road to the cabin. I giggle and can't wait to hear their stories of sweet surprise, hoping dearly that no hungry bear follows my wake.

At the river, I'm stymied. Currents are too swift for me to manage with my bike. If only . . . A splash grabs my attention; movement in the river. A hiker crosses toward me, stoops to reboot, and startles as I introduce myself. In broken English, he tells me he is Bernd, from Germany, going camping. "Could you please help me get my bike across?" I ask.

Bernd wades back into the rapids holding my bike aloft, as I traipse behind. He's shivering, and skinny as string. I nod to him to follow me. "Wormwood; whip," I demonstrate. "Get warm." I lean toward a thicket of salmonberries and hand him some. "Good to eat." He wolfs them down greedily. I point upriver, do a house pantomime, then wiggle my fingers like legs, and pat my stomach. "Come visit when you hike out."

At the cabin, I light the stove, launch a soup, tidy up, and await the return of the guys. I smirk, eager for the candy report. The men trundle in, silent about the surprise. I can't stand the suspense any longer. "How'd you like your sweeties?"

"What sweeties?" asks Ed, puzzled.

"Duh. The ones I left every hundred yards along the road, smack in the middle. There's no way you could miss them. Left about five dozen treats."

"There weren't any," insists Jim.

"You're kidding. Bet some blackie has a toothache by now."

"What about that German dude we met? The one in the berry bushes?" starts Keith.

"Looked awful sheepish," adds Gordon.

"More like he was hiding, not merely eating berries."

"The hiker?" I say. "He's the angel who helped me get my bike across Rocky River."

"Must have thought he was in heaven, finding all that candy."

"I've invited him to stop by for a meal."

"Can't wait to get hold of that creep."

"You guys need sweets bad."

"Great idea, Jan; we'll go to Seldovia. More sweeties."

"And a turkey," adds Keith. "Mmm, hot turkey with stuffing."

"And beer," pipes Jim. "My mouth's like cotton."

Their list grows. Before soup is even ready, Keith and Pete are town-bound for supplies. They stall at the local watering hole, the harborside Linwood bar, and catch a large Alaskan buzz. Their partner in drink is Steve Hughes, who is also in town on a grocery run. They swap stories and laugh like hyenas.

"Best get back," they decide.

As Keith and Pete pass Red Mountain junction, a roar shatters the valley serenity. They jump aside as a bee-yellow maniac zooms by on a motorbike and caroms into the alders. Steve Hughes emerges from the brush, belly-laughing. "I can't miss that turkey. Have to see what Jan and Ed are up to."

The three arrive full of Seldovia spirits and town tales. Pete describes a gal in heels and finery. "Keith was kind of giving her the eye, then he realized she was no lady."

"The town cross-dresser," Ed says. "Great person, and very civic minded.

Simply likes to get dressed up now and then. No one seems to mind."

"I felt like a turkey making eyes at a guy," says Keith.

"Not surprised, he's better with makeup than I am," I reply. "Now, speaking of turkey. . . ." The cabin becomes an aromatherapy center, emanating scents of roasting turkey and baking bread. As all nears perfection, we hear a timid tap.

Pete answers. "You!" he yells.

"The sweet thief," screams Keith.

Gordon grabs Bernd's sleeve. "Get in here. Sit." Steve sticks a cold beer in his hand and sets another plate on the round-spool table. Bernd is shell-shocked: the cabin aromas, all the bodies, the cold brews.

We stuff ourselves with Thanksgiving favorites. Pete's finale is a mulled berry drink, "Gagne's Grog," he tells me. "All the berries you gathered on the way home, Jan, simmered to juice, with a bit of honey, cinnamon, and a nip of rum."

"Weren't you planning to make pie with those, Jan?" asks Ed.

"This is liquid pie, Ed. And a must for the book," I insist. "But perhaps I'd best test again." The cabin reverberates with laughter. Then the floor swells with bodies; Bernd and Steve join the sleepover.

At departure time, all sign the guest book. My brother Jim writes: "Words cannot describe the way I've felt since we landed here. I wish I could find a way to bottle this feeling and take hits off it whenever it's needed. Only one taste of it and I'm an Alaskaholic. I couldn't believe my eyes when I saw all these salmon in the river. That type of fishing has always been a dream of mine. And I've never seen so many friendly people in all my life."

Keith adds his thank you: "You have given me a whole new outlook on a different type of life. I am so happy—really happy—finally. Yeah!"

Ed and I are happy too. New friends remind us of the wonder of the wild river we drink from, the salmon in the pools, the world we call home.

Christmas Cheer ⌒

First frosts hurry us to Homer; Ed's task is interior cabinetry in both Charlotte's cabin and Gardensong. Mine, again, is doing edits. Summer field trials alter recipes; there are appendices, credits, and the book's index to craft as well as products to prepare for Christmas fairs and family gifts.

Ed's sister Anne always does the twelve days of Christmas; each December, two cartons arrive, chock-full of gifts, tree ornaments, note-paper, homemade cookies, wool socks, sweaters, and quality housewares. Santa Anne even remembers Maxwell with chewie toys and treats. Near Anne's Maine home, bargain outlets cluster like beehives: L. L. Bean, Patagonia, the Gap, Banana Republic. Anne stuffs her Santa sleigh with factory closeouts. Homer's shops, meanwhile, offer wallet-challenging artisan originals. We double-check our list: twelve goodies for Anne, gifts for our moms, and for my dad, siblings, nephews, and nieces. Slowly, our boxes fill with Rocky River Grizzly Balm, massage oil, herb tea, lotion, bath salts, syrups, and jams, plus home-smoked salmon and Ed's cotton-wood bark carvings.

Mossy's winter solstice party is a potluck feast of salmon and moose steaks and wild berry deserts. The music is live, with guitar duets by Mossy and her brother Atz, songs by her sister Sunrise, and a yodeling solo by Jewel.

Christmas day will be at Rocky River with buddies Marina, Glen, and Doug. We cross the bay on the *Water Rat* and transfer goods to the three-wheeler's trailer. "Hope the tires don't blow," says Ed. "That trailer is fuller than a tick on a hound-dog's back."

Washouts spin trouble; the trailer's tires free-wheel. Ed applies more throttle. The rubber grabs. The trailer totters like a town drunk and wobbles its way to the summit. Ed finally disappears from sight. We meander slowly on foot. With each mile, worries melt. The Windy sings her river-song. Glenn points to tracks in the mud where the creek skips across the road: lynx.

Past the alders, smoke rises from the chimney. Ed already has the barrel stove roaring in welcome. Glenn heads to the woodpile to split spruce to refill the wood box. Doug fills water jugs. I prep pie crust while Marina starts moose stew. "Where'd you get the moose, Marina?"

"Road kill. Had a call from the troopers to salvage a cow moose that got hit by McNeil Canyon. About five hundred moose fatalities this year statewide from cars; we were lucky to get on the register to get one."

Ed puts away supplies and lights candles for the chefs. A new smell enters the cabin potpourri: moose stew, spruce resin, blueberry pie and . . . the musky aroma of cannabis. Ed passes the pipe. "Bit of blaze, Jan?"

I inhale deeply. "Bit different here than New Hampshire; all that Yankee 'live free or die' bull, when all the time they'd rather die than allow freedom to choose. Alaska's so much saner. Here we can smoke pot legally in the privacy of our home."

"To Alaska," puffs Glenn.

"And friends," adds Doug.

The pipe passes, tongues wag, bellies laugh.

"We need a Christmas tree," says Marina. "Let's go shopping."

"The cabin's small; I don't want one too broad."

"Hate to cut a prime spruce," says Ed. "Let's find a spot where trees need thinning."

Our driveway is lined with alders with volunteer spruce emerging in the understory. "How about that one?" I ask.

"Puny," says Glenn.

"Not very well shaped," adds Doug.

"Perfect," proclaims Ed. "It's dying for want of light and space. It'll tuck right into the corner of the cabin sweet as pie."

Ed gets his way. The guys build a stand to hold the scrawny tree. Meanwhile, Marina and I pop corn in the cast iron skillet. We douse one batch with melted butter, salt, and nutritional yeast, and Rocky River Land-and-Sea-soning. We nibble popcorn as we string unflavored kernels on fishing line, interspersed with red rosehips. Spruce cones become hanging ornaments. We cut aluminum foil into strips for tinsel.

Ed opens the door to toss the old maids to the Steller's jays. "It's snowing," he announces. "A picture-perfect Christmas."

Presents pile under the tree and stack high on the counter. "Whose is that?" asks Marina, pointing to the biggest box, slathered with postage stamps.

"Check it out," I say. She holds the box to the candle light: *To Max Schofield, Red Mountain Alaska.*

"It's from Max's buds in Washington, D.C.; he's got quite the fan club from when we last road-toured."

On Christmas morning, Max grabs his parcel and starts the show. He hooks a tooth into the fold of the paper and lets it rip; a chewie bone sized like a dinosaur rib rolls out.

We delight in our treasures, perfect bush-living gifts: outdoor wear, headlamps for night skiing, and a Cognac for warming winter nights.

Christmas present quickly fades to Christmas past. "Hate to get back to work," moans Marina. "My office at City Hall doesn't even have a window. It's dark when I start work, and dark when I leave."

"I'd best not complain then about a bit of editing. Sometimes I feel in a tunnel with the book, but I do get to see the light of day."

We head Homerward with a lighter trailer and bodies stuffed with turkey and treats. The three-wheeler tows the trailer effortlessly through the new snow. As we climb the divide between the watersheds, snow climbs from ankles to knees. At the pass, drifts rise mid-thigh. The bike stalls. We split forces, half pushing, half towing. Every foot gained is tedious and painful.

We've far too much gear to abandon the bike, and no packs to carry it all. We had glibly expected the weather to hold. Our only option is to push on, step by grueling step. "I'm hotter than a pig on a barbecue," says Ed.

"Me too." As I speak, wind rustles from the south. "Crap." I grow anxious, knowing hypothermia now stalks us. As we push on, light fades, and the wind gains intensity. "What I'd give for a nap," I say.

"Don't you dare, Jan. We have to keep going."

"I'm so tired."

"Soon we'll be out of this; starting to drop elevation now."

At the mill, the road is passable. We pile back in the trailer atop our gear. The bike revs to life and speeds on. The *Water Rat* sits at the dock, crusted with snow. Snow is falling again, whiteout conditions.

"We'd best spend the night on the boat," says Ed. He points to the sardine-can bunks.

"It's as cold as a fridge in here."

The noise of a motor carries across the water. The sound grows in intensity. "Who can be out on a night like this?"

Round Two ⌒⋅

"Halloooo," resounds on the water, drifting through the storm. "You folks okay?"

The voice is familiar; it's Marsha. I holler back. The *Harlequin* emerges and Marsha ties up to the *Rat*. "I heard voices over here and decided to check things out."

"We're fine, Marsha. Weather's too bad to cross; we'll spend the night on the *Rat*. What are you doing out in the whiteout?"

"Christmas at the Christians'. Come join in. Stay at my place afterwards, if you don't mind the floor."

"Will it be okay? The Christians don't know we're coming. And we've nothing baked."

"No problem, I've heaps. Hop in my skiff." We pile aboard. Marsha motors slowly, struggling to discern sea from shore.

Christmas lights in Little Tutka Bay welcome us like a lighthouse beacon. Marsha sets out fenders and ties up. Floating sections of dock sway in the sea; Ed steadies me as we bob our way to shore. Steep stairs lead to a hot, bright room. The cabin is chockers with bodies, the tables with food. Kids race on Christmas adrenalin and adult voices babble over the din. Carols play in the background. Heavenly smells waft around us: prime rib roast with Yorkshire pudding, wild mushroom gravy, stuffed silver salmon, bear stew.

We feast, chat, and catch up on community happenings. We meet the Osgoods, who've opened a wilderness lodge at the headlands between Big and Little Tutka Bays. Live carols drown out chats.

"On the first day of Christmas, my true love gave to me . . ."

The sea of voices bellow local answers: ". . . a spruce hen in a spruce tree . . . two Steller's jays . . . three salmon swimming . . . four wild geese a laying . . . five gallon buckets."

We collapse with laughter. "Hey Ed, wonder if six rolls of Visqueen are up next?"

"And seven rolls of duct tape?"

Joy floats through the room. We sip Marsha's cranberry cordial and let out belts a notch. We're stuffed with contentment.

"Sauna's hot," announces our host. The mob heads for the hot box. Another Christmas potpourri blasts our senses: spruce wood, human sweat, steamy eucalyptus. My head reels, dizzy with drink, dazed by the changing of our worlds. We were sweating from struggle hours ago in icy wind and are now happily wet again, this time from turkey-baking temps.

The dessert table is like a casino buffet. Ed's eyes glow like a jackpot machine. Rows of pies line up: pumpkin, apple, and our favorite, Jakolof Bay blueberry.

Morning at Marsha's home starts with blip-blip sounds and espresso aromas. We jump-start with a stout Euro-style cuppa laced with fresh cream. She piles porridge into pottery bowls; oats swim with raisins, nuts, brown sugar, and cream.

My eyes fog as we turn tail for Homer. Ed notices.

"What's the matter, honey; why so glum?"

"Work time again, Ed. That's fun, too, but this is so very special. Hate to see it end."

Trail of Blood ∽

Back at Gardensong in Homer, we resume tasks. Ed splits firewood while I strip varnish from my heirloom wood icebox. Stew is on the boil atop the Vermont Castings woodstove. Max woofs for entrance. His stump tail wags; his eyes gleam like glowing coals.

"Did you see something interesting in the pawprint news, Max?" I ask him. "Or was there another spruce hen in the yard?" In answer, he flops on the sheepskin rug by the fire and emits his catlike purr. I smile. "You're such a teacher, Max," I babble on, "content wherever you are."

My attention shifts. Another layer of varnish yet to strip. Memories peel as I work, remembering this very icebox at Dad's woodland camp. The background noise alters. I spin about and freeze like a deer in car headlights.

Max's stomach is bloated. "Oh Maxie, have you done it again? Eaten my bread dough? But I haven't made bread today." I kneel at his side. "Belly ache? Did you get in the compost?"

Max moans and extends his legs. They remain rigid. I stroke his body.

His body temperature ebbs and his flesh stiffens to glacial cold. Ed enters, sees me by the corpse, eyes in flood tide. "Oh Janzie. I'm so sorry." He crouches and wraps me in a hug, his eyes moist. We sit, numbly stroking the deceased dog. Noise intrudes.

"Where's that humming coming from?" I ask irritably.

"I don't hear anything. Folks up the way with their stereo blasting?"

"More like church music. And the volume's still going up."

"Still don't hear anything. But I'm deafer than a haddock."

"Max's body feels warmer," I say.

"And softer."

Max's eyes flutter open. He shakes, struggles to his feet, and waves his tail. Ed gapes. "Woo woo," he says, Ed's succinct code for the unexplainable. I nod in agreement.

In the morning, Max bounces in the snow, hard at play, but halfway into our walk, he collapses. Ed races home for the sled; we ferry Max back, and head to Ralph Broshes's office, our vet since seal days. The verdict is grim: abdominal bleeding, borderline anemia, cloudy X-rays. All are signs of tumors of the spleen. "These meds," says the vet, "will help reduce inflammation. You may want to contemplate surgery."

The meds give Max a reprieve. He begs for his daily walk. "Beach?" I ask him. It's his favorite. Max darts after seagulls and sniffs tidal treasures. He returns to me bearing a prize, an old cow hoof. As he begins to gnaw, blood spurts profusely from his mouth. I load him into the van, race to the vets.

"Another symptom of tumors," proclaims Ralph. "This makes Max's surgery risks extreme." He prescribes more medications.

"What do we do now?" Ed asks.

"Wish we knew the answer. Now I wonder . . ."

"Uh-oh, better light my pipe. What are you thinking now?"

"Remember Ellie Vande Visse from Palmer, whom I met when I was doing plant interviews around the state?"

"The lady who went to Findhorn community in Scotland to learn how to communicate with nature spirits?"

"Uh-huh. I wonder if she can talk with dogs. It'd be great to know what Max wants to do."

"Give it a go, Jan. Anything's worth a try."

I call Ellie in Palmer (an hour north of Anchorage). She is keen for a visit to Homer, and an opportunity for interspecies communications. While she regroups from her six-hour drive, we chat about her new organic market garden. "I do all my gardening like we did at Findhorn," she says. Findhorn, founded in the sixties, became world-famous because of its huge vegetables grown in windswept sand. "What made Findhorn unique," Ellie tells me, "is that the founders gardened by asking the plants themselves what they needed."

"And you do all your gardening by talking to plants?" I ask.

"Yes, there's intelligence in all of nature. Dorothy Maclean, one of Findhorn's cofounders, used her intuition to contact plant intelligences that she called devas, another name for angels."

"So they're like guardian angels for plants?"

"Yes, and there are devas for animals too; every species on earth has devas."

"And you can communicate with these devas? You must be psychic."

"Oh no," laughs Ellie. "This requires no special skills, only a willingness to listen and a desire to communicate. In the morning when I'm fresh, we'll do a tune-in to find out more about what Max needs."

As we head to bed, blood seeps from Max's lip. Whimpers wake us at 4 A.M. We dash downstairs.

"Max's bed is soaked red."

"But his lip is dry now," says Ed. "He seems okay."

"Wonder what he saw? He's not a barker."

"Think it was the death angel?"

"Maybe. Certainly hope Ellie has some answers."

Tune-in ⁓

After breakfast, Ellie prepares. "We'll both tune in, Jan, and ask Max's angel to reveal his needs."

"I'll help if I can, but I don't know how effective I'll be. You're the one skilled with this."

"Everyone can do it. All you need is intention and willingness to listen. Not everyone gets words; some get pictures or automatic writing. Often I hear musical soundtracks. Don't discount anything. Take notes on whatever impressions you get. We'll put the pieces together afterward."

We sit in silence, breathe deeply. "Love and light," Ellie begins, "overlighting angel of dog beings, our highest selves, Max's highest self. We are here on behalf of Maxwell. We ask for guidance as to his highest good. How can Janice and Ed assist him at this time?"

"This is stupid," I think. I notice my thought, and breathe into my resistance. My heel itches; I reach down and scratch it. Heel. Heal. Words jump in my head like popcorn in hot oil. Heel. Achilles heel. *Achillea.* Yarrow. "Yarrow," I write. "Hmm, staunch-wort. Stops bleeding. That's logical."

I follow the popping thoughts. My pen doodles hearts. Hearts? Yarrow and what? What plant has hearts? Shepherd's purse does. Another styptic plant, its heart-shaped pods shout its presence.

"What did you get, Jan?" Ellie asks.

"Herbs: two herbs that are high in vitamin K to help with Max's clotting problems. And you?"

"A song verse; it kept repeating over and over:

This old man, he played nine,
He played knick knack on my spine,
With a knick knack paddywack, give this dog a bone . . ."

"What's that supposed to mean, playing knick knack on a spine?"

"Maybe a chiropractor? Let's ask more about your herbs, Jan, to check if your images are correct, and if so how to dose Max."

Ellie addresses the devas again. This time my hand races across the page: "Yes, both yarrow and shepherd's purse are appropriate for Max, as well as red clover. Make a strong tea and add half a cup to his food and water."

"All I heard, Jan, was the melody repeating. I felt like I was being a support to help your connection be strong. Now unless you've more questions, let's thank the devas and end the connection."

We hang up the phone line to devic realms, brew water for human and doggie teas, and have a farewell lunch. Ellie has a long drive back to Palmer; I've a town trip at hand for red clover from Homer Natural and inquiries into chiropractors. I schedule an appointment with one and launch Maxwell's newest program.

As days and chiropractic adjustments pass, Max bounces with vitality. We forget his problems; our own life is a mess. Ed has gutted Gardensong's makeshift kitchen. The workbenches have shuffled to the dining nook. A camp stove sets on plywood atop two sawhorses. Dishes and pots pile in boxes. Upstairs, it's equally messy. Book notes strew across the floor. "I'll make you a built-in desk, honey; you'll have wall-to-wall files," Ed promises. "As soon as I finish the kitchen."

"Oh Ed, I know you'll do it when there's time, but you're flat out with the kitchen cabinetry. I'm overwhelmed with the book deadline, and it's so hard to work in these conditions."

Ed returns from his hardware run, beaming. "Grab your book notes, Jan; we're moving. Wait 'til you see your new office."

The Vision ⁓

Home, for the next two months, is a seaside octagon house ten minutes from Gardensong. The owners are "outside" in Arkansas and Missouri buying antiques for their business. I've spacious tables to spread my notes, bay vistas for inspiration, and an in-house landline to the publisher. Steps away is a secluded beach for Max's daily play.

As our projects progress, Max's play dwindles. He grows listless, and thrusts his body between my hands and moans.

"Damn cancer must be back."

"Remember that healer you called when Mossy was going to put Surprise down?"

"Jack Epperson. I forgot about him." Jack answers my plea. He places his hands a foot apart above Max's sides. "Feel, Jan, like this." I mirror Jack's movements. My palms burn like fever.

"That's inflammation," says Jack. He stops talking and rests his hands on Max's belly. Max purrs contently. Twenty minutes later Jack has me feel again. I hold my hands as before. "Cool as the inside of a cucumber. How'd you do that?"

"It's love energy. It's the same energy Jesus ran, only he was a master. But mothers run it automatically every time their baby falls. They rub the booboo and it feels better. You can do this too; hold Max with love energy."

A week later, the newest vet tests return. The vet is bewildered. There are no signs of internal bleeding, no anemia. All is normal or above.

We drive to Gardensong daily to work. Today I'm putting the finishing touches of varnish on the icebox. Ed has spread natural oil with Varethane on the newly installed spruce-slab countertops. The house reeks fumes; doors are open wide for ventilation.

Ed dashes to town for more building supplies. I take a tea break by the roaring woodstove, on the sheepskin rug, and stroke Max's belly. The fire flickers gently through the glass plates of the Vermont Casting's doors. An image shimmers: a lane of fire, twenty feet of glowing coals. My brain splits and wrestles with my sight. There's me, fascinated by the fire-show; and me, the disbeliever, clambering to make sense. The image persists and fogs only with footsteps on the deck.

"Ed."

"You're pale, Jan; what's the matter?"

"Fire."

"Here? You put it out?"

"No, I saw fire, like a lane of hot coals."

"Must be the fumes, Jan. Maybe we'd best call it a day, and get back to the octagon while everything airs."

The next day I drive to the library for more research material. I flip through the bin of best bets, and add a book by a New Mexico acupuncturist to my pile of takeouts. After dinner, we sit and read. I flip randomly through the book, and freeze. Ed glances up. "What, Jan? See a ghost?"

I hand him the book.

"Firewalking? Is this what you saw yesterday?"

I nod.

Marina arrives and interrupts our chat. We set a date to blend herbs for our newest seasoning. "I almost forgot," she says, as she goes to depart. She rummages in her car and picks up a book. "Check it out, Janzie; I think you'll like this. This guy Robbins teaches NLP."

"What's that, a National Leadership Program?"

"No," she laughs. "NLP stands for neuro-linguistic programming; it's about repatterning nerves and creating new habits and beliefs."

I dive into the book, fascinated by how fat, bankrupt Tony Robbins changed his life, health, and fortune with his NLP exercises. I flip pages, then stop and scowl.

"What's up, Jan?"

"It says that Robbins teaches people to walk on fire. Bizarre how it keeps coming up. That vision with Max, the book from the library, and now this."

"Think you're being prepared for something?"

"Remember all those other weird things I thought were premonitions? Nothing came of the cry of the forest or my stalking hawk and eagle gifts. Mere chance. I wonder if this really means something or if it's simply another dead end?

U Turn ~·

The next day, Ed drives to Homer to make a bank withdrawal. "Your account is empty," the teller tells him.

"Can't be," Ed argues. "I've saved all the money from my sourdough sales. Haven't taken anything out."

"Zero balance," she insists, as she scrutinizes the computer records. "It was taken out by the Internal Revenue Service."

Ed vents like a volcano and fumes about the unfairness of Infernal Revenue grabbing his money. "You need Rocky River," I tell him. "Go take a weekend and unwind. I'll stay here and work on my book."

Ed goes across the bay. With no construction dust happening, I hang out at Gardensong. Friends well know our faint track across the meadow, the planks through the swamp, and the weave through the alders to our cabin tucked into the furthest corner of the property. Our home is like a home in the Russian community. Friends walk in without knocking. But today the door reverberates. Max lets out an uncharacteristic growl. I glance to the window. "Relax, Max. Men in suits. Must be Mormons with some Godtalk."

As I open the door, Max rushes forward, his pointed nose thrust to crotches. I grab his collar and glance down, into black shoes so shiny I can a silver reflection. Badges.

"IRS. We're looking for Ed Schofield."

"He's not here," I stammer.

My heart roils like a roller coaster, one that's derailed.

"Where is he?"

". . . ah . . . uh . . . Red Mountain."

Oh Godmother, why'd I say that? Put the tax bloodhounds on Ed's scent to Rocky River.

Later, we hear from Herb that two men in Brooks Brothers suits wandered up Red Mountain valley. We can only imagine their long climb up the switchback and the six mile tramp through washouts to Herb's trailer and beefalo cows. They don't find Ed. But what we find in the mailbox is a letter. I grab it before it becomes fire starter. "The IRS is threatening to take our property. We need help, Ed. This is serious."

"See Judy Lund," friends tell us. "She's an accountant. Judy used to work for the IRS. She'll know what to do."

Judy coaches us how to respond to restore harmony with the IRS. Ed reenters the tax system. I sigh in relief.

Crossing the Divide ⁓

Spring brings a return to the growing comforts of Gardensong and to cabin routines. Twice weekly we fill five-gallon buckets with free water from the grocery store spigot. We cleanse daily via sponge baths at the sink. Once each week we visit the Laundromat; while our clothes wash we freshen our bodies in the back room with a four-dollar "family" shower.

"Gads, I miss Rocky River."

"Me too, Jan. The music of the river, the magic of the valley."

". . . the magic of the sauna. A sauna would be so nice here in Homer."

"Someday. I'm too busy now."

"But I'm finished with the icebox project. What if I build one? All you need do is coach."

I draw up plans for an eight-by-eight insulated wooden box, and order rough-cut timbers for a deck, walls, and roof. Stick by stick, I haul supplies to our eastern boundary. I heft the generator and Skil saw into the wheel barrow and wheel it across the field.

The generator purrs into action, signaling Ed the way a food gong signals a crew. He races to the scene, takes out his pipe, tamps tobacco, and watches. I wrinkle my nose at my first cut. "Oops, not quite square."

"Here, like this, Janzie." Ed takes the saw, and corrects my cut. He powers through the next two-by-six, and the next. Without a word, our roles revert.

Ed is at home as master builder. I'm well-practiced at board's end. With him at the helm, our sauna progress steams ahead. We raise the walls, frame the roof, insulate, and install windows. We add vents for circulation, build the door, and line walls with fragrant cedar. In the center of the room, we install a made-in-Minnesota sauna stove; its sides and top widened for filling with rocks. The day of christening arrives. Friends launch a Gardensong tradition of communal Sunday saunas. All bring a dish for a potluck and come for a sweat.

With sauna functioning, and book progressing, life feels sumptuous. Our only damper is Max's growing distress. His pains grow more frequent and crushingly intense. He thrusts himself between my hands several times daily.

"We can't let him suffer, Janzie," Ed says.

I take Max for a walk in the spruce. I blather freely, thanking Max for his time in our life. "You lucky dog; your life has had more adventures than many humans. And you've been such an unconditionally loving friend."

He stares back at me. I swear he knows. And I know too. It's time. We drive Max to town and hold him in our arms in the van. The vet joins us. Max purrs contentedly when the killing thumb slides forward. He sighs and relaxes.

We drive home, eyes like burst water pipes. Ed builds a wooden coffin while I assemble Max's toys and find a comforter to line the box. We dig a hole on the knoll above the pond. Ed reads Mary E. Frye's classic 1930s bereavement poem, "Do Not Stand at My Grave and Weep."

> Do not stand at my grave and weep;
> I am not there. I do not sleep.
> I am a thousand winds that blow.
> I am the diamond glints on snow.
> I am the sunlight on ripened grain.
> I am the gentle autumn rain.
> When you awaken in the morning's hush
> I am the swift uplifting rush
> Of quiet birds in circled flight.
> I am the soft stars that shine at night.
> Do not stand at my grave and cry;
> I am not there. I did not die.

Despite the gentle words, we weep. The loss is crushing. Our next Sunday sauna is extra hot. I struggle to dry the grief that splashes like rogue waves.

My spirits lift when Sue Christiansen, my friend since Swift Creek times, arrives. Sue is so upbeat, always reminding me of the importance of following my joy. But tonight, even Sue isn't herself. She must be dampened by my sads.

Post sauna, I'm busy arranging platters of food on the spruce countertop when Sue says grimly, "Have you heard the news about Rocky River?"

"What news? Did something happen to the cabin?"

"No, the cabin's fine."

"Then what?"

"KBBI aired that the Seldovia Natives sold timber rights. All the old growth across the bay and the trees at Rocky River are going to be clear-cut."

PART FOUR

Devil's club
(Oplopanax horridum)

*"I speak on behalf of the ancient ones.
The life of the tree is the life of the people."*

Axing News ~

The news rips my guts; my knees wobble. Rocky River? Clear-cut?
I imagine Grandfather Tree, a waterfall sentinel for over three centuries,
falling to an ax. I see our forest turned to slash, salmon waters silted and
barren. I rant against logging, greed, and shortsightedness.

"Didn't you say you'd logged your land back in New Hampshire?"
asks a new sauna visitor. "How can you possibly be anti-logging?"

"Yankees selectively harvest trees like garden veggies," answers Ed.
"They cull only the largest hardwoods that are in danger of getting red-
heart-rot at the core. Every ten years you get a harvest."

"New saplings and wildflowers sprout in the light patches," I add.
"And deer and other wildlife browse all the new growth. Everything thrives
because of the selective logging."

"And the wood is all processed locally by little mom-and-pop mills.
But Alaska rapes and pillages its forests," continues Ed, "cuts the whole
damn forest down, and sells it on to Japan. Then we buy it back as plywood or chipboard."

"Everybody gripes about the Amazon rain forest," I say, "and raping it
to grow beef for burgers. But this is the same thing. The forest across the
bay is old-growth temperate rain forest. It can never be replaced. And it's
not solely the forest that's ruined. Those slopes are steep. Cut those trees,
and with the Gulf of Alaska rains the rivers and creeks will be sewers,
filled with silt running off the hills. There won't be a salmon left in the
whole area. They can't spawn in silt."

"But they clear-cut for a reason," protests our guest.

"Money," responds Ed. "We need a bigger picture than money pock-
eted for today; we have to look at the impact on coming generations.
Now down in New Zealand, there are sustainable tree farms; you can

harvest foot-diameter trees every twenty years. Do you know how long it takes to grow a spruce that big in Alaska? Over a century. If you clear-cut Alaskan old growth, even your great-grandkids won't get a harvest."

Ed turns to me, pain tensing his face. "How can anyone do this, Jan? Destroy a world-class resource like Rocky River?"

"How can this be?" we quiz Sue. "The Natives do own the timberlands at Rocky River, but across Kachemak Bay is state park land, isn't it? How can they sell trees in the park?"

"Be at Bidarka Inn tomorrow at the lunch meeting," she answers. "It will explain the situation, and how the Natives ended up with in-holdings, private lands within state park boundaries."

"How many in-holdings do they have?"

"Twenty-five thousand acres from the Island Peninsula near Halibut Cove to Tutka Bay."

"That's nearly the entire Homer viewshed."

"Yep, the view that wooed us all to stay, the one that hits you like Cupid's arrow. Sight of the most beautiful place in the world."

I grab for a seat, still reeling. I'm doubly devastated. Max's death. And now Armageddon for the bay. All this beauty to be laid waste, ruined forevermore. All for the sake of a one-shot cash infusion to one small group of folks. It isn't fair. It can't be.

Our guest departs. Ed pours a stiff brandy. I take a pull. "The cry of the forest," I say. "Maybe I really did hear it."

"Why you?"

I shrug my shoulders. "Why anyone?"

"You love this land so passionately, Jan. Maybe love is the communication link. Don't you wonder sometimes, Jan, if there isn't some loving force, call it God or Spirit or Universal Intelligence, that watches over us? And that knows what's coming in our lives and sends us messages to prepare us?"

"Certainly feels that way," I pause. "There's been so many weird happenings that felt like premonitions. And the timing is so strange, with Max dying, creating a void. Maybe this is our firewalk: getting involved in politics, doing what we can to resolve this environmental nightmare. Maybe this is what it's all about."

"You're right, Jan. We have to get involved. And it's time . . ."

"Time?"

"Yes, time to get a telephone."

Into the Fry Pan ⟿

Long-faced locals pack the meeting at the Bidarka Inn. Fisherman Ken Castner leads the meeting and provides the backstory; we time-travel to 1971 and the passage of ANCSA, the Alaska Native Claims Settlement Act. The bill, he tells us, was signed into law by President Nixon to resolve aboriginal land claims in Alaska. ANSCA gave Natives title to forty-four million acres, a ninth of the state, and cash compensation of over nine hundred million dollars. Twelve regional Native corporations and two hundred village corporations were created to administer and oversee the settlements.

Ken explains, "Locally, Seldovia Natives applied for Jakolof Bay lands, and got its selection nixed by the state of Alaska. Their next choice was thirty thousand acres in and adjacent to Kachemak Bay State Park. At that point, the park was merely theoretical. The land was still owned by the federal government. The Native claim took precedence over the State of Alaska's claim for parkland."

The meeting's goal is to form a coalition of citizens, united in efforts to permanently secure the heart of Kachemak Bay State Park. "We need to get the State of Alaska, Seldovia Native Corporation, and the timber corporation to the negotiating table," Ken says.

I raise my hand. "What about the forests of Rocky River?"

"Rocky River and the Island Peninsula forests are outside Park boundaries," Ken replies. "They will have to be addressed by other means."

"What other means?" I ask.

Ken shrugs.

The meeting is the beginning of a citizen mobilization. A name for our group is chosen: Kachemak Bay Citizen Coalition (KBCC). Ken asks for volunteers to cochair the Coalition.

I raise my hand to ask what a cochair is.

"Nominated," says a voice in the crowd.

"I second the motion," echoes another.

I look at Ed, eyes wide, mouth gaping like a trout snatching a fly.

"Do we have another volunteer for cochair?" Ken continues. Roberta Highland, one of the realtors who helped us find our Gardensong land, deliberately raises her hand.

I second the motion, relieved to have a partner. But I feel dazed. What am I getting into? Ed has warned me time and again: "Stay out of politics, Jan. The way to change the world is to change our world."

But now our world and others' world have collided. Perhaps there's no separation after all. I feel catapulted from a cannon, from Rocky River recluse into frontline advocate. The meeting ends. Roberta and I stay behind for more briefings with Ken. I struggle to memorize the players and untangle the script.

Twentieth-Century Times ⌁

For the first time in seven years, we've a landline, a direct telephone link to the outside world. The telephone at Gardensong teleports us, warping serenity and seclusion. The ringing becomes like the barking of noxious dogs. But despite the disruptions, we're glad for the tool, so essential for the work at hand.

Roberta and I split the task lists. We call legislators and talk until we're hoarse. We chat with the timber company, the Native Association, the Department of Natural Resources. We go to meeting after meeting after meeting.

The phone drags the state-capital politics of Juneau home to the dinner table. Work with the Coalition devours time the way bears gobble berries. There is endless research; getting up to speed on MOUs (memorandums of understanding); studying timber plans. We orchestrate mailings, diddle with details.

Life is a never-ending list of "to do's":

- place ad in the *Anchorage Daily News*
- place ad in *Homer News*
- write up an action alert
- get ticket for flight to Juneau
- prep presentation to legislators
- meet with Anchorage Coalition group
- help with fund-raiser
- schedule meeting with Alaska Environmental Assembly (AEA)

The AEA's director, Bill Glude, donates accommodations in his Juneau hillside home for our visits to the state capital. Bill, too, escaped from the Lower-48 rat race, and moved to remote Talkeetna to live simply and sanely. When his beloved wilderness became a "resource for extraction," Bill catapulted to the frontlines of environmental action. "Alaska isn't a place to drop out," he says. "It's a place to drop in."

Like Bill, I am now sizzling in the frying pan of politics. Coalition work expands. School kids write letters to legislators. Fellow Coalition activist

Anne Wieland organizes meetings in Anchorage. Phone trees schedule mass calls to Juneau. We're full steam ahead from early morning until late at night.

Normally, my head shuts down the second it hits the pillow. Now it's plagued by worms of worries. I inhale deeply and count sheep. Sheep exhale as spruce trees. I can't stop thinking about Rocky River. I picture those eight thousand acres of virgin forest laid waste.

I chat with friends, seeking comfort and ideas. Lawyer Ginny Espenshade hands me a magazine. "Check out the article about land trusts. They are spreading like wildfire in the Lower 48." I read and learn that land trusts are nonprofit organizations that work with willing land owners to buy and preserve land for conservation purposes. Each of the over eight hundred land trusts works to preserve wildlife habitat, historic properties, and special places.

I write to the author of the article for more information. She responds with a packet on how to form a land trust.

"Could this," I ask Ed, "be a vehicle to help save Rocky River and resolve other issues in the area?"

"Don't know; let's get more input."

We call a core group and schedule a meeting to discuss forming a land trust in Homer. "What are the hot issues facing our community?" I ask the group. I record responses on a large flip-pad.

"Clear-cutting," sounds off first. The logging threat is on everyone's mind.

"Declines in the moose herd," says Roberta. "Last year record numbers of moose starved to death. Moose need to shift from bluff to bench for feeding and calving. Property development and folk's roaming dogs are disrupting their corridors. And last winter's deep snows didn't help matters either."

"More and more newcomers," continues Ed, "are drawn here by the wildlife, but then raze their property to raise their house. They strip native trees and plant lawns and cultivars. But moose depend on all those willows and native plants."

"What else?" I ask.

"Fisheries loss. Remember all the mom-and-pop crab operations on Homer Spit? When you could buy three fat Dungeness or Tanner crabs off harbor boats for five dollars? And now all of Kachemak Bay's crab and shrimp fisheries are closed."

"And these good old days," adds Ed, "were only five years ago. Once Jan and I had company so we dropped a crab pot off the end of the Spit to make room in the boat. Two days later, it was chockers with twenty-two king crabs. And now there are none. Homer is changing like lightning. Unless we do something, we'll all lose the quality of life that drew us here."

A hand goes up. "We're losing Homer's history too. Inheritance taxes are forcing sales of family homesteads. The land gets taxed at its subdivision potential, and kids have to break land up solely to pay tax."

After hearing the concerns about loss of the special qualities that make Alaska unique, I start to explain our options to save them. "Land trusts," I say, "have tools like conservation easements which help preserve places with historical or ecological significance. With a conservation easement on a homestead, for example," and here I read: "'. . . land remains in private ownership, but selective rights surrender to the land trust and bind the property. If a property, for example, can't be subdivided, its tax value alters.' Families can rest, knowing their homestead will exist for all generations."

Heads nod. Questions flow. I answer the best I can with my limited knowledge. We're all keen to know more and to learn if the greater Homer community has interest in such an organization.

"We'd need to form a nonprofit organization," says Jack. "Talk to Judy Lund."

"The tax accountant," I gulp. "Yes, I'll give her a call."

In Land We Trust ◡

Judy Lund urges me to schedule a meeting with the Alaska branch of the Nature Conservancy to discover if they've any ideas or support to lend us. I phone the Anchorage office and set a date to meet with director Susan Ruddy.

Susan is buffed like a model for a photo shoot. Her nails are polished, every hair obedient, clothes simple elegance. I shake my ponytail in determination to mask my nerves. Susan rises and smiles and extends her hand. I drag my calloused hands from my hips and meet her firm handshake. Her gentle manner puts me at ease. Susan is already up to speed on the timber sale. I describe the key issues we've identified.

"A local land trust would be an asset, Jan. Rather than compete with the Nature Conservancy, it will complement it. But to be effective," she warns, "you'd have to help us advocate for legislation to allow conservation easements, a critical land preservation tool not yet legal in Alaska. Form a steering committee and organize a public meeting in Homer. Educate the public. Make certain there's sufficient community support for such an organization to survive."

Back in Homer, I phone everyone in the core land-trust group to help organize a meeting to educate Homerites about land trusts and conservation easements. "Call the Senior Center and find out if we can use the hall," suggests Judy. "My husband Rob will be happy to do artwork for fliers to advertise the meeting." Rob draws a bald eagle perched in a spruce, gazing at the big Kachemak view. The date is set; fliers are printed and posted.

Leading the public meeting has defaulted to me. How, pray tell, do I open the meeting; something witty? Dramatic? My mind rattles like a can of marbles. There's so much mental noise I can't think clearly.

"Breathe," I remind myself. I inhale deeply, letting oxygen expand from abdomen to upper chest. As my breathing slows, my mind settles. I ask Spirit to please help. But all I can imagine is the meadow surrounding the Rocky River cabin. "It's not time to be thinking about plants," I argue silently. "I need an idea to begin the meeting." The image persists.

To open the meeting, I walk from person to person, dropping Homer wildflower seeds in each hand. "The land trust," I say, "reminds me of . . . a seed. And each of you is like the sun," I tell my neighbors. "The force is with you, the power to grow this seed of an idea into fullness. This is the seed of habitat, habitat for all, for all times."

Judy fields questions and asks for volunteer candidates for a board of directors for the land trust. I stretch my neck further on the guillotine of community service and raise my hand. Phew; other hands rise too.

We pass out membership forms. Twenty-five dollars for an annual family membership. One thousand dollars to be a lifetime member. "Let's put our money where our mouth is," says Ed. "It's our quality of life that's on the line." We sign away two thousand dollars to the newly fledged Kachemak Heritage Land Trust (KHLT). Members elect a board of directors; I become the first president. The Nature Conservancy lends support to our efforts, backing passage of conservation easement legislation. My mentor Susan Ruddy walks in high places with ease, her manner gracious and nonabrasive. She focuses on benefits to Alaskans, and models win–win style meetings. The easement bill passes in the legislature.

The land trust gets a call to meet with homesteader Yule Kilcher, his family, and their attorney. Yule, Mossy's father, is a Homer icon, overseer of a 613-acre homestead. He is keen to have his homestead continue in perpetuity.

I meet with Yule and tell him, "The Kilcher homestead would remain in private ownership; but certain development rights—like the right to subdivide the property—would be surrendered to and monitored for compliance by KHLT." Yule's keen to keep his homestead whole.

We explore a homestead map; Yule marks zones traditionally farmed or grazed and zones of significance for wildlife. We circle the areas best suited for clustered family dwellings. We explore ways to meet land trust and federal criteria for preservation, while allowing desirable family activities to continue. It is obvious this will require far more than a single meeting.

The land trust board meets to discuss ramifications of accepting our first easement; they detail the trust's annual responsibility of monitoring, costs of monitoring, the need for a monitoring fund, and the need for a baseline study of the land. There is so much to learn.

Sue Christiansen secures office space in a historic home along Pioneer Avenue. The room is sized like a walk-in closet and Quaker plain. But we're elated by the economical base to house volunteers, as well as by the donated desk, file cabinets, and telephone.

Sue is my ally, pumping me up daily with her unflagging enthusiasm. Each morning, we focus, inhale deeply, and exhale with attention. "This land trust," begins Sue, "is a vehicle for the highest good. May this organization be a shining light for the community. You, Jan, are motivated by service. All the board is motivated by service. We focus on the highest and the best in everyone."

"You, Sue, are a beacon of hope," I add. "You attract people to the Kachemak Heritage Land Trust by your presence. You are selfless in your actions. You are a tower of light."

Then we set to work. Other volunteers appear. Mary Griswold becomes our right arm. Dan Delmissier, owner of Quiet Sports, sponsors a trails meeting. "We have to take action or our trails will be lost," warns Dan. "More and more newcomers are blocking access to historic ski and hiking tracks." Input flies so fast, I struggle to cope. The pond that was my life has swelled to an ocean. My education fast-tracks.

My book, thankfully, is now at the publishers being typeset, allowing me a respite from editing. Alaska Northwest Books recommended using a three-word title, with two of them being "Wild Plants." Ed and I bantered title ideas for hours: *Foraging Wild Plants, Harvesting Wild Plants, Learning Wild Plants, Using Wild Plants.* We finally settle on "Discovering." It fits our experience about all of life right now; each day we gain awareness of something we didn't know before.

Today's discovery revolves around observation of fauna rather than flora. I join Dave Holderman, the Fish and Game biologist from Harriet the Seal days, as he radio-tracks moose. "We'll follow their migration routes," Dave says, "from their blufftop winter feeding grounds to calving grounds below."

Dave drives me to Skyline Drive above Homer and hands me snowshoes. I strap on the webbed pancakes and strike off in Dave's footsteps. Dave powers over hills and down through gullies, weaving through willows and alders. I toddle behind, struggling with the lift-step-lift-step snowshoe samba. I'm swamped in sweat and we've barely begun.

Dave lifts his beacon, picks up a signal, and strides like a wolverine on track of prey. While I pause for water and second wind, Dave describes how moose depend on these routes and that over two hundred moose calve in the seven-mile stretch of flatlands between Fritz Creek and downtown Homer.

Back at the office, Dave supplies me with facts documenting moose corridors and feeding grounds critical to the future of moose in the community, and asks, "Will you be at the meeting for the Bradley Lake Moose Mitigation Fund?"

"What's that?" I ask, embarrassed. My knowledge of Bradley hearkens back to the helicopter landing in the front yard at Swift Creek to survey the wilderness hydro site. I've some vague idea of power generation for points north.

"The Bradley hydroelectric project is displacing moose habitat, thus this fund will mitigate damage by purchasing critical calving grounds for protection in perpetuity. Attend the Anchorage meeting," says Dave, "and encourage them to use funds to benefit the Homer herd."

In the KHLT office, we're in the midst of yet another grant proposal; Sue, once again, is pulling an all-nighter. Even double-espresso fails my best efforts to keep pace. My head jerks. "Got to get some shut-eye, Sue. I'm no use to you right now. But I'll be good as gold in the morning."

Once Upon a Friday ⟿

I have a nightmare. An oil tanker rams the rocks and splinters its hull. Crude oil smears the sea. Birds preen blackened feathers. Otter fur mats with slime. Carrion stench lures bears to dine, and die. Eagles scoop oil-tainted bounty, and swoop no more. With each tide, death's talons sink deeper. Salmon lie belly up in the sheen. Seaweeds glisten. Sea anemones, weathered veterans of three hundred Alaskan seasons, perish in a single tide.

With each surge, king crude conquers territory. It advances relentlessly north, and smears every cove. Sheen bathes beaches. Tar balls lurch onto shores and puddle with the sun. Ooze suffocates tide pools, paints decorator crabs, slimes sea stars. The crude monster is insatiable.

In towns, fists pound tables: "Pick up the damn oil now." Mouths scream fury at big oil, big greed, piss-poor government, and single hulls on tankers.

The nightmare intensifies. I struggle to waken but night dreams and day are inseparable. The din of radio and the texture of newspaper between my fingertips grounds me. I blankly stare at Good Friday news. 12:26 A.M., March 24, 1989. A tanker is run aground in Prince William Sound.

Captain Joseph Hazelwood of the *Exxon Valdez* has radioed the traffic center reporting the incident: "We've fetched up, ah, hard aground, north of Goose Island, off Bligh Reef and, ah, evidently leaking some oil and we're gonna be here for a while and, ah, if you want, ah, so you're notified."

Leaking "some oil" equals nearly six million gallons, from initial impact, but millions more still hemorrhage into clear waters. My eyes blur as I read: "the worst oil spill in North American history."

Exxon flies in: Texans in three-piece suits, armed with promises bigger than six guns. "We made the mess, we'll clean it." In Homer, Exxon executive Wiley Bragg addresses the packed auditorium and babbles about unfortunate accidents, of doing the best we can. The crowd fries with frustration.

Questions fly: "Where is Exxon's containment boom? The one you've promised in case of emergency? This is an emergency. Where the hell is it? The oil is spreading for God's sake. Do something."

"It is in operation in Prince William Sound," replies Bragg.

"More. We need more. We need it now."

"More. Now. More. Now." The crowd forms a chorus.

Exxon's singsong refrains: "No boom. No boom."

"No boom?" Locals rage. "We'll fricking build it ourselves." Ed jumps into the fray, teamed with Robert Archibald, Chile Willie Condon, Doug Caldwell, and others. Four days later, one hundred bodies stage on the end of Homer Spit, armed with chain saws, sledge-hammers, and come-alongs. Their mission impossible: build a boom, corral the oil, save the bays.

Homer Spit is home to horizontal trees: piles upon piles of spruce slated for shipment to Japan. Klukwon, the timber-harvesting nemesis, converts to savior to save the bays. The log pile it owns becomes stockpile for the boom-building, with logs free for the taking.

Like a childhood game of "Simon Says," the boom-building crew follows the leaders. Schofield flattens a length of Sitka spruce. The crew answers with a chorus of chain saws. Archibald attaches a water-soluble, oil-resistant curtain to the log; the crew unfurls fabric. Condon adds an anchor chain to keep the curtain vertical; the crew swings chain. Caldwell leads the volley of hammers. Boom log after boom log builds.

The skinny four-mile spit, home base to the log stockpile and boom operation, sticks like a sore thumb into the sea. The boom crew juts into the limelight and directly into Exxon's craw. The crew is noisy. Visible. Vocal. Ed tells the Associated Press: "I've been working construction crews for twenty years, and this is the hardest-working one I've ever seen. They're not doing it for money. They're working from the heart. The energy here is unbelievable. We're not going to let anyone stop us."

News releases lure more local and global volunteers. The boomers labor fifteen- to sixteen-hour days, not even leaving the site for meals. Team leaders broadcast a radio appeal; within an hour volunteers arrive with steaming cauldrons of stew, cartons of bread, cases of fruit, and flasks of tea and coffee. As the crew gains fame, Exxon gains notoriety. Volunteers having to build a boom is public proof that Exxon can't cope. Alaskans do it better.

Exxon jumps, and dumps the boom-crew volunteers onto its payroll. Wages start at $16.69 an hour. Ed has free rein for supplies. The boom gang needs clamps, now! No clamps left in Homer? No clamps statewide? Exxon charters a jet to the Lower 48 for a planeload. Money's no object.

Exxon-funded programs spring to life daily to attend oily needs. A bird rescue forms. An otter center springs up in Little Jakolof Bay. Sue drags me to an interview at the Bidarka Inn with Exxon chief Wiley Bragg. I leave dazed, with the position of coordinating communications between Bird Rescue, Otter Rescue, Fish and Wildlife, and Exxon. My salary is $250 per day.

Wiley directs me to get an office in the Bidarka Inn. Instead, I choose a rented room away from the Exxon infrastructure, and stock it with a thrift shop desk, chairs, and file drawer. The Animal Recovery/Rehabilitation Information Office now operates with me, overwhelmed, at the helm. Each day I cloister in the office at 5 A.M. and crawl home at midnight. Most days I forget to eat. There's too much to be done. Land trust work goes into suspension. The oil crisis grabs all hands.

Volunteers flood to the office. They map the area, each responsible to patrol a beach for fouled birds and otters. "I need rubber gloves for volunteers picking up oiled animals and carcasses," I tell Wiley.

"No money for rubber gloves," he insists.

"But gloves are cheap."

"Who do you think you're working for, the community?"

"Yes," I argue, "for Exxon and the community. Aren't the needs the same? What do you want me to do with the flood of volunteers? Folks need to help. All they need is basic supplies."

"Send them home."

"I can't," I insist. "You'll have war on your hands. These people care."

Each night in bed, before we collapse, Ed tells me of the Homer Spit scene. He tells of chartering yet another jet to Los Angeles for more clamps. "It's not fair, Ed." I gripe. "I'm glad you're getting what you need, but it's so flagrantly political. It's only because you're on TV. Exxon won't even give me rubber gloves to pick up its damn oiled birds."

"They don't want them picked up, Jan. Every drop of oil, every dead bird is evidence."

Wayne Watson, on leave from Exxon's rival petroleum conglomerate, British Petroleum, volunteers to coordinate beach monitoring. Volunteer Tia works the computer data base. Pat helps in the office. The phone rings like a phone-a-thon. I spend hours in Wiley's waiting room, waiting for the ax of disapproval. The incongruity between Ed's Santa Exxon and my

Scrooge Exxon grates. It has to be true, Exxon doesn't want evidence.

Back in the office, I meet Sach Bowe, a volunteer on the outer Gulf of Alaska coast. "It looks like the tanker went aground right here, Jan," he tells me. "Here's what it's like at Gore Point." He shows me photos.

I excuse myself. I hide on the toilet and bawl. "Please God, not Gore Point."

Gore Point ～

I cry, remembering Gore Point as it'd been last summer. "The ultimate," Achim, our window-making friend, promised. And he'd not been exaggerating. We'd flown to the southern Kenai Peninsula coast to Gore Point, the triangular wedge fronted by the Gulf of Alaska and sided by Port Dick, located within the boundaries of Kachemak Bay Wilderness Park.

"Look at the bald eagles in the nest, Jan," Ed pointed, "and look at the black bear." I pointed back; a mountain goat, coming off the cliff onto the beach, headed our way.

"Even with all our Alaskan travels, I've never seen wildlife like this. *National Geographic* specials aren't any better."

"Yeah, this place is beautiful in every way except for the weather."

"Yeah. Here comes another squall. Better join Achim."

Gore Point's beach curves, scoops driftwood like a net, and tosses logs into piles ten feet high. Our tent nestle in the logjam, sheltered from Gulf winds.

"Weather is what makes this place," insists Achim. "Keeps it wild."

After the squall, I forage through flotsam. "Glass fishing floats, and check out this bottle."

"Japanese writing. Delivered by the North Pacific currents, Jan. They catch everything, and sweep it onto the beach."

Now Gore Point has snagged a new catch, Prince William's oil. The photos make me heave: a volunteer crew sunk to their knees in crude. In front of them, death row: four dead sea otters; six hundred and seventy-two seabird carcasses.

"When we first arrived here," says Sach, "there were live otters, seals, sea lions, and birds, but with each tide there is more oil and less life. An Exxon cleanup crew came in, all in spanking new white Tyvek jumpsuits."

"It's about time," I say.

"Yeah," he interrupts. "Well as soon as they started to work, helicopters landed filled with newsmen. They shot wads of footage so the Lower 48 can see what good work Exxon is doing up in Alaska. As soon as the helicopter flew off, the workers packed up. Evacuated. Gore Point has been orphaned, Jan. Unless the oil is picked up, it will only get worse."

I make calls to the media. Everyone's up to their ears in stories. I get no response.

Dirty Waters

My next call is from Pete Gagne, my brother Jim's buddy.

"Pete? You're in Alaska?"

"I flew up from New Hampshire to help cleanup efforts. I'm on an oil recovery boat out on the Gulf. Exxon took our shovels away. They told us we were picking up too much oil."

"How can you be picking up too much oil? Isn't that what they're paying you to do? "

"Supposedly. Now we're scooping sludge with kitchen spoons. They won't give us any tools."

"That's ridiculous."

"But true . . . And that's only half of it. The oil we've already collected is supposed to be shipped to Oregon to a toxic waste site. How come the boats are back in a couple days, empty? Where are they taking it? Are they dumping it at sea?"

I'm struck dumb, and dumber still as the center gets more calls. There are reports of boat workers getting nosebleeds, nausea, and burns; rumors of low-flying airplanes at dusk, and strange pellets found on deck in the morning that no one can explain. Sandee Elvsaas, Seldovian director for Veco, Exxon's hiring agency, rings me distressed. Crews sent to the Gulf of Alaska healthy are returning violently ill. Her head office insists they're fine, and doesn't want them to see doctors. Her own brother, Tim Burt, who has been steam-cleaning oiled boats is now suffering agonizing headaches. He was in perfect health before working with the hydrocarbons.

The Homer boom wings into phase two: deployment. Ed and Chile Willie have a new assignment, to monitor the boom at Port Dick. To shift the boom in the dramatic Gulf of Alaska tides, they require a small rubber raft with motor.

"No," responds Exxon.

"It's only three thousand dollars; we can't do our job without it."

Exxon, instead, spends over three thousand per week for a skiff and skiff operator to shift Port Dick's booms. "Exxon overkill," says Ed, "using dollars like diapers to clean up the mess."

Meanwhile, back at the center, my repeated requests for basic supplies plunge me in black waters. I'm fired.

Life after Exxon ⁓

Our office, the Animal Recovery Coordination Center, appeals for help. The Kenai Peninsula Borough responds, paying our office rent, and buying desperately needed supplies. Well-equipped volunteers now patrol beaches and scoop tar balls and tarred birds.

On the Gulf, Ed has more Exxon hassles. Every three weeks, as each Texas boss masters the reading of tide books, and thaws to the hardworking Alaskan crews, he gets exiled south. New honchos from Texas fly in, clad in cowboy boots and gold watches. They touch down in helicopters and spit policy to the weathered workers.

Onshore, as greasy crews scrape oiled rocks, the Department of Environmental Conservation slams workers with warnings: it's illegal to pee or poop in the forest. So, while tides splash crude and swamp life, workers halt to build outhouses.

Ed and Willie face a federal wildlife officer. She's hip on environmental standards, here to assure that workers toe the line. The Port Dick leaders roil. "You're fighting the wrong dragon. Get on Exxon's case, not ours. Help clean up the damn mess. Save beaches, save the fisheries."

Exxon flies in to inspect the efforts. As Ed takes the Texans on tour, they get an eyeful: naked bodies exiting the Port Dick sauna, the wash spot for oil-grimed crews. Gossip streams. News of Schofield's nudie camp hits Homer. But far more crude than nude dominates Port Dick. Boat bumper stickers say, "Shit happens." Each tide delivers more. Each day, the slime shifts, crashes onto rocks, paints the world brown.

Despair is in the air; eau de oil, eau de carrion. "It's a mess out here, Jan," Ed writes me. "Eagles eat oiled birds and die. Otters drop like flies. Picking up the dead does little. It's the oil that needs to get picked up. Feds have their head up their ass, need to stop picking on the workers and get cracking at Exxon."

Homer surveyor Billy Day, employed by Alaska Fish and Game, notes that Exxon is not cleaning up Port Dick beaches, so he mobilizes citizens into the Homer Area Recovery Coalition (HARC). HARC targets Mars Cove, two hundred feet of beach in Port Dick's West Arm. Volunteers bag oiled gravel and stockpile sixty-three thousand pounds of oiled residue. Alaskan barge operator Chris Lopez, on the Exxon payroll to transport oiled waste, collects the load from Mars Cove. Exxon fumes and threatens to terminate Chris, telling him, "There's to be no collection of unauthorized oil."

Unable to dispose of more oil, Billy pools brainpower with his brother Bob and an environmental engineer. There has to be a better way than bagging slimed beach and taking it south for disposal. Day and company devise a prototype of a portable beach machine. Its mission is to wash oiled gravel and rocks on site. The test of the prototype works. But Exxon refuses to fund a single machine. "It works too well," insists Ed. "Believe me. Exxon doesn't want evidence."

The State of Alaska funds four beach-cleaner machines. Volunteers pour to Mars Cove from Homer, statewide, nationwide, and beyond. Nearly three hundred helpers clean Mars Cove. Fundraisers cover volunteer necessities.

I've not seen Ed in weeks. Pilot Bill Decreeft donates the empty seat on his supply plane so I can visit him briefly. Headphones dampen the roar of his DeHavilland; the *Out of Africa* soundtrack serenades my ears. The music weaves with Port Dick vistas as I glimpse the Gulf. From the air, all looks like the handiwork of God on the day of creation. I press my face to the window and hide my tears of joy.

But on the beach, I sob in pain. As I walk hand in hand with Ed, the stench of oil bangs my nostrils. "How can you stand this stink, Ed? I feel nauseous breathing even this short time." "Doing what needs to be done, honey," he tells me. He insists he feels fine.

Around us, oil glistens in the sun. Muck strews on seaweeds and eagle feathers. The last time I was here, silvers cartwheeled around the plane's floats as it touched down; humpies choked the creek mouth. Today, an oil boom blocks the mouth. Crews in Tyvek suits scrape oil. The head of the bay is thick with recovery boats and work crews.

As the season changes, Exxon spirals down its presence. Fall storms blast beaches, shuffling sands, and covering crude. Oil sinks below the surface, hiding truth. Wilderness has been violated.

As oil work ends, Ed returns to Gardensong. "Remember that quote, Jan?" he asks me, "the one from *Illusions* that we used to hang in the outhouse? 'Every problem has a gift in its hands?'"

"Richard Bach blew that one, Ed. Can't imagine gifts ever coming from this oil spill."

"Me either. What a shame. Alaska's forever changed."

Once Upon a Box

Days fall back into pre-spill routines. Only now I'm working overtime to clear the backlog of volunteer tasks with the Kachemak Bay Citizens Coalition and the Kachemak Heritage Land Trust. Winter nights fill with meetings, days with community work. Time with Ed is rare and precious.

Spring is heralded by a package slip in our post box. The clerk returns through the door with a rolling cart bearing a cardboard box stamped *Discovering Wild Plants*! My heart flutters. I slit the tape and fold back the white packing sheet. The smell of printer's ink wafts; the sight of purple chives blazing on green blurs. I lift the hardback, wipe my hands on my jeans, and reverently turn pages. Seven years of work sit in my hands. I can hardly see the words, the art, the photos. My lips taste salt.

Book reviews appear. Doors open. The University of Alaska at Dillingham invites me to teach a weekend course, "Edible and Medicinal Plants." The benefits include flights, per diem, vehicle, and salary. I greet staff, tour the University, set up supplies, and scout field-trip locations. Friday evening begins with slides. I'm so busy answering queries I forget my stage fright. In the morning we load into vehicles and drive the outback roads; we stop at fields, muskegs, beach, and river to identify flora and harvest. We return, laden with herbs, to the home economics classroom.

Students strip bark, wash and chop greens, fry herbal egg rolls, bake wild herb quiche, and brew tea for a student potluck. Sunday is a replay: more habitats and harvest, more plants and products. Participants smear salve on nicks and cuts and brew tinctures. The group favorite is undeniably the massage oil.

Northern Nights Massage Oil
1/2 cup cottonwood buds
1/2 cup birch bark (from twigs), peeled and chopped fine
1/2 cup wormwood leaves, chopped coarsely
1/8 cup spruce pitch

Place herbs in top of double boiler, with water in base pan. Cover herbs with 2 cups grapeseed oil. Simmer gently, covered, for 3–4 hours. Strain through clean muslin cloth, pressing well.

Bottle oil, adding essential oils of choice.

Back in Homer, Ed wears an odd expression. "Remember Jan, when we first arrived in Alaska, and camped in Skagway?"

"Yes," I answer, puzzled as to where this will lead.

"Remember when we saw Governor Jay Hammond?"

"Yes."

"Hammond's retired now, and doing a weekly television special highlighting Alaskans doing noteworthy or unusual things. He's arriving with his crew in two weeks for an interview."

"But I only teach people about wild plants."

"That's what I told them. They want an interview."

During the interview, we stroll the Gardensong grounds with Jay and gather greens for a wild supper. A moose and her twin calves browse birch. Cameraman Larry sets up his tripod. As Larry hits the shutter one calf bites the other in the butt. The calves race, chase, spin, and whirl. They dive in the pond, rear and splash. As Larry removes his finger from the shutter, the calves halt antics, yawn, and nap under a spruce.

Jay quizzes us about what brought us to Alaska and how we got into wild plants. We pick Jay's brain about his home across Cook Inlet and about his creation of the Alaskan Permanent Fund. He is personable, approachable, and genuine. He tells us that red salmon, when they are red, taste a lot like lobster. I'd thought that all spawning salmon were mushy and tasteless but he insists that the reds are an exception.

The show airs, accompanied by a feature on Norman Vaughan, a dog-sled driver on Admiral Byrd's 1928 Antarctic expedition. "Dream big, and dare to fail," Vaughan tells the viewers. Vaughan is expert at big dreams. He completed his first Iditarod race at the age of seventy-two and raced it ten more times afterward. He now plans an eighty-ninth birthday expedition to climb Mount Vaughan, the ten-thousand-foot mountain Byrd named in his honor.

We feel humbled being in such extraordinary company. Sharing our love of wild plants feels so pale compared to the acts of extraordinary explorers. Publishing a book opens strange doors. I'm little prepared for the next.

Trial by Fire ⌒

The mail's highlight is an invitation to teach at Breitenbush Hot Spring's annual herbal conference. Besides flights and salary for teaching my workshop on cooking with wild herbs, I'll be free to attend other workshops and activities. I excitedly accept. The teaching contract arrives along with a conference program. A tremor flutters through my body. On Saturday's itinerary is a firewalk.

The conference is an electrifying enclave of green-minded people. "The plants that surround us most plentifully as weeds," says herbalist Susun Weed, "are the most useful of plants. They shout at us to take notice. They beg us to use them."

My wild herb cooking class is well attended. Folks are keen for more. "Do you do any longer programs? We'd love to come to Alaska to study with you." Ideas sprout like seed.

During intermission, I seek out Phoebe Line, the leader of the firewalk. "How did you ever get into firewalking?"

"I had a vision, Jan."

"I had one too," I admit. I describe my bizarre experience with Maxwell as he was dying, and how I saw myself standing before a line of coals. "It feels important for me to be present at the firewalk, but I don't know that I want to walk."

"Be a supportive participant; help sing and drum. No one has to stand on the coals. You must listen to your guidance."

Evening lures me to the hot springs; in the pool is Phoebe's husband. "Why do you walk?" I ask him. "What is the purpose?"

"You walk for a purpose, Jan. You broadcast your request to the universe; what you firewalk for comes true."

"Always?"

"In my experience, yes."

I return to my Breitenbush cabin and locate a book of matches. "What am I afraid of?" I ask myself as the first match ignites.

"Of being burned by the fire."

Okay, I could be burned. Burns heal. "What else?" I ask myself.

"Of everyone else walking successfully and my failing."

Okay, I recognize that fear. I feel it. I release it. "What else?" I persist.

"Of being able to succeed."

Afraid of success? Perhaps success brings its own challenges and responsibilities.

I light match after match until exhausted of reasons, ravings, and rantings. Now, perhaps, I can face the fire and act on the guidance I receive. The moon is full as fifty participants circle around the six-foot pyre of hardwood.

"Firewalking," Phoebe explains, "is intrinsic to most tribal cultures. In the Philippines, entire villages walk on red carpets of coals to honor eminent visitors. Some islanders walk annually to offer prayer and renew connection with Spirit. In our ceremony, we'll each offer a stick to the fire to symbolize an aspect of ourselves that we're releasing. A second prayer stick will honor what we wish to empower, what we wish to come true in our life."

The towering mound of oak, ash, and maple ignites. We begin rounds of singing, chanting, and drumming. "Keep focused on your intent," reminds Phoebe.

One by one we approach the fire. We speak our heart's desires.

"I pray for healing my relationship with my spouse."

Another woman steps forward. "I pray for forgiveness. I'm angry at my father for the way he treats me and my partner. He won't accept that I love another woman."

A young girl cries for healing her dad's cancer.

A young man asks for success in his new business.

I pray for Kachemak Bay, for preservation of the park, and survival of the Rocky River forests.

A rambunctious child hammers discordantly on a drum. He squawks, runs, and yanks my attention. How can I focus with such distraction? Why don't his parents control their brat?

The rhythmic group energy spirals higher. The flames leap moonward.

The heat of the fire sears the front of my body. My emotions settle, soothed by the rhythm of the drums. The group becomes more cohesive.

"Listen to your soul voice," counsels Phoebe. "Walk only if you're guided to. Some of you may only need to be here, and may not need to walk."

Oh good. I can watch.

"Walking on fire can feel either hot or cold, smooth or crunchy. It's an individual sensation."

I don't care. I'm not here to experience it.

Time dances in the flames. The chant continues: "And everything she touches, changes." The stack of logs changes. Red coals glow. My front breaks sweat. Phoebe rakes the inferno to a twenty-foot path. She strides across confidently. She halts in the center, and scoops coals with her bare hands into a fiery shower. She walks again; on her heels is that raucous child, now silent.

This is so impossible.

The singing builds. The energy rises. More walkers emerge from the circle. I watch, enraptured. "It's impossible. But it's possible."

"Take my hand if you wish," offers Phoebe. She walks around the circle of singers. Hands form a human chain.

"Do I walk?" I ask myself.

"Yes."

I grab an open hand. I follow my peers. The coals scream on my soles. I return to the circle. My feet tingle like nettle stings, the frosty earth so delicious.

The singing builds. The rhythmic drumming mesmerizes. We cheer as more walkers cross the cauldron.

The energy pulses and intensifies. "Do I walk again?"

"Yes," says the voice.

A child of eight walks confidently. I follow behind. The coals are now fiery granola; sparks leap from the pressure of my soles.

Phoebe changes the mood. She sings as she demonstrates. "You put your left foot in, and shake it all about." One by one we soak limbs in the path, and shake them in the coals. The fire burns to a dark haze. The rake redresses the path, bringing the hottest coals to the surface. Walkers return. The energy crests again.

"Do I walk again?" "Yes," answers the voice, "but only for the joy of being one with the fire."

I walk, solo, armed with my sistrum, a leather and bell instrument given me by Marsha Million: ". . . an Egyptian ornament, Jan," she'd told me, "symbolic of fire and joy." I shake the sistrum and walk confidently across the coals. My fear is gone. My need to prove anything is done. The coals are cool clear water under my feet. The tingling's gone. I'm joyous, ecstatic. I can't wait to do this again.

"Every single time you walk, you must ask," reminds Phoebe.

I ask. Of course it will be yes.

"No," says the voice.

I argue. I want to walk.

"Keep your thirst for the fire. Be still."

I watch as others walk. I cheer their success. I am impatient being on the sidelines, but comforted by the promise: firewalk prayers always come true. Kachemak is safe.

Dragon's Den 〜

Following the firewalk, opportunity knocks. Alaska Northwest Books writes, asking if I will do a story on Kachemak State Park. It will be published in their "On the Rim" supplement in their next issue of *Alaska Geographic.*

Ed laughs. "See, Jan. Predicted you'd be writing for *Geographic* someday."

"You only goofed up the first word Ed. *Alaska Geographic*, not *National Geographic*. But no matter. I'm happy the situation in Kachemak Bay will be getting more exposure."

The *Geographic*'s article weaves together Kachemak Bay State Park history, a who's who of the players in the land trade/buyback, a timeline of happenings, and photos, including one of Dad, leaned against Rocky River grandfather spruce.

Months later, in the lair of legislators in Juneau, the firewalk surety vaporizes. Battle lines are drawn: wallets versus wilderness. A team of volunteers from the Kachemak Bay Citizens Coalition—including retired teacher Anne Wieland, spunky Mary Pearsall, and I—begs legislators for $25,000,000 to save the bay.

Anne lures eyes to her photograph album. Mary explains how Seldovia Natives came to hold title to the centerpiece of the Park.

"If it's private land, we can't do anything about it," barks the dragon.

"Yes," says Anne, "except for the Memorandum of Understanding signed by Seldovia Natives; they agreed to exchange these in-holdings for state lands of equivalent value."

"Then why hasn't the trade been done?"

"Controversies over value; Seldovia gave up trying. Now they've sold their timber rights; clear-cutting is imminent."

I, meanwhile, tempt legislators with fiscal facts. "Over two hundred thousand visitors come to Kachemak Bay each season, drawn by the view, the wilderness, the fishing. The bay's bounty snags over six million dollars annually. Slash the wilderness and you slash tax revenue."

We plop fat packets of signatures on the desk: thousands of names and addresses of voters from Ketchikan to Barrow, and friends of Kachemak Bay from Tasmania to Finland. Mary reads aloud letters from school children. "Save the Bay. Don't let them cut all the trees. Please keep Homer beautiful."

"This is a win–win proposition for all," we tell each legislator. "The Native Association is willing to sell the land. The timber company is willing to sell its timber rights. The people of Alaska want the park to be whole. Vote 'Yes' on the House and Senate appropriation bills."

We target committee leaders, instrumental in moving the bill through the review process and to the floor for a vote. In some offices, the legislator before me wears an expression of bored resignation. I feel all he's hearing is, "Blah, blah, blah, Senator, blah, blah, blah."

Some offices, like that of Representative Mike Navarre, fire us with hope. Navarre views the purchase of the Kachemak Bay in-holdings "as an investment in Alaska's future . . . a small price to pay when viewed in the long-term impacts on tourism, recreation, education, commercial and sport fishing, and the environment."

Nightly, we tally our avid supporters, count how many neutrals we've encountered, and identify where we need to focus.

The next day I sit in front of the desk of Ketchikan Republican Robin Taylor. Taylor towers above me, roaring like a chain saw. "We don't need more parks. We need jobs. Logging means jobs."

Anne and Mary return from equally discouraging visits with Lloyd Jones.

"It'd be easier to get stumps to support us," I whine.

"We'll never convince them," says Anne. "But their voters might." We ignite the phone tree. "Call friends in Southeast. Have them harangue their legislators. Vote yes, vote yes, vote yes."

Republican leaders hold the park bill hostage. "Unless the Ketchikan hospital is funded, we won't move Kachemak Bay to the floor for a vote." The legislative clock ticks.

Phone lines increase pressure. Neutrals turn positive. The legislative scoreboard edges upward. The clock ticks. D-day comes, D-day goes. I hide in the corner of a Juneau café, and scratch a letter to my sister.

Dear Doris,

After umpteen hundred volunteer hours, thousands of dollars, and tremendous effort on the part of people all over the world, the Kachemak Bay Park buyback bill died yesterday in the final hours of the final day of the legislative session. Two Senators held the bill hostage in committee. They never allowed it to make it to the Senate floor where sufficient votes lay to pass the bill. Despite the fact over a thousand people called in that one day to the Senator, he wouldn't let it loose.

So we're all licking our wounds. It feels like a funeral around here. Ed's been great, keeping an even perspective on this, and helping me cope through this grieving. Everyone involved has such a passion for this wild land. The news feels like death.

In the Wake of Disaster ⌇

In Homer, Coalition members meet and mourn at Bidarka Inn. "We can't let everything end this way. We can't."

"Is everyone here game for another round?" asks Ken Castner. Hands raise unanimously. I raise my hand again. "I'll help too. But first I need to take some time to handle personal matters. I'll be back in a month."

Home at Gardensong, Ed and I make a "to do" list. "Need to oil the Rocky River cabin again, Jan. Every time we get there these days, all we do is work on it. And if we go anywhere else we feel guilty for not getting to Rocky River. It might be time . . ."

"Forget it, Ed. Rocky River is home."

"But maybe we could find someone who would love the cabin as much as we do. Didn't Sue Christiansen say she wants a place by a river, with cottonwoods? Rocky River has all that."

"Sue," I pause. "With her, Rocky River would still be in the family. She's like a sister to me."

Sue comes for Sunday sauna. She's ecstatic about acquiring Rocky River.

Monday's mail brings an invitation to teach Elderhostel at Katmai National Park. "I'd give anything for more herbal training," I tell Ed.

"Check this out," he says, as he hands me a flier.

It is from Rosemary Gladstar, the inspirational herbal teacher I studied with in California. "She has moved to Vermont and she's offering a two-week teacher training. If I did her program, I could visit family, too."

"Go for it, Jan."

I schedule flights and mail a deposit check. Rosemary's class stretches participants like Play-Doh. Our gaggle of green women study class structure, planning, advertising, and brochure writing. Rosemary videos us as we conduct herbal presentations; we laugh at our bloopers, and learn to identify and eliminate 'isms' such as twirling our hair, and stalling mid-sentence. We fret about ever being able to pronounce botanical names accurately. "Even botanists don't always agree with their pronunciation," Rosemary consoles us. "Say them with confidence and all will be well."

A sweat lodge ceremony led by her husband Karl closes the event. We enter a turtle-shaped lodge that, Karl tells us, represents the womb of mother earth. The lodge is made of willow saplings, topped by blankets. The Native American ceremony is to celebrate our rite of passage, our graduation from the program, and to prepare us for reentry to the world.

He forewarns that the ceremony will consist of four rounds, or endurances, each lasting about thirty minutes. Fire-hot rocks will be added to the central pit with the beginning of each round. Each round will have a different focus and different prayers; some are personal, some for community.

Karl drums and rattles and guides us in chants. As the ceremony proceeds, heat blasts. I press nose to the earth and gasp for breath. I plead to

Spirit. "Please save Kachemak Bay. Please make the Park whole. Please free me to do my herbal work."

When the final round completes, I exit, and plunge into cold water. I resurface revitalized. It's time to go home.

On deck in Homer is a call to Kenai Peninsula Borough to register my new business, Gardensong Herbs, as a school. I must meet with the Kachemak Heritage Land Trust to get current on events; and with Kachemak Bay Citizens Coalition members for yet another round of Save the Bay.

From the Heart ～

Life's a juggling act, only with too many balls in the air. Kachemak Heritage Land Trust grows faster than a springborn moose calf. I'm still president of the board, still working sixty-hour weeks as a volunteer. Sue Christiansen is now employed as director. Mary Griswold is queen of the volunteer force.

KHLT completes the very first conservation easement in Alaska. The Kilcher homestead is now permanently preserved. The land trust receives its first land gifts: waterfront acreage in Neptune Bay, plus ten acres of premier moose-calving habitat adjacent to Beluga Lake. Atop Homer bluff, volunteers build the twelve-mile Homestead Trail. World Wildlife Fund backs our new "adopt an acre program" to acquire critical habitat.

What niggles like a devil's club prickle is that the work being done by Kachemak Bay Citizens Coalition (which Roberta Highland and I still cochair) can only address land within state park boundaries. Still at risk for clear-cutting are eight thousand acres of Rocky River valley, as well as forests of the Island Peninsula surrounding the nonprofit Center for Alaskan Coastal Studies.

I speak to Native Chief Fred Elvsaas regarding the possibility of a conservation easement with the land trust, to preserve these forests for recreation, education, and ecology. He invites me to attend the association board meeting, plus meet with John Sturgeon of Timber Trading.

"Oh Sue, what can I say? How do I convince money-minded men that the forest is important?"

"Speak from the heart, Jan."

I hope Sue is right. I fly to Kodiak Island for the meeting and stand, shaking, before the Native board of directors. I project a slide of my dad leaning against Rocky's grandfather spruce. "I speak on behalf of the ancient ones. The life of the tree is the life of the people." Native stories weave with ecology, the relationship of old-growth forests to the health of the salmon population. I speak of life at Rocky River and the flood, of trees holding soil on steep slopes, of erosion that would result from clear-cutting, of counting tree rings of cabin logs. "It will be more than ten generations before your descendants have forests like these. What if you keep it all: the forests, the fish, the river quality, the recreation? What if your children and all your grandchildren can keep it all?"

I speak of the mechanism of the conservation easement and the idea of a win–win solution. My brain buzzes and warns me that what I'm proposing is nuts; it tells me that corporations count today's dollars, not tomorrow's future. I persist.

The board agrees to discuss the proposal. I fly to Anchorage for round two. Next is my meeting with Timber Trading Company president John Sturgeon. I cower before his skyscraper office. My stomach is a mass of knots. I escape to the rest room, and dose myself with Rescue Remedy, a floral essence I've learned about that helps to calm nerves.

I speak from the heart. John speaks with his board.

Ups and Downs ～

Much to my relief, the old-growth forests outside the park boundaries get a reprieve. Timber Trading Company announces it will donate these timber rights to Kachemak Heritage Land Trust and the Center for Alaskan Coastal Studies for land conservation purposes. Their gift, however, depends upon state purchase of TTC's remaining timber rights within the park boundaries.

More than ever, the nonprofits need clones, and cash to fund operations. For the Trust, Sue uses fun to raise funds; she orchestrates a costume ball. Land's End hall jams with porky pigs, dancing trees, prancing moose, all vying for prizes donated by community supporters.

Anne, Mary, and I return to Juneau to lobby for the Citizen's Coalition. Our arms fill with signatures from Save-the-Bay campaigns throughout Alaska. We show legislators our full-page newspaper ad that includes quotations of support by Governor Walter J. Hickel, Representative Mike Navarre, Senator Arliss Sturgulewski, and an extensive lineup of politicians, businessmen, artists, and supporters. "The people of Alaska, the people of the world," we emphasize, "want the Park whole. Please vote yes."

But Senators Taylor and Jones are again bad news bears. On April 29, 1992, the *Anchorage Daily* headlines blast: "Kachemak Timber Bill Hits Snags—Senators: Bill Won't Reach Floor Unless Other Projects Are Also Funded."

We head to the movies for comic relief. Bill Murray plays a newscaster in *Groundhog Day,* trapped in a time loop, reliving a dreaded event over and over. We hoot. Our Juneau plotline feels all too similar. Will we, like Murray, finally have a happy ending?

With the legislature in its final day, our phone tree ignites the capital; lines ring incessantly. Aides can do little but answer calls from our supporters. The message sounds loud and clear. *Save the Bay.*

The bill breaks, limps from committee to the floor. The House votes . . .
Yes.

We hold our breath as it goes to the stubborn Senate.

The Senate votes . . .

Yes.

We leap in the air. Clap. Hug. Cry. We've accomplished a miracle. We've done it! We've all done it.

We link arms and dance a jig. Our three years of work have paid off!

A legislative aide enters, face grim.

"Come on, join us. We've won."

The aide shakes her head.

"What's up? Why the sad face?"

"Hickel."

"What about Governor Hickel? He supports us."

"He's unhappy with the budget. He's going to red-pen it."

"But not the buyback," we insist. "Hickel even backed our ad. He's with us. He can't red-pen Kachemak Bay. We've won."

Red Ink

Anchorage Daily News *headlines blare:* "Veto Kills Timber Buyouts. Hickel's Capital Budget Cuts Disappoint Environmentalists."

The blanket veto slices $76 million from the legislature-approved budget. The red pen slashes Kachemak Bay. The park logging will take place. The agreement with Timber Trading Company is defunct; Rocky River and the Island Peninsula will also be under the knife. All our work . . . for nothing. We hold each other and bawl. We return to Homer to process this death.

Ed and I head across the bay. I sit, twirling an eagle feather. "I'm so bummed. Here I am turning forty and my whole life is a mess."

"The big four-oh isn't that bad, Jan."

"It's not my age. It's everything. I want to teach about plants and here I am spending all my time doing volunteer stuff. And for what? What's the use?"

"Oh honey, you're looking in the mud. Look at how much has been done."

"But Ed," I say, sweeping my hand, "the forests. Without these trees, there won't be any fish. This place will be like Alaska's Gulf Coast hell. Everything's turned to shit. I don't get enough time with you. And I'm not making squat. You're the one earning all the money these days, building that new house for Robert and Roberta."

"That's okay, Jan. What you're doing is important."

"But I want to contribute, Ed. And my time's not my own. No writing. No time for teaching."

"Honey, you need to take a bit of time for you."

At the Rocky River cabin, we savor the solitude we once owned. I spot Sue's Celtic runes on the shelf in the bedroom. I open the cloth bag and pour the runes onto the floor, face down. "Sit with the runes in silence," Sue had told me. "Focus. Be specific with a question."

"Higher Self: do we try again with the park buyback?"

I flip a rune; it looks like a hawk stepped on the tile with an inked foot. I shudder, remember the hawk that tailed me moons ago. The rune guide opens to the bird track symbol. I read, "Feoh, the rune of impending fertility and success."

A bush line calls me to Marsha's. We hike, gather kelp, and talk about her expanding water taxi business and my disappointments. Later, I sit solo on Little Jakolof Point and gaze at otters at play in the bay. A bald eagle swoops from its nest in the Sitka spruce. I hear music. But there's no one in the Cove other than Marsha; and no one on the water either.

"Okay, angels. . . . What does this mean?" I ask.

"A promise."

"What kind of promise?"

"We want you to write this story."

"I don't want to write about me."

"It's not about you. It's about everyone."

"I won't do it."

"We want you to do it."

"I'll only do it if . . ." I tell them my conditions.

Pickles ⁓

While I'm at Little Jakolof Bay, Ed has guy time with his teammate from the spit boom job, Bob Archibald. Joining them is outsider Mark, keen for fly-fishing on the Rocky River.

Ed hits Seldovia for groceries, then meets Bob and Mark at the dock. "What's in this?" asks Ed as he hefts a large suitcase. "Feels like feathers."

"Shoes," says Mark. "My loafers, tennies, rubber boots, slippers, lace-ups."

"Going bush, you know," says Ed, exasperated. "Never mind, load up the van. We'll get this heap in the bike trailer at the head of the bay."

"Look what else that idiot brought," Bob whispers. "A gallon of dill pickles. Damn city slickers."

"That's mine," Ed says sheepishly. "Love all those P foods, you know: pies, pasta, pickles. Can't have a day without pickles. You'd better carry them, Bob. They might get broken on the bike trailer."

"Okay," Bob says reluctantly. "But I'll feel mighty stupid carrying pickles."

"Never know. They might come in handy."

Ed drives off in the three-wheeler at the mill, leaving Bob and Mark on foot. On the switchback by Wolverine Creek, Bob and Mark meet a hiker. He's bent over, poking with a stick at scat.

"Bear," Bob tells him.

"Good thing I've got a gun for protection. Aren't you packing anything?"

"Don't need a gun, I've got pickles."

"Pickles?"

"Where you from, boy?"

"California. I'm fresh out of university; up in Alaska to see the world."

"Don't they teach you anything in school?"

"Heaps. But not about pickles."

"If a bear hassles you, all you need do is get up a tree. And when that bear opens its mouth down below, you drop a pickle down its throat."

"You're joshing me."

Bob looks to Mark and winks. "Bob's telling God's honest truth," Mark chimes in. "Has to do with the bear's system and the acidity in the pickles."

"Yep, drops them on the spot. You want some pickles to carry with you?"

"I've got the gun thanks, but next time I might get me a jar."

"You'd best do that. Safest thing you can have in the wilderness. And if you're hungry you can eat them. You can't eat bullets."

Groundhog Days ～

The Coalition regroups in Homer. "Bad news," says Ken Castner. "Juneau has a new cast of legislators. We're back to ground zero. Everyone needs to be educated all over again."

"Seldovia Chief Fred Elvsaas," adds Sue, "says there is mutiny on his board of directors. Strong opposition is growing to the buyback. The board wants to log. But he promises to get them on step for one final round in Juneau."

Ken's good news is that the Exxon Trustee Council, composed of federal and state government agencies, now has $900 million in civil fines available for use in habitat restoration. He notes, "These are dollars the state can't abscond into general funds. Who's game to replay this all again?"

Our hands wave like flags. The Coalition's back on deck, back to Juneau.

We wade through bureaucratic channels with the trustees; from them we seek $7.5 million toward the buyback.

On December 12, 1992, the *Anchorage Daily News* headlines read: "Environmental Rules Block Kachemak Land Sale."

KBCC meets again, with Ken explaining how the panel of trustees was within a hair's breadth of approval when two of its six members balked. They decided to study the parameters more, to evaluate whether the timber rights buyback in Kachemak Bay qualified for funds. The phone tree ignites. Calls batter the trustees. Kids flood them with pleas to save the trees.

On January 20, 1993, the headline announces: "Spill Panel OKs Timber Buyout."

We win a round. Trustees approve $7.5 million toward the Kachemak Bay timber purchase. This will combine with $7.5 million the state has now allocated toward the land purchase. The deal is now shy $7 million.

We increase the pressure. The phone tree expands. Calls statewide, calls worldwide, hammer the legislative offices. The legislative aids are again inundated. Anne Wieland, Mary Pearsall, I, and a host of other Coalition supporters return again to Juneau. We canvass the halls. A number of our key supporters have left office, and our foes remain. We sit through hearing after hearing. We testify and alert those at home. The phone tree activates before each hearing. The pressure mounts.

Each voice counts, but the legislators, we find, respect group power.

More and more associations back the Coalition drive. Groups scream for passage of the bill, and funding of the final $7 million.

The legislature enters its final days. The clock ticks madly. The bill's still stuck in committee. The night before adjournment, I visit friend Jane Bell. "Why so glum, Jan?"

"The bill's stonewalled again. Exactly like last time. No matter what we do, we can't get this thing through. It's like it's trapped in a psychic web."

"Want me to try? I've been working with a battle energy release process. It repatterns energy surrounding conflicts."

"Huh?"

"It's energetic architecture," explains Jane. "When you build a home, the blueprint dictates the result. The same thing happens with events, Jan. Change the blueprint and you change the result."

"I don't know that I understand it, Jane. But I'll try anything. I'm desperate for this to end. We all need to go on with our lives."

"First we need to send blessings to all who have engaged in the process, including gratitude to the unseen helpers. We have to thank the land itself. We ask to clear conflict and stagnation and repattern the entire negotiation process, so that everything is neutral and energized."

"Great, do it. Do whatever you can. I'm ready for change."

I drift to sleep, dreaming of duels. I waken to news headlines: "Kachemak Bay Buyout Ends an Eighteen-Year Battle. Funding Means Saws Stay Silent in Kachemak Bay State Park."

Word spreads like forest fire. We have won. We have all won. We truly have accomplished a win–win. The battle energy has released. The firewalk prayer has come true. And now, I realize, with a sinking feeling, I must pay the price. I have a promise to keep, a story to tell.

⟿ Epilogue ⟿

"So whatever became of the gold bar?" persists Ellie, who has now heard the whole story that she asked for.

"Ed kept burying and unburying the darn thing for years; he was worse than a dog with an old bone. When the shovel handle broke, he stuffed it under the Homer cottage, and covered it with an old shingle."

"Right on top of the ground?"

"Yeah. So I figured its days were nearing an end. Soon afterward he stopped at Randy's yard sale to buy his kayak, and left owning the entire yard. He traded the gold bar for Randy's five acres, cabin, and kayak. I was so relieved. Gold is nothing but a metal headache. You fret about it, its market value, where to store it. No one can steal a cabin. And with land, you can grow crops or harvest wood to keep you warm. We kept Randy's place for rental income for a few years, then sold it to a local artist."

"So that was the end of the gold bar. What about your promise?"

"It was to write this story if my firewalk prayer came true and the park was made whole. I've long said that when people lead, leaders follow. I wanted Spirit to prove to me that this is true."

"And the people led?"

"Absolutely. Everyone from kids to seniors. And the leaders followed suit. Now we only need to decide what else we truly want. And to lead our leaders until we have it."

~ Postscript ~

Shortly after working on the Exxon Valdez *oil spill cleanup,* Ed and two other men in the Red Mountain postal area alone were diagnosed with non-Hodgkin's lymphoma. In the hospital for yet more tests, dressed in an embarrassing gown, Ed looked at me with conviction. "I'm not ready to go, Janzie. Let's find another way."

Ed's way brought ten years of remission. We altered our diet to macrobiotics, eating mainly whole grains, sea vegetables, fresh greens, and Alaskan salmon. He quit his pipe and did fortnightly acupuncture treatments. We both did a ten-day Avatar course to explore and change beliefs that might be contributing to the illness. "Thanks to the Avatar tools," said Ed afterward, "I feel more Source, more able to create the life I prefer." Ed restored his relationship with two of his daughters. The youngest had carried his photo in a matchbook for years, always hoping to someday find her father; her wish came true.

⁓ Ed's Legacy ⁓

As a child growing up in Massachusetts, one of Ed's favorite hangouts was Walden Pond, and his model for manhood was Henry David Thoreau. Like Thoreau, Ed believed implicitly in going confidently in the direction of his dreams, and daring to live the life he imagined. He believed it essential to step to the music of your own drummer.

Outside of rare moments like the "cooties" scene at Swift Creek, Ed and I lived harmoniously. But a decade after the oil spill, our hearts beat rhythms of new dreams, dreams that led ultimately to my rehoming in New Zealand, and to Ed alternating life between Alaska and New England until his death in 2003.

Ed's legacy endures in finely crafted homes, beautiful daughters, and memorable words. "You can do it," I still hear when I hit a hard spot. "Live now. Remember Janzie, you've got to live free, or die."

～ Appendix One ～

Kachemak Heritage Land Trust

Kachemak Heritage Land Trust continues its mission of preserving critical habitat, and recreational and cultural land, for public benefit. More than three thousand acres on the Kenai Peninsula are now permanently protected through conservation easements and donations of land for conservation.

KHLT's publication *Living in Harmony with Moose* assists folks to coexist with their moose neighbors. KHLT volunteers built and maintain the "Homestead Trail" and "Calvin and Coyle Nature Trail" and an observation platform near Beluga Wetlands. KHLT also conducts a summer program for residents and visitors that includes guided nature hikes, beach walks, wetland tours, and visits to properties protected by KHLT conservation easements.

See www.kachemaklandtrust.org for additional information, an events schedule, and membership information.

This book supports Kachemak Heritage Land Trust's "Two Bits for Land" program; two percent of author royalties fund ongoing land conservation on Alaska's Kenai Peninsula.

∾ Appendix Two ∾

Wake of the Exxon Valdez

Writing about the spill some twenty years later still stirs nightmares. Exxon's Good Friday oil spill in Alaska crucified the environment. And the pressurized hot water wash, used to clean beaches, also wiped out much surviving beach life—like clams and kelps.

Unlike the religious Easter story, with death-to-life resurrection in three days, rebirth and recovery of oil-affected species will take decades. Sea otters, harbor seals, Pacific herring, and harlequin ducks are among those still classified as "not recovering." For some species—like loons and the shy murrelets—the full extent of injury and recovery may never be known.

According to Exxon estimates, 14 percent of eleven million gallons spilled into Prince William Sound was reclaimed. Other sources indicate up to thirty-eight million gallons were spilled, and likely less than 5 percent of the oil was reclaimed. The spread of the oil covered ten thousand square miles; its reach from Prince William Sound to Kodiak is comparable to a spill spreading from New York to Cape Canaveral, Florida. More wildlife was killed by the *Exxon Valdez* than by any other spill in history.

Following the *Exxon Valdez* spill, two major lawsuits by the State of Alaska and the federal government charged Exxon for *damage to the environment*. Exxon pled guilty. Though punishable by up to $8 billion dollars, Exxon received a $25-million criminal fine, $100 million in restitution to the state and federal governments, and a $1-billion civil settlement (including a $100-million optional reopener clause) payable over ten years. Seven million of the civil settlement, earmarked for habitat restoration in oil-affected communities, helped preserve the heart of Kachemak Bay State Park.

But the hearts of many spill-affected Alaskans remain broken. They still anger at the fact that Exxon had a lapsed alcoholic in command of a vessel. That the fisheries and their livelihoods collapsed in the years following the spill. That oil tankers operating in treacherous Alaskan waters lacked safety features like double hulls. That emergency equipment wasn't available as promised to corral and skim oil during the good-weather window immediately surrounding the spill. That the spill spread. Its aftereffects resound decades later.

Fishermen, Natives, and others affected by the spill banded together to sue Exxon for *punitive damages*. The 1994 Alaska Court's award of $5 billion *punitive* (and $289 million *compensatory*) was reduced by the 9th Circuit Court to $2.5 billion (compensation that would have averaged $78,000 per claimant). But Exxon's continual appeals kept all in limbo. In 2008, the U.S. Supreme Court slashed the punitive award, ordering Exxon to pay $507.5 million (equating to $16,000 per fisherman). Exxon is now challenging the court mandate to pay the twenty years of interest to claimants.

What also remains unsettled is the ongoing toll on human health of both the oil spill and the cleanup. Ed was but one of the *Exxon Valdez* spill workers who suffered lymphoma following work in oiled areas. His years of exposure to construction chemicals make his work on the oil spill an "unprovable" link, but in Cordova, Dr. Riki Ott, Ph.D., has documented extensive lists of oil spill cleanup workers suffering cancers, chronic headaches, nosebleeds, rashes, and liver and kidney problems following hydrocarbon exposure. My personal interview with Sandee Elvsaas in Seldovia detailed the experience of her brother Tim Burt (p. 338) who, says Sandee, "was in great health until he steam-cleaned

Exxon-oiled boats. The hydrocarbons triggered unbearable, unstoppable headaches. Six years later, with Tim still in agony and unable to work, doctors upped the potency of his pain medication. The very next day, Tim, fogged by pain, took his usual number of pills, forgetting that their individual potency had been significantly altered. Tim died. Despite his pain," continues Sandee, "Tim wasn't suicidal; he was keen to live. His sudden death was hard enough for the family to bear. And what happened next gutted us all. Exxon confiscated Tim's body to test his organs. Six months later, we were still begging for Tim's body so we could have a funeral. Exxon kept stonewalling us, insisting they needed Tim's body for yet more tests. But when we requested Tim's tissue samples, Exxon insisted they'd lost them. None of us had money to legally challenge Exxon to get Tim's body back. Then someone called my sister in Juneau, telling her someone was being buried in our family plot. It was Tim, being dumped in a grave. None of us even got to be there. Exxon never even gave us an apology."

It's true that the *Exxon Valdez* spill was an accident. Exxon didn't intend to spill oil into Prince William Sound. Exxon paid money for cleanup. And Exxon paid its criminal and civil fines to the state and federal governments.

But what I hunger to see, still, is full punitive damage paid to affected Alaskans, apologies and compensation to families like the Elvsaas family, new technologies that reduce our dependence on oil, and in the realm of seaborne oil transport, full installation of double hulls on tankers, long before the court-mandated 2015 deadline. (Less than one-third of Exxon tankers have double hulls, as of 2008.) The spill can't be undone, but a safer, saner future can be created.

Profits, meanwhile, soar for Exxon, the most prosperous corporation in history; CNN reports that in 2008, Exxon-Mobil netted $10.89 billion in its first quarter; its prior quarter yielded $11.66 billion, equivalent to earning $1,385 per second. Less than two months of profits would have paid all claimants the original court-mandated award. The revised damages will cost less than five days of profits.

For additional information on the *Exxon Valdez* spill, visit Web sites:

- www.wholetruth.net
- www. soundtruth.info
- Alaska.sierraclub.org/issues/forests/sound-truth.html

or read:

- *Sound Truths and Corporate Myth$, The Legacy of the Exxon Valdez Oil Spill,* Dr. Riki Ott, Ph.D., Dragonfly Sister Press, 2005
- *Not One Drop*, Dr. Riki Ott, Ph.D., Chelsea Green Publishing, 2008

⁓ Final Thanks ⁓

Memory can be like a dusty attic, swept clean only with collaborative effort. I'm deeply thankful to everyone who chatted and wrote, reliving events and filling in gaps. Thanks, too, to Rocky River journals left by countless guests, to Sandy Unsworth's travel journals, and Helen's Broomell's *Solo on the Yukon* tales. Deepest thanks to one and all, in front lines and behind the scenes, who contributed to this work, and who helped keep Kachemak Bay the amazing place that it still is today.

Thanks, too, to Marina Schaum and Ellen (Ellie) Vande Visse for reading the first draft and urging me forward, and to Gordy Vernon for grounding himself in New Zealand and breathing life into dry places. Countless helpers have made suggestions and critiques that have aided this memoir to evolve.

Thanks, too, to the crew at Graphic Arts Center Publishing Company, and to editor Laura O. Foster, for assistance in taking this manuscript to finished form and helping me fulfill my promise.

⁓ Note on Names and Place-names ⁓

In most cases, identities used in this work are as named. Fictitious names, used to preserve privacy, include Maples and Blueberry Hill in New Hampshire; Tony of the gold bar story; Lucia, Ed's ex-wife; Sara, who saw Ma Russell's ghost; and Ted of Camellia Drive, Florida.

～ Recommended Reading ～

Ewing, Susan. *The Great Alaska Nature Factbook*. Portland, Ore.: Alaska Northwest Books, 1996.

Klein, Janet. *A History of Kachemak Bay, the Country, the Communities*. Homer, Alaska: Homer Society of Natural History, 1981.

Hulten, Eric. *Flora of Alaska and Neighboring Territories*. Stanford, Calif.: Stanford University Press, 1968.

Schofield, Janice. *Discovering Wild Plants. Alaska, Western Canada, The Northwest*. Portland, Ore.: Alaska Northwest Books, 1989.

Schofield, Janice. *Alaska's Wild Plants, A Guide to Alaska's Edible Harvest*. Portland, Ore.: Alaska Northwest Books, 1992.

Springer, Susan Woodward. *Seldovia, Alaska*. Littleton, Colo.: Blue Willow Inc., 1997.

The Homer Foundation. *Kachemak Bay Alaska*. Homer, Alaska, 2005.

The Alaska Geographic Society. *Where Mountains Meet the Sea: Alaska's Gulf Coast*. Volume 13, Number 1, 1986.

The Alaska Geographic Society. *The Middle Yukon River*. Volume 17, Number 3, 1990.

⁓ About the Author ⁓

A passion for nature and animals, coupled with a love of travel, led Janice from New Hampshire to the wilds of Alaska. She and her husband, Ed, left behind the congestion of the East Coast to follow their dream and build a log cabin in the Far North woods. Environmental pressures of impending clear-cuts of old-growth forests combined with the *Exxon Valdez* oil spill led them into community action that included the formation of Alaska's first land trust.

The desire to know Alaska's plants intimately inspired the writing of *Discovering Wild Plants* and *Alaska's Wild Plants* and led to a twenty-year career teaching edible and medicinal plant classes. "There's abundant wild food and pharmacy in our own back yards," says Janice. "And the plants are amazing teachers, revealing themselves to us. They help us 'live freer' in terms of economics, and healthier by eating with the seasons, and connecting to life's cycles."

Janice's present life cycle involves residence in New Zealand, where she's discovering plants of the Southern Hemisphere. She and her husband, Barry Eaton, operate a bed and breakfast (barrye2000@xtra.co.nz), and studio. Their kiwi pets have ranged from Kai the singing Labrador to pet lambs and magpies and a small herd of haflinger-cross sport ponies.

～

Printed in the United States
140683LV00001BB/2/P